CYBARIS®
AN INTELLECTUAL PROPERTY
LAW REVIEW

Volume 6   2015   Issue 1

EDITOR-IN-CHIEF
Sarah A. Howes

EXECUTIVE EDITOR
Adam E. Szymanski

NOTES & COMMENT EDITORS
Nadja Baer   Christopher Bayliss   Katherine Boyle

STAFF
Mihajlo Babovic   Joseph W. Dubis   Brian Jarvis
Chelsea Ganske   Kelly Fermoyle   Anthony Marshik
Nodira Ismoilova   Vincent W. Rotty   Anthony Salmo
Caitlin Kowalke   Jaime Sekenski   Brian Smith
Molly Littman

FACULTY ADVISOR
Ken Port

2015

Cybaris®, an Intellectual Property Law Review, is published two times per year by the students of the Intellectual Property Institute of William Mitchell College of Law at 875 Summit Avenue, Saint Paul, Minnesota, 55105. Telephone: 651-290-6425. E-mail: eic.cybaris@wmitchell.edu.

Manuscripts: Cybaris®, an Intellectual Property Law Review, welcomes unsolicited manuscripts. All manuscripts submitted for consideration should be double spaced, with citations placed in footnotes that conform to THE BLUEBOOK: A UNIFORM SYSTEM OF CITATION (19th ed. 2010). Please forward all submissions to the Cybaris® Editorial Office at the address listed above.

Opinions expressed in Cybaris®, an Intellectual Property Law Review, do not necessarily represent the views of the publication, its editors, the William Mitchell College of Law, or any person connected therewith.

CYBARIS®
AN INTELLECTUAL PROPERTY
LAW REVIEW

Volume 6   2015   Issue 1

FOREWORD

KATHRYN E. WAGNER[1]

Rapidly developing technologies over the past twenty years have increased both the demand for and the easy access to copyrighted works. While increased demand and access should be beneficial for both creators and users of these works, such easy access has led to the creators' contributions being devalued under the guise of the public good. This access defies the traditional paradigm of permissions and licenses mandated under the Copyright Act. Instead, such access has bred a culture that expects immediate, free access to the works. At Volunteer Lawyers for the Arts in New York, we witness firsthand the hardships that individual creators face in order to exploit their works and support their artistic endeavors. For many, the current copyright regime gives no practical answer.

With an active debate brewing as to whom the Copyright Act should serve, law must follow and lawmakers should seek new legal structures to manage the changing landscape. Beginning in 2013, the Copyright Register, Maria A. Pallante, called to update the U.S. Copyright Law and urged Congress to make it more functional in the 21st century.[2] Emphasizing the need to serve the public interest, the Register has stated that Congress has a duty to provide for authors, as part of the public, and should focus on the creators needs:

---

[1] Kathryn E. Wagner is Executive Director of Volunteer Lawyers for the Arts (VLA). Prior to joining VLA, Ms. Wagner was Vice President and Counsel for the National Music Publishers' Association, serving as a legal advisor for the litigation and policy initiatives of the association. She practiced in the litigation group at Pryor Cashman LLP, specializing in intellectual property and complex business transactions. She holds a law degree from Tulane University, where she served as editor-in-chief of the Tulane Journal of International and Comparative Law. Ms. Wagner would like to thank Inbal Golany, VLA legal fellow, for her assistance with this piece.
[2] Maria A. Pallante, *The Next Great Copyright Act*, 36 COLUM. J. LAW & ARTS 315, 324 (2013).

Thus, [the next copyright act] must confirm and rationalize certain fundamental aspects of the law, including the ability of authors and their licensees to control and exploit their creative works, whether content is distributed on the street or streamed from the cloud.[3]

To that end, Congress is conducting hearings[4] and has directed the Copyright Office to prepare a number of formal studies[5] on issues related to copyright owners' control of their works. For example, in 2014, the House Judiciary Committee, Subcommittee on Courts, Intellectual Property, and the Internet, held a hearing to address the debate regarding the expansion of fair use that followed emerging technologies.[6] The hearing further called to reexamine the application of the "transformative use" standard,[7] which has been in the center of the fair use expansion debate. The Subcommittee also held a hearing covering moral rights, termination rights, resale royalty, and copyright term.[8] At this hearing, Congressman Jerrold Nadler introduced the American Royalties Too (ART) Act,

---

[3] *Id*, at 323.

[4] *Moral Rights, Termination rights, Resale Royalty, and Copyright Term: Hearing before the Subcomm. on Courts, Intellectual Prop., & the Internet of the H. Comm. on the Judiciary*, 113th Cong. (2014) [hereinafter *Moral Rights*]; *Copyright Remedies: Hearing before the Subcomm. on Courts, Intellectual Prop., & the Internet of the H. Comm. on the Judiciary*, 113th Cong. (2014); *Chapter 512 of Title 17: Hearing before the Subcomm. on Courts, Intellectual Prop., & the Internet of the H. Comm. on the Judiciary*, 113th Cong. (2014). For roundtable examples, see Study on the Right of Making Available Comments and Public Roundtable, 79 Fed. Reg. 10571 (U.S. Copyright Office Feb. 25, 2014); Music Licensing Study, 79 Fed. Reg. 25626 (U.S. Copyright Office May 5, 2014).

[5] OFFICE OF THE REG. OF COPYRIGHTS, U.S. COPYRIGHT OFFICE, COPYRIGHT SMALL CLAIMS (2013); OFFICE OF THE REG. OF COPYRIGHTS, U.S. COPYRIGHT OFFICE, RESALE ROYALTIES: AN UPDATED ANALYSIS (2013); OFFICE OF THE REG. OF COPYRIGHTS, U.S. COPYRIGHT OFFICE, COPYRIGHT AND THE MUSIC MARKETPLACE (2015).

[6] *The Scope of Fair Use: Hearing before the Subcomm. on Courts, Intellectual Prop., & the Internet of the H. Comm. on the Judiciary*, 113th Cong. (2014).

[7] *Id.*

[8] *See Moral Rights, supra* note 4, at 4.

incorporating recommendations from the Copyright Office report on resale royalties. This report recognized that current law does not provide the same protections to visual artists that exist for other creators protected through current copyright law.[9] Further, the Subcommittee held two hearings in June 2014 addressing music licensing under the Copyright Act.[10] In conjunction with these hearings, Representative Doug Collins, along with many supporting co-sponsors, introduced the Songwriter Equity Act (SEA) proposing revisions to Sections 114 (i) and 115 of Title 17.[11] Moreover, the Copyright Office recently released an extensive music licensing study after receiving public comments and holding roundtables to debate current issues facing the industry.[12]

This volume of Cybaris®, an Intellectual Property Law Review, presents a range of issues that serve to inform those debating the next great Copyright Act.

Alma Robinson discusses the recent developments in the effort of promoting a regulatory scheme for resale royalties in California and its effects on transactions in the United States. Robinson further draws the justifications for enacting a federal resale royalty act. California's experience with enforcing its resale royalty act and the pending Ninth Circuit decision of its constitutionality will serve to inform the national debate.

---

[9] Press Release, Representative Jerrold Nadler, Rep. Nadler Welcomes New Report on Resale Royalties for Artists (Dec. 13, 2013), *available at* http://nadler.house.gov/press-release/rep-nadler-welcomes-new-report-resale-royalties-artists.

[10] *Music Licensing Under Title 17: Part One: Hearing before the Subcomm. on Courts, Intellectual Prop., & the Internet of the H. Comm. on the Judiciary,* 113th Cong. (2014); *Music Licensing Under Title 17: Part Two: Hearing before the Subcomm. on Courts, Intellectual Prop., & the Internet of the H. Comm. on the Judiciary,* 113th Cong. (2014).

[11] *See* Songwriter Equity Act of 2014, H.R. 4079, 113th Cong.

[12] COPYRIGHT AND THE MUSIC MARKETPLACE, *supra* note 5.

Niels Schaumann, following up on his earlier work on the subject, provides a strong opinion in favor of the legitimacy of appropriation art as a non-infringing practice, building on its "transformative" nature. The fair use doctrine, as Schaumann explains, has undergone significant change, particularly in the area of appropriation art. Schaumann suggests that Courts should give deference to appropriation art when analyzing its legitimacy to appropriation artists' lack of protections, which applies narrowly to works of visual art.

Amanda Schreyer's article highlights the expansion of creative works that require the protections of the Copyright Act. Schreyer brings a thorough analysis of the protection for fictional characters, and describes the legal protections available to creators of fictional characters, as well as the limitations on the owner's rights in his characters. With Internet fan blogs and comic cons becoming increasingly popular, the effectiveness of the legal protections for fictional characters comes into question, and should also be considered as part of the broader copyright reform.

Jared R. Sherlock further demonstrates how far copyright protection might go, as he brings an in-depth discussion on whether a magic performance can be copyrightable. Sherlock explains that magicians have been struggling to protect their creative works—the secret behind their illusions—through intellectual property law, and at the same time attempting to keep it secret, in order to maintain their profession. This has led to lack of protection, as traditional intellectual property law requires public exposure. Thus, Sherlock proposes that instead of protecting the secret, a magician's performance should be protected under copyright law.

Mihajlo Babovic identifies a growing concern for many engaging in social media websites' Terms of Service agreements that affect the exclusive rights granted to authors by the Copyright Law. Babovic argues that since such agreements counter the purposes of the U.S. copyright law, they should be declared unconstitutional and thus prohibited.

Caitlin Kowalke explores the legal ramifications of the music industry's recent shift into the online distribution market. Kowalke relates the inadequacies artists face in lowered royalty compensation to the newfound accessibility consumers are presented with through digital downloading. While statutory changes have been presented, no reformation efforts have stemmed artist losses at a pace quick enough to keep up with changes in technology. Additionally, Kowalke addresses the likelihood future online music markets will be structured as more widespread streaming services, in following current television trends such as Hulu and Netflix.

Creators from the various art disciplines greatly contribute to society, and thus, their works should be valued accordingly. Unfortunately, the Internet diminishes the value of creative works, as it lacks proper protective mechanisms for online content. Many view creative work available online as free for use without recognition that such use infringes upon copyrighted work. To prevent this growing misconception, a copyright reform is necessary, both from a legal perspective as well as from a social one. The initiatives of the Copyright Register, and the fact that it is taking into account all sides to the current issues, are important and crucial steps in the reform. This Cybaris® issue adds to this review highlighting the need for better legal protections for artists, and the positive social implications such protection will have.

THE EFFECTS OF EXPOSURE ON THE ECOLOGY OF THE MAGIC INDUSTRY: PRESERVING MAGIC IN THE ABSENCE OF LAW

JARED R. SHERLOCK [†]

[†] B.A., Saint John's University, 2011. The author is an American magician and producer who tours nationwide and abroad performing over 150 shows a year at theaters, corporations, and fairs. His work has been featured by *The Wall Street Journal Online*, *MSN Money.com*, and *Magic Magazine*. The author would like to thank William Mitchell College of Law; Editor-in-Chief Sarah Howes for her instruction, confidence, and her inspiring and altruistic leadership in the discipline of Arts Law; the editors and staff members of the William Mitchell College of Law Intellectual Property Law Review for their talents; Roger M. Lindmark for his generosity in founding the Lindmark Fellowship that enabled this research; his family (Tina, Russ, and Corben) for their humbling support and encouragement; and Olivia for her unconditional love. For more information, please visit JaredSherlock.com.

I. INTRODUCTION

Magicians have gone to great lengths to protect the methodologies and designs of successful magic effects through the practice of secrecy. Magic is "part science and part showmanship."[1] Magicians are sworn to ethical codes created by professional civic organizations that passionately urge practitioners not to reveal the science behind a piece of magic.

A vulnerable resource, magic secrets are depleted when they are abused.[2] Industry practitioners labor in a dead space of intellectual property law. Operating in such an unprotected space has forced industry insiders to endure a great number of domestic and international exposures. If a magician's illusion is deceptive and original, it is eligible for protection under United States patent law. However, to earn this protection, the magician must meticulously explain how the effect is accomplished. By attempting to legally hide and protect their secrets, magicians would paradoxically make them available to the general public and other competitors. According to Professor F. Jay Dougherty, "[t]he ideas behind an illusion and the devices and useful methods used to implement it are not protectable by copyright. Words and short phrases are not viewed as sufficiently original to merit copyright protection."[3] This is a

---

[1] JIM STEINMEYER, HIDING THE ELEPHANT: HOW MAGICIANS INVENTED THE IMPOSSIBLE AND LEARNED TO DISAPPEAR xx–xxi (1st ed. 2003).

[2] *See* Jacob Loshin, *Secrets Revealed: Protecting Magicians' Intellectual Property without Law, in* LAW AND MAGIC: A COLLECTION OF ESSAYS 123, 140 (Christine A. Corcos ed., 2010).

[3] F. Jay Dougherty, *Now You Own It, Now You Don't: Copyright and Related Rights in Magic Productions and Performances, in* LAW AND MAGIC: A COLLECTION OF ESSAYS 101, 102 (Christine A. Corcos ed., 2010); *see infra* Parts II.D.5, V. *But see* Teller v. Dogge, 8 F. Supp. 3d 1228, 1233 (D. Nev. 2014) ("The mere fact that a dramatic work or pantomime includes a magic trick, or even that a particular illusion is its central feature does not render it devoid of copyright protection.").

challenging reality, as "[c]opyright law thus fails to protect the most common expression of magicians' intellectual property—live stage performance—as well as magicians' most highly valued intellectual creations."[4] The magic secret is a distinctive kind of intangible resource that defies established economic theory of intellectual property law. Exposure reveals the secret, and thereby damages its value. This unsupportive legal atmosphere severely hinders practitioners' incentive to invest in and cultivate new ideas when they can be easily repossessed and duplicated by a competing player in the industry without legal ramifications.

This Note proposes that protecting a magician's performance—not the secret from disclosure—is practicable and effective in safeguarding a magician's finances, morals, and secrets. Part II explores the nature of intellectual property law in the magic industry, its history, and its practitioners.[5] Part III profiles some of magic's most influential figures in exclusive interviews.[6] Part IV examines United States intellectual property law and the limited protection it currently affords magic secrets.[7] Part V discusses a recent court ruling in favor of copyright protection for magic.[8] Finally, Part VI summarizes the impact of intellectual property law on the ecology of the magic industry and emphasizes the advantage practitioners preserve by attempting to protect their performances, instead of their secrets.[9]

---

[4] Loshin, *supra* note 2, at 131.
[5] *See infra* Part II.
[6] *See infra* Part III.
[7] *See infra* Part IV.
[8] *See infra* Part V.
[9] *See infra* Part VI.

II. BACKGROUND OF INTELLECTUAL PROPERTY IN THE MAGIC INDUSTRY

A. Brief History

A form of theatrical entertainment referred to as stage magic, not to be confused with paranormal activity, presents seemingly impossible feats called magic effects, tricks, or illusions for the pleasure of a live audience. Indeed, anthropological writers agree in titling magic a "pre-science," and its origins can be traced to ancient tribal rituals.[10] Over time, magic has transformed from a practice associated with mystics to that of contemporary entertainers. Magician Teller[11] explains it well:

> Magic is such a superb theatrical form, it's intrinsically just about the most powerful, simple piece of theatrical language that you can use. You go to see a work of art because you want to see something that will amaze you and put you deeply in touch with someone else. But before this idea of touching someone else's heart, there is this fundamental impulse of all art to be amazed. You go to be jarred out of the real world, and be profoundly amazed by what you are seeing.[12]

One could argue that magic is the art that most directly addresses that impulse. If what an audience experiences when they go to see a magic show does not

---

[10] *See* MARCEL MAUSS, A GENERAL THEORY OF MAGIC 15, 19–21 (Robert Brain trans., Routledge, 2d ed. 2001) (1902).

[11] Born Raymond Joseph Teller, Teller is an American magician, writer, New York Times bestselling author, and he is the silent character in the world famous Penn & Teller show.

[12] Telephone Interview with Raymond Joseph Teller, Magician and Illusionist (Aug. 6, 2010).

look miraculous or evoke feelings of amazement, then the magic performance has failed. The late Robert-Houdin[13] was quoted in saying, a magician "is [just] an actor playing the part of a magician."[14] Illusion inventor and designer Jim Steinmeyer[15] says this famous line serves as an important reminder that a magic effect is a "supernatural" short play.[16]

Magic practitioners, much like actors, produce their work for the pleasure of an audience. Generating some level of amazement and amusing an audience directly impacts the bottom line. The ability of a magician to successfully manipulate an audience's perception is contingent on their capacity to conceal the ideas, inventions, and methodologies behind their magic effects. Thousands of careful psychological choices and intricacies characterize and encircle a magic performance. The ideas and methods of the art that make magic possible originate from several professions within the industry. The following is an overview of the terms and introduction to the different players in the magic industry, followed by a glance at the dynamics of innovation within the business of magic.

---

[13] Jean Eugene Robert-Houdin is a renowned French magician born in 1805 and considered to be the father of modern magic. *See* STEINMEYER, *supra* note 1, at xiii, 6.

[14] F FOR FAKE (Janus Film 1973) (quoting JEAN EUGENE ROBERT-HOUDIN, THE SECRECTS OF CONJURING AND MAGIC: OR HOW TO BECOME A WIZARD 43 (Louis Hoffmann ed. & trans., Cambridge Univ. Press, 2d ed. 2011) (1868)).

[15] The "celebrated 'invisible man'—inventor, designer and creative brain behind many of the great stage magicians of the last quarter-century." Teller, *'Hiding the Elephant': Now You See It . . .* , N.Y. TIMES (Dec. 7, 2003), http://www.nytimes.com/2003/12/07/books/review/07TELLERT.htm l).

[16] Telephone Interview with Jim Steinmeyer, Professional Magician (July 27, 2010).

B. The Players

The four key players in the magic industry are inventors, designers, builders, and performers. Many of magic's large stage illusions and apparatuses rely heavily on scientific principles to accomplish the desired visual. The inventor of a scientific principle employed in a magic effect is rarely a magician, but rather an engineer, psychologist, or inventor. Henry Dircks'[17] "Pepper's Ghost"[18] creation perfectly differentiates the role of an inventor from the other players in the world of magic. A designer draws up a plan or model integrating the scientific principles with a custom designed apparatus[19] (or for close-up artists, existing materials such as playing cards) to achieve the desired visual effect.[20] Designers sometimes employ the same (or similar) principles and methods within different apparatuses to create very different illusions and visual dramatic works. The plan drafted by the designer is then crafted and assembled by a builder.[21] Lastly, a magician, actor, or production company

---

[17] Born in Liverpool in 1806, Henry Dircks was a civil engineer, patent examiner, and part-time inventor whose most famous invention, the Dircksian Phantasmagoria, gave theaters the ability to create the visual of a ghost appearing onstage. STEINMEYER, *supra* note 1, at 25.

[18] Pepper's Ghost was originally known as the Dircksian Phantasmagoria, but was later purchased by and named after Royal Polytechnic Institution chemist and professor John Henry Pepper. Pepper's Ghost made its public debut on December 24, 1862. The resulting visual of the principle behind Pepper's Ghost can still be experienced today in Disney's "The Haunted Mansion" ride in Orlando, Florida. *See* STEINMEYER, *supra* note 1, at 25–43.

[19] For example, a cabinet that a volunteer enters which aids in the visual of solid matter of one person or object or thing penetrating the solid matter of another person, object, or thing.

[20] For example, the effect of production, vanishing, transposition, transformation, penetration, anti-gravity, attraction, invulnerability, creating a physical anomaly, telepathy, etc.

[21] Builders of magic props and equipment are generally very skilled carpenters and metal workers.

produces or performs the magic. The four
aforementioned players are most commonly individual
parties contracting one another as subcontractors.[22]

C. Developing and Sharing Secrets

Leading performers work very hard to get original
material; it is not an idle luxury for them. The
application of a magic effect's method (the science
portion) generally originates from an illusion designer.
Inspiration may or may not be provided or
commissioned by a magician or theatrical company.
This idea or method is then translated to a paper draft
that can be interpreted by an illusion builder, much like
an architect drafting a blueprint for a construction
contractor. The illusion builder then procures the
necessary materials and constructs the prop or
equipment as directed by the drawing. The finished
product is then re-acquired by the illusion designer,
inventor, or purchased by the commissioning magician.
It is not unusual for this sensitive process to span
months, years, and even decades.[23]

---

[22] On rare occasions, a magic practitioner will assume the role of
designer, builder, and performer. For example, Daniel Summers is an
American magician and illusion designer; he is widely considered one
of the finest designers and builders of illusions in the world today. *See*
DANIEL SUMMERS ILLUSION DESIGN, http://www.danielsummers.com
(last visited Nov. 24, 2014).

[23] Preeminent illusion designer Jim Steinmeyer graciously
accepted naive phone calls and emails from me throughout my
adolescence inquiring about his creations. In 2010, as I was an
undergraduate student, he shared the interview cited in this article.
See Telephone Interview with Jim Steinmeyer, *supra* note 16. In 2011,
at twenty-two years old, I flew to Los Angeles to meet with him and
express interest in performing one of his original illusions. In 2012,
Mr. Steinmeyer invited me to commission one of his new creations
entitled *Grand Larceny*. After I paid a royalty fee directly to
Steinmeyer for the performing rights, he designated world-renowned
Santa Paula-based illusion builder William Kennedy to construct the
first model. As the purchaser, I paid Mr. Kennedy for his materials

To further profile the innovation ecology at work in this enterprise, one must consider the various levels of how magicians share their ideas. Every magic secret has its own inherent value; this value determines the level at which the idea may be communicated from one practitioner to another.[24] Jim Steinmeyer brings the concept vibrantly to life:

> To really understand magic, you need to nudge past the tyros at the magic shop and sidle up to the old professionals standing in the corner, who aren't interested in the five-dollar plastic envelopes stuffed with instructions, but are whispering in a weird sort of shorthand—the names of past masters, the precise moment they chose to "accidentally" drop a silk handkerchief on the stage and pick it up, or the particular bend in their thumb as they cut a deck of cards in preparation for a shuffle.[25]

Jacob Loshin's essay in the book *Law and Magic* illustrated that secrets are shared through three channels: popular magic, common magic, and proprietary magic.[26] The first channel, popular magic, describes "five-dollar plastic envelopes stuffed with instructions,"[27] as well as beginner children's magic sets, novelty items, and magic that is affordable and accessible to most skill levels. The second, common magic, is the largest of the three channels with the

---

and labor to build the apparatus (as well as its travel road cases) on a mutually agreed upon timeline. The finished illusion was delivered to my Minneapolis residence in May of 2012.

[24] *See* Telephone Interview with Jim Steinmeyer, *supra* note 16.

[25] *See* STEINMEYER, *supra* note 1, at xix.

[26] Loshin, *supra* note 2, at 127.

[27] STEINMEYER, *supra* note 1, at xix; *see* Loshin, *supra* note 2, at 127.

widest selection of material. With materials ranging in difficulty from novice to advanced, common magic can be found in books, videos, journals, at club meetings, conventions, and it is the magic practiced by both hobbyists and working professional practitioners.[28] The final channel of magic, proprietary magic, is the most deceptive and innovative magic shared selectively among the world's most prolific practitioners. This material is often intended to be built and performed exclusively through permission from the inventor or designer.[29] Due to the level of secrecy involved, proprietary magic is the most vulnerable of the three to exposure.

The beginning of the 1900s marked the golden age for magic as a vibrant and innovative profession that was taking the world by storm. The most famous theaters in the world were advertising the next great deception by groundbreaking showmen like the Davenports,[30] David Devant,[31] Harry Kellar,[32] Howard Thurston,[33] and Harry Houdini.[34] Ideas and

---

[28] Loshin, *supra* note 2, at 127.

[29] *See id.*

[30] Ira Erastus Davenport (1839–1911) and William Henry Harrison Davenport (1841–1877) were "[t]wo Buffalo, New York brothers who originated the controversial cabinet séance act and presented it on stages around the world." STEINMEYER, *supra* note 1, at xiii.

[31] David Devant (1868–1941), a British magician, "[r]espected among his peers for his mix of skill, creativity and . . . natural performing style on stage." *Id.* at xiv.

[32] Harry Kellar (1849–1922), "[a]vuncular, business-like and beloved by his audiences, this touring American magician proudly filled his program with the finest illusions from London." *Id.* at xv.

[33] Howard Thurston (1869–1936) was "[t]he successor to Kellar and America's favorite magician from 1908 to 1936; Thurston was known for his easy rapport with children and a wonderful speaking voice." *Id.* at xvi.

[34] Harry Houdini (1874–1926) was known as the "[b]rash, dynamic American vaudeville performer who started as a magician and

methodology became infectious, spreading from conjurer to conjurer in the advent of civic organizations and publications. Institutions galvanized the sharing of ideas. London's Magic Circle was founded in 1905, shortly after the founding of the Society of American Magicians in 1902.[35] The International Brotherhood of Magicians, now the largest magic organization in the world, opened shortly thereafter.[36] In the height of the vaudeville era, these organizations gave rise to an explosion of books, magic shops, organization networks, clubs, and other more exclusive networks such as Hollywood's members-only Magic Castle, home of the Academy of Magical Arts.[37] In addition, magic magazines were being published worldwide; ideas flowed freely and the magicians' little world was getting smaller and smaller all the time.

D. Stealing & Exposure

The most successful practitioners became acutely sensitive to the advantages to be gained through the exclusive ownership of new ideas.

> In the late 1870s, during one of Buatier deKolta's[38] early successes in Paris, he was

---

achieved his greatest success as an escape artist; he made an elephant disappear at the New York Hippodrome in 1918." *Id.* at xiv.

[35] *Our History*, MAGIC CIRCLE, http://www.themagiccircle.co.uk/about-the-club/our-history (last visited Nov. 25, 2014); *History of the S.A.M.*, SOC'Y AM. MAGICIANS, http://magicsam.com/about-s-a-m/brief-history/ (last visited Nov. 25, 2014).

[36] *See History*, INT'L BROTHERHOOD MAGICIANS, http://www.magician.org/about/history (last visited Nov. 25, 2014) (opening in 1922).

[37] For more information on the Academy of Magic Arts, Inc. and the Magic Castle, interested readers can view the organization's website. *About the Academy*, MAGIC CASTLE, http://www.magiccastle.com/ama/index.cfm (last visited Nov. 25, 2014).

[38] Joseph Bautier deKolta (1848–1903) was "[a]n ingenious French

performing his flower trick. He deftly
twisted a large sheet of stiff paper into a
cone and shook it gently, revealing that it
was filled to overflowing with pastel tissue
flowers, which cascaded out of the cone
and into an upturned parasol. DeKolta
had every intention of keeping his secrets,
but one night at the Eden Theatre a slight
draft from the wings wafted several of the
flowers beyond the footlights, and they
tumbled off the stage. A magician in the
audience reached down to pick one up
and rushed from the theatre with his
discovery: an important key to the trick
was the ingenious construction of each
paper flower. For the next hundred years,
the famous deKolta flowers could be
purchased for a few dollars at magic
shops. [39]

Magicians are notorious for developing greed and
thirst for secrets, acquiring as many as possible, and
protecting them diligently. While uncommon, deceit
and espionage can be found in the roots of many
successful, professional magicians and illusionists from
the last two hundred years. Most practitioners agree,
however, that the looting of a few secrets does not have
a devastating effect, as the secret—or the "scientific"—is
only one half of what an audience is paying to witness.
The other half is the presentation. Jim Steinmeyer
emphasizes this notion by coining the description of
magic as "part science and part showmanship."[40] This
philosophy compliments magic as an art, but it is

---

magician who began his career with sleight of hand magic and later
invented a number of trendsetting mechanical illusions such as The
Vanishing Lady." STEINMEYER, *supra* note 1, at xiii.

[39] *Id.* at 161–62.

[40] *Id.* at xx–xxi.

important to remember that the magic presentation simply will not be effective if the feat does not fool its audience. Therefore, one could reasonably argue that practitioners are equally dependent on the secret and the presentation. While the industry seems to collectively agree that the pilfering of secrets has no widespread, negative fiscal effect, one could argue a different and equally damaging observation: an audience goes to see a work of art to see something fresh and new, not the same old thing again. Stealing indicates a lack of creativity in the art of conjuring; magicians who steal want all of the attention, but do not have anything to say. Teller candidly aligns with this idea:

> Old wine in new bottles! It's a lame excuse for a rampant lack of creativity, a rampant lack of courage and a rampant lack of guts. I am disgusted by the amount of imitation. The first few years of most any performer are imitative, but then you find your own voice or you get into real estate, or finance management. With magicians, the majority spend their life pursuing an imitation of the very first thing that they fell in love with, that is to say some dork in coattails producing cards, and that is a real problem. That means that these are people with no ideas, no personality, and no stage presence.[41]

Teller is not the first esteemed professional to passionately contribute to this perspective. Guy Jarrett, Howard Thurston's illusion designer, was always cynical about what was happening to magic. Jarrett wrote:

---

[41] Telephone Interview with Raymond Joseph Teller, *supra* note 12.

> I have spoken personally to every
> magician . . . and there is not a single one
> with the desire or ambition to become
> great, or famous, or to earn real money. . .
> . Not a single one has guts or ideas or
> imagination. They just got hold of a
> bunch of tricks and walked out on stage.
> So, they are only a bunch of drug store
> magicians.[42]

These responses illustrate the magic industry's
sparse patience for stealing another's act, material, or
secrets. Several notable incidents from magic's history
seem to suggest that exposure is a greater threat to the
ecology of professional conjuring. Years of practice
ensure the proper performance of a routine onstage to
protect the effect's secret. Magicians and illusion
designers work tirelessly to see to it that their
investments survive the test of time by scrupulously
defending their secrets. With the belief that the prop
and routine are their intellectual property, especially
sensitive magician owners will retire exposed pieces of
magic. A friend of the revered late nineteenth century
American magician Harry Kellar once recalled an
emotionally charged example of this type of behavior:

> One season Kellar was using a beautifully
> made, expensive, trick box in his
> program. At one performance, a spectator
> from the audience happened to indicate
> that he knew how the box worked. After
> the show, Kellar took the box out to the
> alley behind the theatre and smashed it to
> pieces with an axe. "Now we'll build a new
> one that no one will figure out," he told

---

[42] STEINMEYER, *supra* note 1, at 214–15.

his mechanics.[43]

Proprietary magic is expensive to replace. Only magicians with great resources and capital can react in this way. While most of the exposure takes place among the ranks of common magic, several historical incidents have placed physical and emotional stress on practitioners of proprietary magic.

E. The Discoverie of Witchcraft

Rather ironically, it was discovered that magic's first global exposure originated from a friend of magic, Reginald Scot, in 1584. Mr. Scot published a book entitled *The Discoverie of Witchcraft*[44] that offered great detail on how to accomplish a number of magic effects, including tricks such as the Cups and Balls routine that still remain popular today.[45] This exposure was not without reason. In the height of the Salem Witch Trials, Mr. Scot published this text to stop the inhumane persecution of magicians by the orders of religious authorities.[46] Mr. Scot's actions aided the rebuttal of magicians accused of being witches, and his writings arguably served as the first textbook for magicians. King James—the one that we now celebrate on our Bibles— ordered a decree that all copies be burned to extinguish the resistance against the witch-hunt.[47] As a result, few

---

[43] STEINMEYER, *supra* note 1, at 168–69.

[44] REGINALD SCOT, THE DISCOVERIE OF WITCHCRAFT (Reprint ed., 1972).

[45] *See* Loshin, *supra* note 2, at 128.

[46] MAURINE CHRISTOPHER, THE ILLUSTRATED HISTORY OF MAGIC 23 (1st ed. 1996).

[47] DANGEROUS IDEAS: CONTROVERSIAL WORKS FROM THE WILLIAM L. CLEMENTS LIBRARY, *Reginald Scot, The Discoverie of Witchcraft (1584)*, http://clements.umich.edu/exhibits/ online/bannedbooks/entry2.html (last visited Nov. 26, 2014).

original printings survive today.[48]

1. R.J. Reynolds

The R.J. Reynolds Tobacco Company exposed more magic to a wider audience than Reginald Scot could have imagined with its Camel Cigarettes 1933 advertising campaign entitled, *It's fun to be fooled . . . it's more fun to know*. Historian Mike Caveney documents in his 1994 *Magic Magazine* contributing article "The Camel Cigarette Wars: 60 Years Later" that the R.J. Reynolds's advertisements ran in "full color" to over 1200 American newspapers for a duration of eight months where the graphics showed illusions followed by descriptions of how they were accomplished.[49] The advertisements exposed an illusion of American magician Horace Goldin,[50] famously recognized as "sawing a lady in half."[51]

> Outraged, Goldin sued R.J. Reynolds alleging 'unfair competition,' but the court quickly dismissed his suit. Observing that Goldin had patented his illusion, the court explained[:] "Certainly [Goldin's patent] is a clear and detailed exposé of the secret to the public by the plaintiff himself. Any one who cares to can rightfully and lawfully procure a copy of said patent, containing a full detailed and diagramed explanation of the trick. . . ." And, it should be added, any cigarette

---

[48] *Id.*

[49] Loshin, *supra* note 2, at 129 (citing Mike Caveney, *The Camel Cigarette Wars: 60 Years Later*, MAGIC MAG., Apr. 1994, at 28, 28).

[50] Horace Goldin (1874–1939): "[a]t the turn of the 20th century, this American illusionist and vaudeville star was best known for the whirlwind pace of his act; he later became famous for performing the illusion, Sawing a Woman in Half." STEINMEYER, *supra* note 1, at xiv.

[51] *Id.*

company   can   then   publish   that
explanation in the newspapers for all to
see.[52]

2. *The Houdini Historical Center*

As the former home of the world's most well-known
magician Harry Houdini, Appleton, Wisconsin has
become a national magic hub featuring famous annual
conventions and the Outagamie County Historical
Society, home to The Houdini Historical Center. In
2003, the Outagamie Society's new director, Kimberly
Louagie, shocked the magic world when she formally
announced that they would be featuring a new exhibit
entitled, "A.K.A. Houdini," that would offer the general
public the ability to learn and participate in a selection
of Houdini's most coveted secrets.[53] Eighty-nine-year-
old Houdini advisor to the worldwide organization the
Society of American Magicians and Honorary Board
member to the Outagamie Society, Frank Dailey[54] said
in his letter of resignation: "I regret very much that the
memory of Houdini must be so desecrated. I'm certain
that his memory will live on longer than either of us, or
the Outagamie County Historical Center."[55] Supporters
of the exhibit argued that the secrets are revealed in a
way that challenges the participants to understand and
appreciate the skill required to perform these feats of

---

[52] Loshin, *supra* note 2, at 131–32 (quoting Goldin v. R.J. Reynolds
Tobacco Co., 22 F. Supp 61, 64 (S.D.N.Y. 1938)).
    [53] Meg Jones, *Unveiling Houdini Magic Trick Causes Museum
Controversy*, MILWAUKEE JOURNAL SENTINEL, Apr. 14, 2004, *available at*
http://www.jewishworldreview.com/0404/ houdini_magic_trick.asp.
    [54] Frank W. Dailey (1919–2012) was the President of the National
Society of American Magicians from 1983–84 and later became the
historian for the organization for many years.
    [55] Letter from Frank Dailey to author (Nov. 6, 2003) (on file with
author) (referencing Letter from Frank Daily to Outagamie County
Historical Society (2003)).

magic.[56] But magic leaders like David Copperfield[57] and
Frank Dailey campaigned strongly to stop the exhibit,
and they were not alone.[58] In December of 2004, a mere
year and half after the opening of the exhibit,
Outagamie executive director Terry Bergen announced
a decision to suspend the Houdini Historical Center
membership program as a result of financial challenges
attributed to low patronage.[59] The once booming tribute
to one of magic's most influential icons was now
forecasting a very bleak future.

3. *The Masked Magician*

Interestingly enough, Outagamie representatives
defended their actions through comparisons to the
exposures of the wildly popular Fox Network series,
Magic, Secrets Revealed.[60] Val Valentino, an alleged
American magician, illusionist, and actor, gained
notoriety by starring in the magic specials as the

---

[56] Associated Press, *Magicians Angry Over Unveiling of Houdini's Secret*, FOX NEWS (June 2, 2004), http://www.foxnews.com/story/2004/06/02/magicians-angry-over-unveiling-houdini-secret/ ("Museum officials . . . insist the exhibit—set to run for [ten] years—doesn't reveal anything not already available in books and on the [I]nternet. They also say people will appreciate magic more by knowing the secrets.").

[57] David Copperfield (1956–present), "[n]amed Magician of the Century and Magician of the Millenium." *See generally David Copperfield: Biography*, DAVIDCOPPERFIELD.COM, http://www.davidcopperfield.com/html/pdf/dc_biography.pdf (last visited Nov. 28, 2014).

[58] Associated Press, *supra* note 56.

[59] *See generally* Dean E. Murphy, *With Sadness, Houdini Artifact Collector Puts It on the Auction Block*, N.Y. TIMES (Oct. 29, 2004), http://www.nytimes.com/2004/10/29/national/29houdini.html?page wanted=print&position= (discussing financial challenges for the Outagamie organization).

[60] For basic information on the series, please see *Breaking the Magician's Code: Magic's Biggest Secrets Finally Revealed*, IMDB, http://www.imdb.com/title/tt0207261/?mode=desktop (last visited Nov. 28, 2014).

Masked Magician. Fox's specials were produced and sold successfully in large quantities, capturing worldwide interest.[61]

4. Shadows

The audience gazes upon a single rose resting upright in a small vase, its shadow cast upstage onto a white paper easel backdrop.[62] Illuminated by a single lamp, Teller begins to delicately and deliberately cut the shadows of the petals with a gleaming metallic knife.[63] Perfectly timed with his articulate cuts, the rose's real petals fall from the stem—petal by petal—in a seemingly impossible fashion.[64]

Part of his original repertoire since the 1970s, *Shadows* is widely considered Teller's seminal contribution to the art of magic.[65] In March of 2012, a friend sent Teller a YouTube video uploaded by Dutch magician Gerard Bakardy performing his own rendition of the trick—entitled *Rose and Her Shadows*—and offering to sell the method.[66] When Bakardy refused Teller's settlement proposals, which offered to pay Bakardy to cease all performances and sales of the trick, Teller filed a suit in federal court in Nevada, alleging copyright violation and unfair competition.[67] The

---

[61] Paul Brownfield, *Fox Isn't Disillusioned as Masked Magician Series Ends*, L.A. TIMES (Oct. 31, 1998), http://articles.latimes.com/1998/oct/31/entertainment/ca-37752 (Airing in November 1997, the first installment of the series drew 24.2 million viewers and was the highest-rated special ever on Fox).

[62] Penn & Teller, *Teller's Shadows Magic Trick*, YOUTUBE (Mar. 16, 2012), https://www.youtube.com/watch?v=etuVHEHF3FM.

[63] *Id.*

[64] *Id.*

[65] Chris Jones, *The Honor System*, ESQUIRE, Oct. 2012, at 139, 143, *available at* http://www.esquire.com/features/teller-magician-interview-1012.

[66] *Id* at 139.

[67] Complaint at 1, 6, Teller v. Dogge, 8 F. Supp. 3d 1228 (D. Nev.

federal court agreed that Teller's *Shadows* was a
dramatic work entitled to copyright protection.[68] The
court granted summary judgment for Teller on all
copyright claims (minus willful infringement) as it
found Bakardy had copied Teller's work.[69] This victory
for Teller marked a legal precedent, as it was the first
time since the Copyright Act was amended in 1976 that
a court held that a magic trick, although only through
its presentation as dramatic work, is eligible for
copyright protection.[70]

Acknowledging these and other exposures, industry
practitioners do not ignore their relevance to the
innovation ecology of the magic industry. However,
there remains a ferocious disagreement about the
damage exposure ultimately has on magic as a whole.
Some see it as a "minor annoyance," stating that
exposure is a catalyst of innovation obligating industry
professionals to invent new effects. Or, as previously
discussed, they advocate that the presentation is equally
important, making the secret simultaneously valuable
and valueless.[71] The other side vehemently argues that
wrongful exposure and stealing takes away one's
competitive advantage. In other words, if someone
writes a book, anyone and everyone can read and use
the literary text and the value of the book is not
depleted, as it is a non-rival resource. The same
principal does not apply to the intangible resource of
the magic secret. When the "Masked Magician" and R.J.

2014) (No. 2:12-cv-00591) (2012 WL 1259288).
    [68] Teller v. Dogge, 8 F. Supp. 3d 1228, 1233 (D. Nev. 2014).
    [69] *Id* at 1235–37.
    [70] Jessica McKinney, *Can Magic Be Copyrighted?: Teller's
Infringement Lawsuit Against Another Magician May Reveal the Answer*, 84
PAT., TRADEMARK, & COPYRIGHT J. 371, 371 (June 2012); *See* Janna
Brancolini, *Abracadabra!—Why Copyright Protection For Magic Is Not Just
An Illusion*, 33 LOY. L.A. ENT. L. REV. 103, 105 (2013).
    [71] *See* Loshin, *supra* note 2, at 130.

Reynolds expose the secret of a magic effect, their intentions of using the secret conflict with the intention of the original magician, and subsequently strip the secret of its value and arguably damage the original magician's competitive advantage.[72]

F. Policy Goals of I.P. Law

Article I, Section 8, Clause 8 of the Constitution empowers, yet limits, Congress to effectuate patent laws "[t]o promote the Progress of . . . useful Arts, by securing for limited Times to . . . Inventors the exclusive Right to their . . . Discoveries."[73] Within these bounds, Congress determines the best way to promote society's welfare.[74] A patent must be "worth to the public the embarrassment of an exclusive patent."[75] Put differently, a grant of patent rights should benefit the public.[76] When such a grant would be detrimental, it should be denied.[77] Congress, with its limited, discretionary power, restricts the grant of a patent to those instances best serving the public.[78] The requirements and restrictions serving this purpose—like disclosure, "the quid pro quo of the right to exclude"[79]—prove troublesome for magicians seeking protection.

---

[72] *Id.*

[73] U.S. CONST., art. I, § 8, cl. 8.

[74] 1 CARL MOY, MOY'S WALKER ON PATENTS § 1:30 (4th ed. 2009), *available at* WestlawNext Moy's Walker on Patents.

[75] Graham v. John Deere Co. of Kansas City, 383 U.S. 1, 9–10 (1966) ("As a member of the patent board for several years, Jefferson saw clearly the difficulty in 'drawing a line between the things which are worth to the public the embarrassment of an exclusive patent, and those which are not.' The board on which he served sought to draw such a line and formulated several rules which are preserved in Jefferson's correspondence.").

[76] MOY, *supra* note 74, at 1:27

[77] *Id.*

[78] Graham v. John Deere Co. of Kansas City, 383 U.S. 1, 6 (1966).

[79] Kewanee Oil Co. v. Bicron Corp., 416 U.S. 470, 484 (1974) (citing Universal Oil Co. v. Globe Co., 322 U.S. 471, 484 (1944)).

III. THE SHERLOCK STUDY

A. R.J.T.

The subject line of the email read, "Re: Sure."[80] He accepted the interview. On a whim, in August of 2010, my imaginative curiosity had drafted a formal interview request to one of the most iconic and influential prestidigitators to ever touch a deck of cards. The body of his email was as direct as his interview; "I'll speak with you" were his only words. I read the four words four times. He actually accepted my interview. Awestruck, I responded with the same terseness, "When would be best for you?" My phone rang almost instantaneously. The caller's location: Las Vegas, Nevada.

I lunged anxiously for the phone. The first words I had ever heard him speak were addressed to me, "Hello, Jared, this is Teller."[81] With sincere humility, he gently advised that I provoke him with questions.[82]

Exceedingly aware of both my good fortune and the finite time at my disposal, I attempted to evoke a candid and accessible answer to my original question. I asked, "Teller, do you believe that industry norms, relationships, codes of ethics, and self-regulating institutions are effective in preserving magic's secrets?" He responded expeditiously, "In regard to preserving magic's secrets in the absence of law," Teller continued, "I truly don't think that someone learning a magic

---

[80] E-mail from Raymond Joseph Teller, Professional Magician, to author (Aug. 6, 2010, 4:51 p.m. CST) (on file with author).

[81] *See* Telephone Interview with Raymond Joseph Teller, *supra* note 12.

[82] Teller is highly regarded by academics and critics alike for his work as a comedian, writer, and playwright and for his contributions to atheism, libertarianism, free-market economics, and scientific skepticism.

secret is going to put anyone out of work. I think that's the only real ethical argument that you could make." There was a major problem with this response. At the time of this interview, I was concluding my tenth and final week of research for the business ethics fellowship that prompted this study. Worse yet, I believed him.

His words unexpectedly shifted my perspective. While magicians have very little ownership over their creations, the magic industry continues to flourish publicly. Exposure of magic secrets may be hindering job creation, but it does not seem to be causing widespread job loss in the magic industry. However, the absence of rules (laws) may be allowing the corruption of honor. Sometimes, the approach to enforcing ethical challenges is by establishing rules, when what should be considered is what type of people inventors and magicians should be.

In my final hours of collecting information on the regulation of intellectual property, Teller's response revealed a new ethical variable concerning the notion of character of a good magician. On August 6, 2010, two years prior to his own suit against Bakardy, Teller's response indirectly suggested that an evolution of creative copyright law might reduce performance theft and could be fiscally and morally supportive to magic's practitioners.

B. Study Design

Though patent law seemingly offers attractive protections—exclusive rights for twenty years from filing[83]—in reality, seeking such protection is fraught

---

[83] Emily M. Hinkens, *Patent Term Adjustment and Terminal Disclaimers: Are the Terms of Patents Being Decided Ad Hoc?*, 94 MARQ. L. REV. 375, 377 (2010) ("In general, a patent applied for today will have a term that ends twenty years from the date on which the patent application was filed.").

with difficulties. Filing fees[84] and statutory hurdles of subject matter,[85] novelty,[86] nonobviousness,[87] and adequate disclosure[88] may act to bar magic practitioners from this avenue. Further still, if the application published before issuance, the disclosure requirement would provide enough detail for enterprising competitors to design around the claims before the inventor acquired enforceable rights.[89] As discussed in the next Part, patent rights fail to protect magic practitioners.

While copyright law will not protect a magician's trick for being a "procedure" or "process,"[90] the recent *Teller* decision suggests it will protect his or her performance. Copyright protection extends to "original works of authorship fixed in any tangible medium of expression."[91] Common protected works include songs, movies, and artwork, but the 1976 Act also provided for the protection of choreographic works like those created by dancers. To register their work with the U.S. Copyright Office, dancers may present either a film

---

[84] *See generally United States Patent and Trademark Office Fee Schedule*, UNITED STATES PATENT AND TRADEMARK OFFICE, http://www.uspto.gov/web/offices/ac/qs/ope/ fee010114.htm (last updated Nov. 4, 2014) (listing fee structure associated with filing patent applications).

[85] *See* 35 U.S.C. § 101 (2012).

[86] *See id.* at § 102.

[87] *See id.* at § 103.

[88] *See id.* at § 112.

[89] *See* William F. Lee & Lawrence P. Cogswell, III, *Understanding and Addressing the Unfair Dilemma Created by the Doctrine of Willful Patent Infringement*, 41 HOUS. L. REV. 393, 405 (2004) (citing Yarway Corp. v. Eur-Control USA, Inc., 775 F.2d 268 (Fed. Cir. 1985) ("One of the benefits of a patent system is its so-called 'negative incentive' to 'design around' a competitor's products, even when they are patented, thus bringing a steady flow of innovations to the marketplace. It should not be discouraged by punitive damage awards except in cases where conduct is so obnoxious as clearly to call for them.")).

[90] 17 U.S.C. § 102(b) (2012).

[91] *Id.* at § 102(a).

recording or a precise description by way of either
written text or accepted "dance notation systems such as
Labanotation, Sutton Movement Shorthand, or Benesh
Notation."[92]

Trade secret law, too, offers no harbor for
magicians, as it is broader yet weaker than patent
protection.[93] Trade secret law maintains "commercial
ethics and the encouragement of invention," holding
that "good faith and honest, fair dealing, is the very life
and spirit of the commercial world."[94] Protecting
anything—kept in confidence—that may yield a
competitive advantage,[95] "trade secret law does not
forbid the discovery of the trade secret by fair and
honest means, e.g., independent creation or reverse
engineering."[96] As with patents and copyrights, the
limits of trade secret law do not align with the needs of
magic practitioners.

As we have seen, neither copyright law, patent law,
trade secret law, moral persuasion, nor industry self-
regulating institutions offer significant protection for
magicians' intellectual property. The research
conducted in this study is exploratory. While exposures
and theft have been well documented, little has been
published on the subject of ethics and intellectual
property in the magic industry. The study being used is

---

[92] U.S. COPYRIGHT OFFICE, FL-119, DRAMATIC WORKS: CHOREOGRAPHY,
PANTOMIMES, AND SCRIPTS (2010), *available at*
http://www.copyright.gov/fls/fl119.pdf.

[93] *See* Kewanee Oil Co. v. Bicron Corp., 416 U.S. 470, 489–90 (1974)
("Trade secret law provides far weaker protection in many respects
than the patent law."). *See also infra* Part IV.A.3.

[94] *Kewanee Oil Co.*, 416 U.S. at 481–82 (quoting National Tube Co.
v. Eastern Tube Co., 13–23 Ohio C.C. 468, 470 (1902), *aff'd*, 70 N.E. 1127
(1903)).

[95] *See* CORP COUNS GD TO PROTECTING TR SECRETS § 1:1
("[G]enerally, a trade secret is any information that is not generally
known and that could give a company a competitive advantage.").

[96] *Kewanee Oil Co.*, 416 U.S. at 490.

most akin to an ethnographic and interview hybrid design as the study uses historical and popular text as a foundation to interview top practitioners in search of narrative based off of their experience to analyze the industry.

C. Results of Interviews

"Magicians are actively taught that innovation has no value. It frustrates the process."[97]

Jim Steinmeyer strongly believes that the challenges associated with preserving magic's secrets in the absence of law is directly related to magicians themselves having no value for the magic secret itself or the art of magic.[98] Mr. Steinmeyer said disappointedly, "[t]he world of magicians does not teach people to value creativity. It's weird that the world of magic does not perpetuate any value for these things."[99]

Lawyer and historian David Ben agrees, "[m]agicians don't value their own heritage and experts. . . . If we won't pay for it, why should the public?"[100] Mr. Ben is speaking in reference to practitioners buying stolen rip-off illusions at a discounted rate instead of paying the originator of the idea.[101] Mr. Ben foreshadows a systematic harm as a result of audience dissatisfaction from witnessing less than impressive performances. Much like a class of adolescent students who see through a teacher's false sense of authority immediately, audiences too will see through an imitative and poorly designed performance with great ease. In presenting this quality of work, these magicians

---

[97] *See* Telephone Interview with Jim Steinmeyer, *supra* note 16.
[98] *Id.*
[99] *Id.*
[100] Telephone Interview with David Ben, Attorney and Magician, Magicana, (Aug. 3, 2010).
[101] *Id.*

cheapen the craft of magic.

Challenging the interview candidates to offer a solution produced as many theoretical ideas and solutions as there are problems. Interviewees spoke humbly from their own areas of interest.

This study's legal source, Jacob Loshin (one of the earliest published authors of an academic legal exploration of the magic industry's intellectual property challenges), suggests the following ideas:

> Judges ought to be more willing to heed the role of norms and idiosyncrasies in the application of IP law. . . . Yet, the issue remains a comparative one, and formal IP law does not fare well in this comparison. Even if legal protection could be strengthened, such efforts would have an unfortunate chilling effect on magic's vibrant and free-flowing marketplace of ideas. Rather than investing in lawyers, magicians might be better off investing in their own institutions.[102]

In agreement with Jacob Loshin, Jim Steinmeyer expresses hope that clubs at the local and national level could heavily incorporate education on the ethics of intellectual property and the value of creativity in their charter.[103] Teller offered a different kind of recommendation to encourage other practitioners to come up with original ideas:

> Hate all other magicians. Salvador Dali said, '[t]he first step of any artist is to

---

[102] See Loshin, *supra* note 2, at 140.
[103] See Telephone Interview with Jim Steinmeyer, *supra* note 16.

learn to hate all of the other artists.' And
hate is a very, very, good fuel for coming
up with ideas. It is a good strong emotion,
and it is not difficult to get. In magic's
case you only have to look at 86% of the
world's performers, and the hate will be
so intense that you will want to go out and
react against that.[104]

While his suggestion is more philosophical than
systematical, it readdresses the notion that the magic
industry needs to approach its ethical challenges not
from a basis of rules and laws, but character and values.
Teller's attraction to this quote may derive from its
intensity; this quote is intended to make those who
adopt it burn with a desire to always be better—a
quality that Teller has practiced in his professional
career since the beginning. When asked whether or not
an individual can teach another to be creative, Teller
did not think so, but he expressed that it can at least be
demanded.[105]

Assuming there were industry practices to provide
the necessary information, is it possible to teach
someone ethical behavior and creativity with the desire
to generate a value for these qualities within the art of
magic? Subpart C of the following section will examine
the feasibility of Jim Steinmeyer, Jacob Loshin, and
David Ben's ideas.

IV. LIMITATIONS OF INTELLECTUAL PROPERTY LAW & THE INDUSTRY'S RESPONSE

A. *Limitations of Existing IP Law*

The previous sections of this study have uncovered

---

[104] *See* Telephone Interview with Raymond Joseph Teller, *supra* note 12.
[105] *Id.*

how the free transfer of ideas positively influences the magic industry's ecology and innovation. Conversely, this paper has also gone some distance to illustrate the challenges and dangers. This section will briefly outline the advantages and disadvantages of three primary forms of IP law.

1. Patents

As discussed above, patent law sets out certain requirements to ensure a net public benefit when granting patent rights. Though a patent proffers the right to exclude others from making, using, or selling for a limited time,[106] a potential inventor must adequately disclose the device to the public.[107] The enablement provision of 35 U.S.C. Section 112 requires the patent to describe the invention in a way that that "one skilled in the art can make and use the claimed invention."[108] One can quickly deduce how this protocol might be successful if it were protecting the manufacturing process of a hammer but counterproductive for the protection of a magic illusion:

> In order for magicians to protect their intellectual property through patent law, they must make their secrets available to the public. They must thus be willing to destroy much of what makes that property valuable. Consequently, few magicians now patent their innovations.[109]

---

[106] 35 U.S.C. § 271 (2012) ("[W]hoever without authority makes, uses, offers to sell, or sells any patented invention, within the United States or imports into the United States any patented invention during the term of the patent therefor, infringes the patent.").

[107] See 35 U.S.C. § 112 (2012).

[108] MPEP § 2164 (9th ed. Rev. 1, Mar. 2014).

[109] See Loshin, supra note 2, at 132. But see U.S. Patent No.

For a conjuror to patent an illusion in the interest of protecting its secret, he would first have to reveal it, which interferes with the conjuror's original purpose of applying for patent.[110]

2. *Copyright*

To secure a copyright for a material is for the originator individual or organization to acquire "the exclusive legal right . . . to print, publish, perform, film, or record literary, artistic, or musical material, and to authorize others to do the same."[111] F. Jay Dougherty[112] explains that copyright law differs from patent law as it does not protect a work's procedure, process, system, or operation:

> The ideas behind an illusion and the devices and useful methods used to implement it are not protectable by copyright. Words and short phrases are not viewed as sufficiently original to merit copyright protection. Common scenes and expressive elements that are indispensable, or at least standard, in depicting an idea are unprotectable 'scenes à faire.' 'Stock' characters, standard character types without original creative delineation, are treated similarly. Copyright has limited application to

---

5,354,238, filed June 7, 1993 (patenting a levitation illusion designed by John Gaughan but famously performed by David Copperfield). Gaughan reportedly filed the patent against Copperfield's wishes.

[110] *See* Loshin, *supra* note 2, at 132.

[111] NEW OXFORD AMERICAN DICTIONARY 376 (2d ed. 2005).

[112] F. Jay Dougherty is the Director of the Entertainment and Media Law Institute and Concentration Program, as well as a professor, at Loyola Law School in Los Angeles, California. *See F. Jay Dougherty,* FAC. & ADMIN., http://www.lls.edu/aboutus/facultyadministration/faculty/ facultylistc-d/doughertyfjay/ (last visited Nov. 29, 2014).

literary and visual material that is utilitarian. Useful methods, processes and articles are all excluded from copyright protection.[113]

Dougherty points out that one could publish and copyright a book that reveals the process of how to accomplish or build a magic effect, but the methodology itself is still not protected.[114] Magic pieces occupy a grey area incapable of a pure and effective classification between expression and function, copyright and patent.[115]

3. Trade Secret

Lastly, magicians have attempted to employ trade secret law to protect their ideas; generally, these too have been unsuccessful. Confidential information or trade secrets are formulas, processes, designs, or specific information that give an individual or organization an economic advantage over competitors.[116] However, this economic advantage is only protectable if strict trade secret stipulations are followed.

Trade secret law stipulates that liability for violating a trade secret is only applicable to individuals or organizations that obtain the secret through theft or an inability to maintain secrecy.[117] An example would be an

---

[113] *See* Dougherty, *supra* note 3, at 102.

[114] *Id.* at 104.

[115] *Id.* at 108.

[116] Kewanee Oil Co. v. Bicron Corp., 416 U.S. 470, 474–75 (1974) (quoting RESTATEMENT (FIRST) OF TORTS § 757 at comment b (1939)).

[117] Donald M. Zupanec, *Disclosure of Trade Secret as Abandonment of Secrecy*, 92 A.L.R. 3d 138, §2(b) (1979) ("[T]here are three elements in a cause of action for the tort of misappropriation of a trade secret: (1) the existence of a trade secret; (2) disclosure of the trade secret to the defendant in confidence, or the defendant's acquisition of the trade secret by improper means; and (3) injury to the plaintiff resulting from the defendant's use of the trade secret.").

assistant or technician who exposes the secret to
another magician. Magicians are able to manage this
requirement modestly through the use of secrecy
agreements.[118] Therefore, should another party simply
discover the secret or acquire the secret in good faith,
trade secret law will no longer protect the secret.

Another stipulation of trade secret law that furthers
the magic industry is that it requires secret-holders to
make efforts to maintain secrecy. Should a secret be
revealed within the confines of an industry, the courts
no longer qualify it as a secret. If the secret is published
in magicians' trade journals, books, or if it has been
shared informally among circles of magicians, it is
likely to lose its protection through trade secret law.[119]
Jacob Loshin explains the magic industry's
incompatibility with traditional trade secret law in
greater detail:

> The fundamental difficulty with trade
> secret law rests on the fact that courts
> tend to view intellectual property as
> inhering in individuals or in firms, but
> not in industries. This stems from the
> traditional conception of trade secret law
> as a means of incentivizing innovators by
> giving them a competitive advantage over

---

[118] David Copperfield requires those involved with his shows to
sign the following agreement: "I . . . understand that in the course of
my employment I may become entrusted with the secrets of the
illusions and magic in the David Copperfield Show. I realize that this
is privileged information and that a great deal of time, energy, and
money has been spent in the development of these illusions. I
promise never to discuss these secrets and methods with any other
person, relative or friend. The secrets of the Magic of David
Copperfield are the proprietary rights of David Copperfield and
under penalty of severe fine I agree to cooperate with my total
secrecy." DAVID COPPERFIELD, SECRECY AGREEMENT (1998) (copy on
file with author); *see also* Loshin, *supra* note 2, at 133.

[119] *See* Loshin, *supra* note 2, at 133.

their direct competitors in the industry.
Yet, the magic community's innovation
ecology works differently. The threat of
exposure results primarily from
competition by industry outsiders, not by
insiders. Disclosure of secrets to
insiders—[that is], to fellow magicians—
thus does not void the intention to keep
something secret. [120]

Should the magic industry desire to seek full
protection under trade secret legislation, practitioners
must be willing to sacrifice the valuable widespread
sharing of ideas between peer magicians and designers
to reduce the chance of ideas leaking to outsiders. The
harsh reality of protecting intellectual property in the
magic industry is that no single method of legal
protection is wholly effective. Trade secret protection
requires the industry to undergo drastic changes to its
already established innovation ecology, patent law
protects intellectual property from theft but not
exposure, and copyright law can protect sufficiently
original routines but not the method, devices, or
operations within the routines.[121]

Yet, the lack of legal protection has only stood as a
minor obstacle for professional magicians as they
innovate and develop their unique craft. Outside the
purview of the law, scholars have observed how
magicians have developed an informal set of industry
norms that have a positive effect on controlling
exposure, limiting industry access to secrets and
punishing violations. The following sections will
explore various ways industry practitioners have gone
some distance in protecting magic's secrets without the

---

[120] *Id.* at 134.
[121] *Id.*

assistance of the law.

B. *Industry Norms*

Magicians quickly gain awareness of informal industry norms that help control exposure of secrets. The industry's informal intellectual property norms are fairly successful at controlling usage and exposure. In a 2010 essay, Mr. Loshin states that the first set of norms exists to credit the inventors: "(1) The first person to publish or prominently perform a trick gets credit for inventing it, [and] (2) [p]eople are encouraged to publish improvements and new versions of previously shared work, but derivative works should acknowledge and credit the original."[122]

The importance of the above industry norms is to promote sharing for a rich innovation ecology in the magic industry. Honor and popularity often come with the invention of a new piece of magic; many conjurors seek to cultivate their reputation through the invention of new routines, methodologies, and presentations. The second set of industry norms Jacob Loshin summarizes governs the usage of new ideas after their conception and creation:

> (1) If a secret method or dramatic presentation has not been widely shared, published, or sold, nobody else can use it.

> (2) If a secret method has been widely shared, published, or sold, it may be used freely.

> (3) If a dramatic presentation has been widely shared, published, or sold, it may be used, but it will be considered bad form to do so without creative adaptation.

---

[122] *Id.* at 136.

(4) If a trick was originally published
or shared but has not been used for a long
time, the person who re-discovers it
should be treated as if she invented it.[123]

The norms that govern a new idea allow the creator to
control whether they will perform the piece exclusively,
as well as promoting the discovery of old, dormant
ideas. Finally, all practitioners understand the most
steadfast rule is to protect secrets from exposure to the
general public.

Loshin argues that any exposure at all damages the
value of the secret as an intangible resource. Incidents
such as the Outagamie Historical Society in Appleton
Wisconsin[124] illustrate these intellectual property norms
being enforced informally. When the museum chose to
reveal its secrets, board members, historians, museum
property owners, and patrons associated with industry
organizations resigned in great numbers echoing the
vow to disassociate themselves from anyone who
betrayed the code of ethics. Financial trouble as a result
of failing patronage threatened the museum in a way
that intellectual property laws could not.

There is widespread disagreement about whether or
not moral persuasion, such as the aforementioned
industry norms, is effective and valuable to protecting
the craft of magic. Narratives from the pages of trade
journals, discovered stories by amateur magician
writers, and private correspondence between
practitioners offers evidence that moral persuasion and
industry norms can occasionally govern and punish
improper use of a magic secret.

Admired American illusionist, and past president of

---

[123] *Id.* at 136–37.
[124] *See supra*, Part II.E.2.

The Society of American Magicians, Walter "Zaney" Blaney[125] shares a personal account of intellectual property theft:

> "[A] company in England, Illusions Plus, was selling still another rip-off of my illusion. When I protested to the owner, James Antony, he told me there was no court in the world, which could stop him from what he was doing. I explained I had no intention of going to court. I instead simply told my many friends in [London's] Magic Circle about it . . . When the word spread, soon Mr. Antony 'had a problem.' As things turned out, there was indeed a court which promptly put him out of business . . . the bankruptcy court."[126]

Often, the top illusion builders make their income solely on the sale of intellectual property. They profit nothing from the performance or the creation of the prop, only the design, process, or device methodology. Mr. Blaney's reputation alone commanded the attention of professional magic practitioners worldwide. In this particular case (possibly coincidentally), practitioners sought affordable creations from alternative reputable dealers. James Antony's bankruptcy halted the manufacturing of his rip-off illusions and subsequently drove magician consumer interest looking to purchase Mr. Blaney's creations back to its original source, Mr. Walter Blaney himself.

---

[125] *See* WALTERBLANEY.COM, http://www.walterblaney.com/illusions/bio.html (last visited Nov. 19, 2014).
[126] Open Letter from Walter Blaney to the Magic Community (Nov. 2002) (on file with author).

The *Chinese Linking Rings* are a classic of magic. In the traditional presentation of the effect, a set of solid metal rings appear to link and unlink, seamlessly passing through one another forming chains and patterns. A few years ago, a very innovative and respected comedy magician (who will remain unidentified) seeking to re-design the effect for contemporary audiences, created a new variation entitled *The Linking Coat Hangers*. This modified variation on the classic Chinese ring routine accomplishes the same visual effect, but is made with coat hangers. After a popular reception from audiences and magicians alike, this unidentified magician began manufacturing and selling the routine for approximately $100 (generally an accepted value for a highly entertaining seven minutes of entertainment). The routine was a hit, and sales were high. Shortly thereafter, a Midwest magic dealer began creating and selling the same routine, defending his decision to do so by claiming that the respected comedy magician did not invent the linking coat hangers. While this is partly true, the linking coat hangers previously existed; it is also partly false as the new linking coat hanger routine employed a completely different method. The inventive magician urged the dealer to stop without success. What finally forced the dealer to stop was a phone call from now deceased magic legend Jay Marshall.[127] The pressure of losing Jay Marshall as a

---

[127] Jay Marshall (1919–2005) was an American magician known as the "Dean of American Magicians." His sixty-year career highlights include being a regular on the Ed Sullivan Show as well as the first person to open for Sinatra in Las Vegas. Douglas Martin, *Jay Marshall, 85, the Dean of Magic, is Dead*, N.Y. TIMES (May 13, 2005), http://www.nytimes.com/2005/05/13/arts/13marshall.html.

The phone call with Marshall was reportedly brief and gentle. Jay explained to the dealer that he had a problem. The unsuspecting dealer's attention was now piqued as he asked what the problem was. Jay went on to casually tell the dealer that he was both friends with

friend quickly ended the sale of the rip-off coat hanger routine. This story reveals the strong social pressure that remains active in the magic community. But like the norms and legal methods mentioned previously in this study, social pressure as an industry norm is unreliable. Violators looking to expose the secret or its manufacture would not be subject to the same social pressure or industry norms; one such example would be a person that is not part of a fraternity of magicians uploading a rip-off of the routine on the Internet.

But respected magic historians like David Ben, Teller, and Jim Steinmeyer argue that the moral authority presented above doesn't mean much of anything.[128] Ben confidently addresses the subject stating that the moral persuasion that exists in the magic industry is unreliable and that the "stakes are so low" that it does not matter.[129] "Most of the large pieces," he says, "are protected from the industry by the dollar value that's assigned to actually create or perform them correctly."[130]

The wildly popular *Masked Magician* FOX special aided in the magic industry's realization that neither law nor industry norms are entirely successful.[131] New

---

him (the dealer) and with the unidentified comedy magician, but that at that moment Jay couldn't be a friend with both of them. The dealer responded quickly and humbly that only two more coat hanger routines remained in his shop, and that once they sold, he would never manufacture one again. Jay Marshall thanked the dealer, and shortly after the coat hangers were once again exclusively sold by the comedy magician. Telephone Interview with Stan Allen, Founding Editor of MAGIC Magazine (Aug. 4, 2010).

[128] *E.g.*, T.A. Waters, *Jim Steinmeyer: Deviser of Illusions*, MAGIC MAGAZINE   (Sept.   1996), http://www.jimsteinmeyer.com/profile/magic.html.

[129] Telephone Interview with David Ben, *supra* note 100.

[130] *Id.*

[131] Paul Brownfield, *Fox Isn't Disillusioned as Masked Magician Series Ends*, L.A.   TIMES   (Oct.   31,   1998),

institutional and administrative strategies in the realm of self-regulation were born.

Self-regulating institutions are popular in industries that operate outside the purview of the law, such as the culinary and fashion industries.[182] The magic industry has only given rise to one such institution: the World Alliance of Magicians (W.A.M.).[133] Founded in response to the most recent major exposure on the FOX network, *The Masked Magician*, W.A.M. founder Walter Blaney recruited some of the brightest minds in magic in an effort to protect the secrecy of magic effects worldwide.[184] The organization saw limited success. Most notably, W.A.M. members persuaded major corporate sponsors of the FOX magic revealed special, such as American Airlines, Coca-Cola, Kellogg, and 3M, to pull their ads from the programming.[135] This action proved financially frustrating for FOX executives in the production of the fourth season.[186] In the end there were only three sponsors remaining, and the rest of the ads were FOX programming commercials.[137]

The members also assembled a book that summarized all of the legal theories that might be used to protect secrecy with the purpose to help the performers, creators, and manufacturers of magic

---

http://articles.latimes.com/1998/oct/31/entertainment/ca-37752.

[182]   *E.g.,*   U.S.   FASHION   INDUSTRY   ASSOCIATION, http://www.usfashionindustry.com (last visited November 19, 2014).

[133] W.A.M. was an organization dedicated to preserving the wonder and amazement of the Magical Arts for the general public, protecting the secrets of the magic profession from exposure, and reinforcing the positive contributions of the Magical Arts to society. WORLD ALLIANCE OF MAGICIANS, http://www.geniimagazine.com/magicpedia/World_Alliance_of_Mag icians (last visited November 29, 2014).

[184] Telephone Interview with Walter Blaney (Aug. 4, 2010).

[135] *Id.*

[136] *Id.*

[137] *Id.*

secrets understand and appreciate the choices available to them. W.A.M. unexpectedly folded shortly after the FOX network cancelled programming of the *Masked Magician* show.[138] In response to why the organization folded, Walter Blaney said simply that in regard to the FOX network, "The need was gone."[139] He added that the second purpose was to protect the inventors, but individual industry practitioners were not interested in supporting the organization financially. Mr. Blaney concluded, "W.A.M. members just ran out of gas in their attempts to solicit capital to sustain the organization's operations."[140]

Developing an industry self-regulation system raises several concerns for professionals who make their living off the sale of intellectual property. Questions arise as to who will legislate, how this legislation will take place, and how the rules will be enforced. W.A.M.'s lack of support from individual practitioners indicated concerns shared presently by some of the most recognized names in magic. Jim Steinmeyer stated candidly in an interview:

> It's only the intellectual property that I make money on. So the notion that [ten] people decide whether I should make money on a creation is frightening to me. I look at the list of names, of the grey beards of our industry, and I say I don't trust them. I don't trust them as a group, I don't trust them to cast judgment on my work. I know my part of this industry very well. I know the history, I know how ideas were developed, and I think I know

---

[138] *Id.*
[139] *Id.*
[140] *Id.*

more about it than those people do.[141]

Lawyer, Toronto University professor, and world-renowned sleight of hand artist David Ben seconds Jim Steinmeyer's anxiety:

> I don't think there are enough people, if there is anyone, who can actually speak with enough authority—from true knowledge—of how ownership of credit should be allocated. I can't imagine it being done. The whole history is so intertwined.[142]

But intricacies of an invention's origin are not the only reason magic's top practitioners are opposed to a self-regulating institution. Professionals feared that a representative body of magicians emotionally (and publicly) opposed to the show would only drum up further interest for the network's specials. As the old adage goes, any publicity is good publicity. Hollywood television tabloids seemed to agree as the notorious TMZ broadcast included coverage of the W.A.M. versus FOX controversy in their programming. Los Angeles illusion designer and manufacturer John Gaughan[143] opposed W.A.M.'s public relations strategy.[144] In a left-

---

[141] Telephone Interview with Jim Steinmeyer, *supra* note 16.

[142] *See* Telephone Interview with David Ben, *supra* note 100.

[143] John Gaughan is an American illusion builder who has spent a career building large-scale illusions for artists like Jim Morrison, Elton John, Michael Jackson, Alice Cooper, Cher, and more. *See generally* Stephanie Rosenbloom, *Magicians Ask What's Up His Sleeve?*, N.Y. TIMES (May 18, 2008), http://www.nytimes.com/2008/05/18/fashion/18magic.html?pagewanted=all.

[144] Telephone Interview with John Gaughan, Illusion Builder and Inventor (Jul. 5, 2010). Gaughan recalled a story of a strip club's grand opening in a rural area of Glendale, California. The club's management made placards complaining about the club in local neighborhoods, and they hired people to picket outside the building.

handed way, W.A.M.'s efforts may have put fuel on the fire. But ultimately, the FOX network specials lost their audience along with their motivation to continue pursuing the project, and so did the World Alliance of Magicians.

Eight out of the nine interviewees for this study, who all hold reputations as one of the industry's top sources of innovative magic and historical analysis, regretfully conceded that they simply have no idea how an industry institution or system that regulates ownership of magic's intellectual property could work. All eight admitted that while they had come to this conclusion, they had done so selfishly. The optimism has simply faded.

Skepticism of who would govern, legislate, and enforce new industry regulations emanate from a time-honored mistrust of other practitioners. Thirst for magic's secrets breeds a dangerous self-interest, even in the most seemingly innocuous conjuror. Jim Steinmeyer adds with a quality of resolve:

> The notion of forming some kind of grand alliance to protect these things within the industry is doomed, because the industry itself wants to steal these things constantly and wants every justification to do that.[145]

Steinmeyer describes an unethical mentality seemingly unique to professionals in the magic industry. In music there are people and organizations that take it upon themselves to protect their work, in magic it is the same people that want to take the ideas.

John remarks with a tone of obviousness that he recognizes is long overdue, "It was free publicity, and everyone bit on it."

[145] *See* Telephone Interview with Jim Steinmeyer, *supra* note 16.

While there is strong disagreement as to whether or not keeping a secret from the public, or from other industry insiders, prevents or provokes systematic harm to the industry's ecology. Everyone enthusiastically agrees that they are in the same business, the business of producing shows so audiences might be amazed and entertained:

> Magic is an art. People work a very long time to invent, create, and perfect the music, choreography, costumes, staging, and assistant work to create a theatrical experience. And when you abuse the one Achilles heel of magic, the secret, everything else is forgotten—it was all for nothing.[146]

While surely an exaggeration, his statement gracefully acknowledges the bigger picture. If there is truth in Teller's belief that someone learning a magic effect is not going to put anyone out of work, and the great majority of practitioners are ultimately under the opinion that their work is about the final presentation, the intangible magic secret becomes only a portion of the overall production value and audience experience. However, as this study suggests, the audience's experience at a magic show is enhanced with their inability to understand how a trick works. Should a conjuror aspire to both protect magic's secrets and entertain, one could argue that it would require the individual to have a fidelity to the art of magic. As a result of this faithfulness, the practitioner would benefit professionally from satisfied audiences and the industry would benefit systematically from an ethically healthier ecology.

As illustrated within this study, preserving magic's

---

[146] *See* Telephone Interview with Walter Blaney, *supra* note 134.

secrets requires discipline and astounding audiences demands creativity, not imitation. Interviews with the industry's top practitioners suggest that imitators, and their lack of creativity, are to blame for damages to intellectual property and the entire innovation ecology of the magic industry. Teller said in his interview that while imitators can be successful, he points out a dangerous side-effect: "The result however, is that because people are at least amazed by their imitation, they credit these magicians as being participants in an art form; meaning that often the people that get into magic are the scum of entertainment."[147] If this is true, there exists a direct correlation between a magician or inventor's creativity and an audience's satisfaction.

C. Difficulties in Applying/Regulating a Professional Code of Ethics

The idea that analysis would help a magician or inventor acquire value for creativity and the magic secret, who does not already possess it to some degree, is a highly questionable one. In the interest of applying this theory, the following discussion section will offer a few thoughts and criticisms to the suggestions of the interview subjects; but please note the observations will be shallow. A comprehensive and philosophical exploration of honor and character is beyond the scope of this Note.

This study suggests that in the absence of law, practitioners' attempts to govern intellectual property by controlling theft and exposure while motivating creativity are polluted by an overwhelming self-interest and complicated by practitioners who allegedly do not value the art of magic or the secret itself. If internal institutions   followed   one   of   Mr.   Steinmeyer's

---

[147] Telephone Interview with Raymond Joseph Teller, *supra* note 12.

suggestions to include ethics education in magician's civil society club meetings, the complication remains whether or not it is even possible to communicate these values, and furthermore, see them put into practice.

1. Feasibility of Ethics Education Governed by Industry Group

Using history as a tool to determine whether this theory is feasible, Teller suggested an examination of Aristotle and Socrates.[148] Aristotle wrote arguably the most lucid analysis that has ever been written about the theater. In the *Poetics*, the theories about drama that he describes are about as accurate as one could be about theories scholars present today about playwriting and theater. But when one looks through his works, they do not include a single play. Similarly, Socrates in *The Symposium* talked about his frustration with finding people who actually knew what they were talking about. Socrates went to the poets, thinking that since they created amazing poems, they would therefore be wise. But since the poets were unable to explain their poems, he concluded that they were unwise. But then again, they were able to compose those poems and Socrates could not.[149] Just as a screenwriter teaches expensive and thought-provoking classes on the theory of screenwriting while having never written a major motion picture, these stories of Aristotle and Socrates serve as a reminder that the actual process of teaching a subjective quality or skill is terribly challenging.

Contemporary comparisons might be the tasks of teaching someone how to be funny, or perhaps harder yet, how to be a good father. There is no quick list to teach either of these qualities; one could offer an individual some rules but mechanically the rules or

---

[148] *Id.*
[149] *Id.*

suggestions would not work. To be funny one must watch comedians, and to be a good father one must watch and experience a good father.[150] To be an honorable magician or inventor, one must watch and experience magicians and inventors who practice their craft with an unwavering fidelity to the art of magic as a theatrical medium.

2. Creating a Code of Honor

When Jim Steinmeyer expressed his desire for magicians to value the magic secret and the art itself,[151] he talked about magicians having an intrinsic commitment to the art of magic, a fidelity to the magic secret, and ultimately a sense of honor. Honor is, more than anything, a standard of conduct and an adherence to what is right. Professor of Philosophy at the College of Saint Benedict and Saint John's University Anthony Cunningham says, "When we talk about honor, there is your honor, there is my honor, and then there is just honor. Honor is much bigger than any of us."[152] This idea implies that when thinking about what type of people inventors and magicians should be, having a strong sense of honor for one's craft demands that one quit at the point where they need to sell out to survive. If Mr. Antony adhered to a code of honor to the art of magic, he would have electively gone out of business before resorting to stealing Walter Blaney's intellectual property.[153]

The complicated temptation, for those that attempt to adhere to this intrinsic commitment, is how a new professional magician with limited resources balances

---

[150] *Id.*

[151] *See* Telephone Interview with Jim Steinmeyer, *supra* note 16.

[152] Interview with Anthony Cunningham, Professor of Philosophy, Coll. of St. Benedict & St. Johns Univ., in Collegeville, Minn. (Aug. 11, 2010).

[153] *See* Telephone Interview with Walter Blaney, *supra* note 134.

the need to make money while simultaneously retaining a fidelity to the art. The pursuit to honor the art of magic must always overcome moments of weakness where a magician might be filled with a begrudging envy of another magician's performance or creation.

The martial arts have accomplished the feat of educating participants in a standard of conduct. Fighters in the martial arts bow before they begin, an act that reminds the participants that they are merely a conduit, a way that the art can be expressed. "In the martial arts you study a code of honor, as the art you are learning could be deadly. The code implicitly states that you will use martial arts only for good."[154]

Should a martial arts master have a fatal move, it is unlikely that she would share the move with her students right away; first she must determine if the students are trustworthy.[155] Once she reveals the methodology to accomplish the move, she must trust the recipient, as she is now unable to prevent the recipient from using the move.[156]

Furthermore, the martial arts comparison might be applied to the relationship between an innovative illusion designer, a magician, and the magic secret or creation. The magician must be trustworthy for the inventor to reveal the methodology to accomplish the new illusion, as the inventor is now unable to prevent the magician from using or protecting the secret improperly or ensure that the resale of an apparatus will include the builder's royalty or the illusion's performance rights. Likewise, magicians adhering to honor would be required to embrace the idea that they

---

[154] *See* Interview with Anthony Cunningham, *supra* note 152.
[155] *Id.*
[156] *Id.*

are merely participants in an art form that is much larger than they are.

3. Challenges

a. Peer Criticisms

Illusion builder and inventor John Guaghan, who believes the magic industry's ethical challenges are much worse in Europe and China, raises a practical concern about excommunicating those who unethically acquire and rip-off intellectual property.[157] Mr. Gaughan shared, reluctantly, "[a] few years ago, I discovered an amusement park in Germany that was using some of my creations. My portfolio revealed that half were properly acquired, and the other half of the props were not obtained from designated builders, nor had they acquired the appropriate performing rights."[158]

Illusion design is a business that generates a very lumpy income from project to project. Mr. Gaughan questions the sanity of turning away such a large client that may produce future business.[159] Daniel Summer[160] agrees, citing a similar story where he ultimately conceded to an unlicensed[161] European builder, by allowing him to continue building substandard reproductions of Mr. Summer's apparatus in return for his full royalty and performance rights.

b. Consumer Perspective

Jim Steinmeyer offers practitioners of magic the following motivation to protect their secrets:

> [M]agicians   are   notoriously   close-

---

[157] *See* Telephone Interview with John Gaughan, *supra* note 144.
[158] *Id.*
[159] *Id.*
[160] *See supra* note 22.
[161] And in this author's humble opinion: shady.

> mouthed, but the real reason we guard our secrets is not to protect them from being known by the audience, but to protect the audience from the secrets. The methods used by magicians are simple and uninteresting. Magicians prize basic, dependable techniques for their illusions, but they also realize the corrosive effect when an audience understands those crude secrets. These bare technical details are terribly deflating.[162]

A magician's craft is created for an audience. They perform for the pleasure of their audience, and the audiences are the people purchasing tickets to their shows. Failure to always act with an audience's interests in mind is not only complacent, but will likely lead to financial instability. Teller argues that there is no value in protecting magic's secrets from an audience, "[e]veryone else in the world will learn magic from a book or from a person. Every person in your audience knows something about magic, and that is whom you are performing for."[163]

Conversely, audiences attend under the pretense that they are to be fooled. Should a magician diligently protect his or her secrets, the audience member's experience will be as they expected. The ethical challenges of preserving magic's secrets appear to affect external consumers very little.

Revealing the secret to an audience has often been

---

[162] JIM STEINMEYER, THE GOLORIOUS DECEPTION: THE DOUBLE LIFE OF WILLIAM ROBINSON, AKA CHUNG LING SOO, THE "MARVELOUS CHINESE CONJURER", at x (2005).

[163] *See* Telephone Interview with Raymond Joseph Teller, *supra* note 12.

compared to the experience of reading a story, getting toward the end of the story, and then someone unexpectedly reveals the ending. Left without details but with knowledge of the ending, the reader has a feeling of the ending having been ruined. Discovering the ending before arriving there on one's own effectively pulls the rug out from the experience. But as this study has illustrated, industry practitioners agree that the secret is only part of the theatrical experience. There is merit in both perspectives. A fictional story has similar qualities. When you tell a child a story, they may say, "that's not true!"[164] They may want to verify the story.[165] Other people who hear the same story won't care; they will be swept up and captivated, provided you can tell it well.[166]

The only question is how many metaphorical television sets should conjurors be expected to have hiding in their home? After all, Teller would lose his competitive advantage if he could not continue producing bigger and better tricks.

V. TELLER WINS

In 1983,[167] Teller registered *Shadows* with the United States copyright office.[168] "The registration describes the piece as 'Dramatic Work and Music; or Choreography,'

---

[164] *Id.*

[165] *Id.*

[166] *Id.*

[167] Teller started to perform *Shadows* seven years before registering the work, meaning the registration was not *prima facie* evidence of copyright validity. Still, enough evidence was brought forward to prove Teller the rightful owner of the performance. Teller v. Dogge, 8 F. Supp. 3d 1228, 1231 (D. Nev. 2014).

[168] Eriq Gardner, *Teller Wins Lawsuit Over Copied Magic Trick Performance*, HOLLYWOOD REP. (Mar. 21, 2014), http://www.hollywoodreporter.com/thr-esq/teller-wins-lawsuit-copied-magic-690347.

with 'Notes: Pantomime.'"[169] The registration included detailed notes of how the trick was to be *performed*, similar to how choreographic notations[170] register a dance performance itself.[171]

Gerard Dogge, a Dutch performer, created two YouTube videos of his own version[172] of the trick, which he entitled *The Rose and Her Shadow*. Additionally, Dogge offered to sell the secrets to Teller's illusions to "customers in various countries."[173] Teller sued Dogge, claiming copyright infringement and unfair competition.[174] Teller then motioned for summary judgment on both claims.[175] The defendant argued that his secret to performing the magic differed from Teller's. The presiding judge responded:

> By arguing that the secret to his illusion is different than Teller's, Bakardy implicitly argues about aspects of the performance that are *not perceivable by the audience*. In discerning substantial similarity, the court compares only the *observable* elements of the works in question. Therefore, whether Bakardy uses Teller's method, a technique known only by various holy men of the Himalayas, or even

---

[169] *See* Brancolini, *supra* note 70, at 105; *see also* Complaint at ex. 1, *Teller*, 8 F. Supp. 3d 1228 (No. 2:12-CV-00591), 2012 WL 1259288, at *3.

[170] *See* Bethany M. Forcucci, *Dancing Around the Issues of Choreography & Copyright: Protecting Choreographers After* Martha Graham School and Dance Foundation, Inc. v. Martha Graham Center of Contemporary Dance, Inc., 24 QUINNIPIAC L. REV. 931, 942 (2006).

[171] The court notes that while "magic tricks are not copyrightable" the dramatic performance surrounding the trick is copyrightable. *Teller*, 8 F. Supp. 3d at 1233.

[172] Dogge added a second illusion, where the vase's water was subsequently poured into a drinking glass to be consumed by the performing magician.

[173] *Teller*, 8 F. Supp. 3d at 1231.

[174] *Id.*

[175] *Id.* at 1230–31.

real magic is irrelevant, as the performances appear identical to an ordinary observer.[176]

This analysis is made stronger by the fact that Teller himself admits to using two other methods to accomplish the same visual effect in previous years.[177] Accordingly, Judge Mahan granted the motion for summary judgment on copyright infringement and awarded Teller attorney fees, but denied summary judgment on the determination of damages and unfair competition.[178] Damages were later contested, but ultimately the court granted Teller permanent injunction for the videos, and $15,000 in damages, $30,000 in costs, and $500,000 in attorney fees.[179] While it is uncommon for a court to grant an award for attorney fees, the infringing magician's many years of delaying this lawsuit compelled the court to award fees in this case.

VI. CONCLUSION

The complexities of magic's ecology and process appropriately occupy a negative space of intellectual property law and the competitive advantages that accompany its protections.[180] But Teller's successful protection of his performance's copyright, while preserving the illusion's secret, marks an important

---

[176] *Id.* at 1236.

[177] *See* Jones, *supra* note 65.

[178] *Teller*, 8 F. Supp. 3d at 1238.

[179] The court has broad discretion in awarding damages, and even though the plaintiff's actions were arguably willful, making the infringement eligible for statutory damages up to $150,000, the court that since the video had very little exposure and a permanent injunction was granted, the court found a "maximum statutory award unnecessary." Teller v. Dogge, No. 2:12-CV-591 JCM (GWF), 2014 WL 4929413, at *4 (D. Nev. Sept. 30, 2014).

[180] *See* Feist Publ'ns, Inc. v. Rural Tel. Serv. Co., 499 U.S. 340, 349–50 (1991) (discussing goals between protecting authors' work and promoting innovation).

shift in copyright's ability to provide theft protection for magicians.[181] The evidence shows that protecting a magician's performance—not the secret from disclosure—is practicable and effective in safeguarding a magician's finances, morals, and secrets.

Meanwhile, magic continues to flourish as prominent magicians headline productions from Broadway to Las Vegas, and thousands of other amateur and professional magicians perform and invent new ideas in the absence of law. Despite many ethical concerns, magicians will continue using their unique theatrical medium to share an intangible beauty that evokes a sense of wonder from their audiences.

> *Listen for the brief pause between the end of the trick and the start of the applause—the split second when the entire audience shares a gasp of genuine amazement, at that moment there's always been an honorable quality in illusion.*[182]

---

[181] *See* Brancolini, *supra* note 70, at 105 (discussing spirit of copyright law and performance theft).

[182] *See* STEINMEYER, *supra* note 1, at 331.

AN OVERVIEW OF LEGAL PROTECTION FOR FICTIONAL CHARACTERS: BALANCING PUBLIC AND PRIVATE INTERESTS

AMANDA SCHREYER[†]

[†] Amanda Schreyer is Of Counsel in the Media and Intellectual Property Group at Prince Lobel Tye LLP in Boston, where she practices intellectual property, media, and entertainment law. The author thanks Jay Kogan, adjunct professor of intellectual property law at New York Law School, whose 2001 article *Trademark Protection for Identity Elements of Character After Copyright Expires* inspired this article, for his invaluable contributions to this article, and without whom this article would not exist.

I. FICTIONAL CHARACTERS AND THE LAW

After 127 years of providing detective consulting services, in 2014, Sherlock Holmes faced his toughest case yet: "The Mystery of the Public Domain." In that case, the Seventh Circuit was asked to balance the competing interests of the estate of the Sherlock Holmes creator with the interests of authors to use the character in new fictional works.[1] Utilizing the existing body of case law on the subject, the court deduced that Arthur Conan Doyle and his estate had exploited the Holmes character as far as copyright law allows, setting Holmes up for new adventures in the public domain.[2]

American intellectual property law is designed to incentivize authors to create new literary, artistic, and other works of authorship; and thus add to America's rich and ever-growing popular culture. To achieve this objective, copyright law, and in fact, the Constitution, affords authors certain exclusive rights in their copyrighted works, including to the original characters contained therein, so that the authors can secure a fair return on their efforts.[3] At the same time, the law limits a character owner's monopoly by (i) limiting the protection afforded to characters to only those that are fully developed; (ii) allowing others to create and exploit similar, but non-infringing, characters that share common traits and stock or genre characteristics; (iii) permitting third parties to make fair uses of characters; and (iv) ensuring that the copyright in protected characters will eventually expire, injecting such characters into the public domain. While character owners have an assortment of legal tools available to protect their work, these legal tools are not absolute; the

---

[1] Klinger v. Conan Doyle Estate, Ltd., 755 F.3d 496 (7th Cir. 2014).
[2] *Id.* at 503.
[3] U.S. CONST. art. I, § 8, cl. 8.; U.S. CONST. amend. I.

public can utilize characters owned by others without the need to secure rights from the owners by way of devices like the fair use doctrine and free speech rights.

Character owners and new creators should familiarize themselves with the legal protections afforded to fictional characters. To best exploit and protect a character over time, character creators should consider legal protections while conceiving and designing characters. New creators should understand how existing characters might impact their ability to create and exploit new ones that are similar to, or reminiscent of, those existing characters. On the other hand, creators and owners of existing characters should be aware of the limits on their exclusive rights, so that they can avoid wasting energy and resources taking meritless actions against perceived infringers.

This article explains the legal protections available to characters, and the limitations on character owners' exclusive rights. Part II provides an overview of the laws available to protect fictional characters. Sections III through V examine specific examples of how various laws have been applied to fictional characters. Section VI addresses the limitations on character owners' rights, and explores the ways in which characters or their constituent elements may be freely used without permission. Finally, section VII offers tips on protecting characters within existing legal parameters.

II. LEGAL BASIS FOR PROTECTING CHARACTERS

Copyright law provides exclusive rights for creative works, including fictional characters that are (1) original, and (2) fixed in a tangible medium.[4] Cases construing the meaning of "originality" generally have required it to mean "independent creation plus a modicum of creativity."[5] The creativity bar is not high.[6] Moreover, while "some original expression" is required, the original expression contributed to a work need not be separable from the work as a whole.[7]

The goal of copyright is to promote the progress of the arts[8] and consequently enrich the public.[9] This goal is accomplished by giving creators an incentive to create by allowing them certain exclusive rights for limited periods of time.[10] By limiting the duration of copyright,[11] the public's interest in an ever-growing, rich public domain is balanced with the interests of creators. By affording copyright owners protection in their works, copyright law also benefits the public by encouraging authors to produce original works. It is not

---

[4] 17 U.S.C. § 102(a) (2012); *see* Balt. Orioles v. Major League Baseball Players Ass'n, 805 F.2d 663, 668 (7th Cir. 1986) (discussing the statutory definition of "fixed" in 17 U.S.C. § 101).

[5] Feist Publ'ns, Inc. v. Rural Tel. Serv. Co., 499 U.S. 340, 362 (1991).

[6] *See* Mazer v. Stein, 347 U.S. 201 (1954); *Balt. Orioles*, 805 F. 2d at 669 n.7; L. Batlin & Son, Inc. v. Snyder, 536 F. 2d 486, 490 (2d Cir. 1976) ("[T]he quantum of originality that is required may be modest indeed . . . .").

[7] Gaiman v. MacFarlane, 360 F.3d 644, 658 (7th Cir. 2004).

[8] U.S. CONST, art. I, § 8, cl. 8.

[9] *See, e.g.*, Golan v. Holder, 132 S. Ct. 873, 889 (2012); Sony Corp. of America v. Universal City Studios, Inc., 464 U.S. 417, 429 (1984); Mazur v. Stein, 347 U.S. 201, 219 (1954).

[10] *See Golan*, 132 S. Ct. at 902 (citing *Sony Corp.* and *Mazur* in support of the proposition that the limited copyright conferred by copyright is meant to motivate authors to create).

[11] 17 U.S.C. § 302 (2012).

designed to let creators avoid "the drudgery of working up something fresh" by simply copying existing works.[12]

Trademark law protects any word, name, symbol, or device that is used to identify the source or origin of a product.[13] Thus, to the extent that any character indicia function to identify the source or origin of a product or service, such character indicia may be entitled to trademark protection.[14] While exclusive trademark rights protect owners by encouraging them to invest in the goodwill attendant with their marks, trademark law is rooted in consumer protection.[15] Just as consumers buy any trademarked goods based on the goodwill of the applicable trademark, the public consumes entertainment products based on the brands associated with such products.

---

[12] Campbell v. Acuff-Rose Music, Inc., 510 U.S. 569, 580 (1994).

[13] 15 U.S.C. § 1127 (2012).

[14] *See* Sony v. Fireworks, 137 F. Supp. 2d 1177, 1198 (C.D. Cal. 2001) (holding that where plaintiffs could not define to what they were claiming trademark rights, nor that the character had acquired secondary meaning as a source identifier, the court could not assess whether there was a likelihood of confusion between plaintiff's and defendant's marks to find trademark infringement by the defendants), *vacated*, 2002 WL 32387901 (C.D. Cal. 2002). Where a character, or its name, is not inherently distinctive, and it is not otherwise protected as a registered trademark, it may still be entitled to trademark protection if it has acquired "secondary meaning" such that the consuming public would associate any third party's use of those elements with the source or origin of the entertainment property from which those elements were derived. Dallas Cowboys Cheerleaders, Inc. v. Pussycat Cinema, Ltd., 604 F.2d 200, 203 (2d Cir. 1979).

[15] James Burrough Ltd. v. Sign of Beefeater, Inc., 540 F.2d 266, 276 (7th Cir. 1976) ("The trademark laws exist not to 'protect' trademarks, but. . . to protect the consuming public from confusion, concomitantly protecting the trademark owner's right to a non-confused public.").

The goal of trademark law is to protect "the purchasing public from confusing desired product with similarly named, labeled, or branded product from a different source."[16] Trademark law also gives trademark owners the incentive to invest in the establishment of brand names and marks, and to maintain high levels of quality control over their products and services.[17] Trademark law can thus "contribute to a favorable climate for expression by complementing the economic incentive that copyright provides to create and disseminate artistic works."[18] Unlike copyright, trademark rights may persist indefinitely as long as the trademark owner continues to use its mark. However, merely registering an image of a character as a trademark does not give the registrant perpetual rights in the image.[19] It is not the recognition of a character image that provides perpetual rights in that image. Rather, it is the character owner's continued use of that image as a source identifier that allows the image to receive trademark protection indefinitely.[20] Copyright protection in a character, in contrast, continues for the duration of the copyright term regardless of whether the copyright owner continues to exploit the work. Copyright owners can let their works go out of print or elect not to publish or license any third parties to publish any new works using a character, and still preserve copyright protection for that character. Trademark law, on the other hand, requires that a

---

[16] Mechanical Plastics Corp. v. Titan Techs., Inc., 823 F. Supp. 1137, 1143 (S.D.N.Y. 1993).

[17] Scandia Down Corp. v. Euroquilt, Inc., 772 F.2d 1423, 1429 (7th Cir 1985); Truck Equip. Serv. Co. v. Freuhauf, 536 F.2d. 1210, 1215 (8th Cir. 1976).

[18] Silverman v. CBS, Inc., 870 F.2d 40, 48 (2d Cir. 1989).

[19] See In re DC Comics, Inc., 689 F.2d. 1042, 1052 (C.C.P.A. 1982) (Nies, J., concurring).

[20] See id. at 1052.

trademark owner continually convey its character to the public to maintain trademark rights in that character.

Another proprietary right that may protect characters from unauthorized use is the right of publicity. Every person, whether famous or not, has a property right in her name and likeness. Some people become famous because of characters they portray or personas they adopt, and the name and likeness of that character or persona can have substantial value. Unlike copyright and trademark law, rights of publicity are state-based (both statutory and common law), and therefore not uniform throughout the country. Generally, the laws prohibit the unauthorized use of a person's name or likeness for commercial purposes.[21] As opposed to the right of privacy, which protects a person's feelings, a person's right of publicity gives the exclusive right to control the commercial exploitation of her name and likeness.[22] Often invoked as a complement to trademark rights, right of publicity laws have been used by individuals to prohibit others from commercially exploiting characters or personas that they portray. Moreover, right of publicity claims will not be preempted by copyright or trademark laws if

---

[21] RESTATEMENT (THIRD) OF UNFAIR COMPETITION § 46 (1995) ("One who appropriates the commercial value of a person's identity by using without consent the person's name, likeness, or other indicia of identity for purposes of trade is subject to liability . . . ."); *Id.* § 47 (1995) ("The name, likeness, and other indicia of a person's identity are used "for purposes of trade" . . . . if they are used in advertising the user's goods or services, or are placed on merchandise marketed by the user, or are used in connection with services rendered by the user. However, use "for purposes of trade" does not ordinarily include the use of a person's identity in news reporting, commentary, entertainment, works of fiction or nonfiction, or in advertising that is incidental to such uses.").

[22] Haelan Lab. Inc. v. Topps Chewing Gum, Inc., 202 F.2d 866, 868 (2d Cir. 1953) (recognizing property right in a baseball player's photograph used on trading cards).

such claims address rights different from those
protected by copyright and trademark, such as persona
or likeness.[23]

III. COPYRIGHT PROTECTION OF CHARACTERS

Copyright provides exclusive protection for original
works of authorship fixed in a tangible medium.[24] The
law does not grant a monopoly over mere ideas,
themes, or concepts; which are in the public domain
and available to everyone.[25] In order to gain exclusive
copyright in a character, character creators must not
only create original works, but must also flesh out their
characters with enough original expression to make
them distinctive.[26] Courts have therefore developed
tests to determine whether a character has reached a
level of distinction to grant exclusive rights to the
unique compilation of the character's traits.

In the 1930 case of *Nichols v. Universal Pictures*, the
Ninth Circuit employed the now oft-cited "sufficiently
delineated" test.[27] Pursuant to this test, if an author has
imbued the character with sufficient original details, the
character will be entitled to some level of protection.[28]
The more highly developed the character, the greater

---

[23] *See* Wendt v. Host Int'l, Inc., Nos. 93-56318, 93-56510, 1995 WL
115571, at *1 (9th Cir. Mar. 16, 1995).

[24] 17 U.S.C. §102 (2012) (corresponding to the language of the
Copyright Act of 1909 Act, § 3) ("That the copyright provided by this
title shall protect all the copyrightable component parts of the work
copyrighted . . . .").

[25] Sega Enterprises Ltd. v. Accolade, Inc., 977 F.2d 1510, 1526 (9th
Cir. 1992) (explaining that copyright does not confer a monopoly over
the underlying idea or functional principle, as that is the domain
under the more stringent standards imposed by patent laws).

[26] *See* Nichols v. Universal Pictures Corp., 45 F.2d 119 (2d Cir.
1930).

[27] *See id.* at 121.

[28] *Id.*

the protection available. In *Nichols*, the court found that the plaintiff's characters were not sufficiently developed and thus not copyrightable because they were merely archetypal characters that often appeared in literature.[29] In his opinion, Judge Learned Hand warned would-be plaintiffs that "[t]he less developed a character in a play is, the less it can be copyrighted; that is the penalty an author must bear for marking them too indistinctly."[30]

Another well-known judicial test for the copyrightability of characters is the "story being told" test that originated in the Second Circuit in 1954. In *Warner Bros. v. Columbia Broadcast Systems*, the court found that a character could only be the subject of copyright protection where the character constituted "the story being told."[31] Pursuant to this test, the character must be more than a "mere vehicle" for the telling of the story, and must actually be the "story being told."[32] Taking a more restrictive view of the copyrightability of a character apart from the work in which he appears, the court here reasoned that because "[t]he characters of an author's imagination and the art of his descriptive talent . . . are always limited and always fall into limited patterns," allowing one author to claim a monopoly over that character would violate copyright law's goal of promoting the useful arts unless the character constitutes the story.[33] In that case the court found that Sam Spade was merely the vehicle for

---

[29] *Id.* at 122–23.
[30] *Id.* at 121.
[31] *See* 216 F.2d 945, 950 (9th Cir. 1954).
[32] *Id.*
[33] *Id.* at 950.

telling the *The Maltese Falcon* story, and thus not copyrightable.[34]

Most courts have declined to follow *Warner Brothers*, suggesting that the proposed "story being told" test was dictum.[35] Others have reasoned that while the "story being told" test may apply to literary characters, it is inapplicable to visual characters.[36] Still others have held that, if the test was ever good law, it is no longer.[37] Other courts have applied elements from each of the foregoing tests, looking both at how developed a character is, and the character's role in the work in which it appears.[38] In *Anderson v. Stallone*, the court held that the characters from the first three films from the *Rocky* motion picture series were among "the most highly delineated characters in modern American cinema, and were *so highly developed* and central to the films that they constituted *the story being told*."[39] A few years later, in *Metro-Goldwyn-Mayer v. American Honda*, the same court found that the James Bond character was both sufficiently delineated and the story being told throughout the sixteen films in which he had appeared,

---

[34] *Id.* In that case, the holding that the character was not protectable under copyright law actually favored the character's creator who wished to use the character in new works after granting exclusive rights to the work in which the character first appeared to a movie studio. *Id.*

[35] *See* Walt Disney Prods. v. Air Pirates, 581 F.2d 751, 755 (9th Cir. 1978); Anderson v. Stallone, 11 U.S.P.Q.2d 1161, 1165(C.D. Cal. Apr. 25, 1989).

[36] *See* Gaiman v. McFarlane, 360 F.3d 644 (7th Cir. 2004); *Walt Disney Prods.*, 581 F.2d at 755; *Anderson*, 11 U.S.P.Q.2d, at 1165.

[37] *Anderson*, 11 U.S.P.Q.2d, at 1165 ("Subsequent decisions in the Ninth Circuit cast doubt on the reasoning and implicitly limit the holding of the Sam Spade case."); *Gaiman* at 660 ("The Ninth Circuit has killed the decision, though without the usual obsequies.").

[38] *See* Metro-Goldwyn-Mayer v. American Honda, 900 F. Supp. 1287 (C.D. Cal. 1995); *Anderson*, 11 U.S.P.Q.2d, at 1166.

[39] *Anderson*, 11 U.S.P.Q.2d, at 1166 (emphasis added).

such that the character was deserving of copyright protection.[40]

A. Literary Characters Versus Visual Characters

Not all characters qualify for copyright protection, and not all characters are treated equally under the law. Pursuant to any judicial test, characters lacking distinctive, original traits or an original combination of distinctive traits have been found to be uncopyrightable.[41] Also, while purely literary characters might be protectable, visual characters (such as comic or cartoon characters) are easier to protect, as their visual embodiments are entitled to protection independent of their literary attributes. This is not to say that characters developed solely by "word portraits"[42] are not entitled to protection. They certainly are, but identifying the protectable elements of purely literary characters presents challenges not applicable to visual characters.[43] In a recent Seventh Circuit case, the court was asked to consider all the protectable traits of the Sherlock Holmes and John Watson characters from an entire series of books and stories.[44] It found that those

---

[40] *Metro-Goldwyn-Mayer*, 900 F. Supp. at 1296.

[41] *See* Olson v. National Broad. Co., 855 F. 2d 1446 (9th Cir. 1988).

[42] 1 MELVIN NIMMER, NIMMER ON COPYRIGHT § 2.12 (Matthew Bender rev. ed. 2014).

[43] *See Anderson*, 11 U.S.P.Q.2d, at 1165 ("As a practical matter, a graphically depicted character is much more likely than a literary character to be fleshed out in sufficient detail so as to warrant copyright protection."); Walt Disney Prods. v. Air Pirates, 581 F.2d 751, 755 (9th Cir. 1978) ("While many literary characters may embody little more than an unprotected idea... a comic book character, which has physical as well as conceptual qualities, is more likely to contain some unique elements of expression.").

[44] Klinger v. Conan Doyle Estate Ltd., 755 F.3d 496, 503 (7th Cir. 2014) ("From the outset of the series of Arthur Conan Doyle stories and novels that began in 1887 Holmes and Watson were distinctive characters and therefore copyrightable.").

characters were distinctive enough to be proper subjects of copyright independent of the stories in which they appeared.[45] While multiple appearances may aid in the development of the character, they are not required for a court to find that a literary character is developed enough to be copyrightable. A district court in Washington had no difficulty in concluding that an anthropomorphized seagull appearing in one book was both sufficiently delineated and the story being told, and therefore copyrightable.[46] But characters lacking visual depiction that are only described in a few lines will likely not be developed enough to be copyrightable.[47]

In the case where a character is solely described in writing, the reader must necessarily use imagination to create a vision of the character in the mind. Each reader therefore could have a different interpretation of the elements combined to create the character, making it difficult to define what makes the character developed. Where a character has a visual representation, however, all viewers receive a uniform interpretation of the character.[48] The Ninth Circuit in *Walt Disney Productions v. Air Pirates* asserted that visual characters should not be subject to the Second Circuit's stringent test applicable to literary characters.[49] It reasoned that the

---

[45] *Id.*

[46] Bach v. Forever Living Prods. U.S., Inc., 473 F. Supp. 2d 1127 (W.D. Wash. 2007). *C.f.* Rice v. Fox, 330 F.3d 1170, 1175 (9th Cir. 2002) ("[T]he magician is dressed in standard magician garb—black tuxedo with tails, a white tuxedo shirt, a black bow tie, and a black cape with red lining—and his role is limited to performing and revealing the magic tricks.").

[47] *See* Olson v. Nat'l Broad. Co., 855 F. 2d 1446, 1452–53 (9th Cir. 1988).

[48] *See* Gaiman v. McFarlane, 360 F.3d 644 at 660–61 (7th Cir. 2004).

[49] 581 F.2d 751 (9th Cir. 1978).

physical and conceptual qualities of a comic book character, apparent through its visual representation, are more likely to be a unique expression.[50] The court then held that Disney's famous graphic characters were protected by copyright and infringed by the defendants when they placed the innocent characters in "adult" situations.[51]

The court in *Anderson v. Stallone* found that the defendant's script treatment for a fourth *Rocky* film was a "bodily appropriation" of the characters portrayed in the first three *Rocky* films—and an infringement.[52] In its opinion, the court evaluated the judicial tests for copyrightability of characters and noted that "[a]s a practical matter, a graphically depicted character is much more likely than a literary character to be fleshed out in sufficient detail so as to warrant copyright protection."[53] Reasoning that the detail with which the characters were developed in the first three films delineated the characters more than sufficiently, and that the characters—as opposed to the plots—are what drove the three *Rocky* films, the court found the *Rocky* characters copyrightable under both tests.[54] Similarly, the court in *Metro-Goldwyn-Mayer v. American Honda* had to determine whether James Bond was a copyrightable character separate from the works in which he appeared.[55] Noting that the law in the Ninth Circuit was unclear as to which test should be applied to a visual character such as James Bond, the court elected to analyze the copyrightability of Bond under both

---

[50] *Id.* at 755.

[51] *Id.* at 755–56

[52] Anderson v. Stallone, 11 U.S.P.Q.2d, at 1166 (C.D. Cal. 1989).

[53] *Id.*

[54] *Id.* at 1174.

[55] 900 F. Supp. 1287 (C.D. Cal. 1995).

tests.[56] Because the character as portrayed in each of plaintiffs' sixteen Bond movies displayed such specific traits—"his cold-bloodedness; his overt sexuality; his love of martinis 'shaken, not stirred;' his marksmanship; his 'license to kill' . . . ."—James Bond was more than sufficiently delineated.[57] Moreover, because these character traits remained consistent throughout the sixteen films even though the character was played by multiple actors, the stories really were about the James Bond character.[58]

B. Component Parts of Characters Can Be Separately Copyrightable

While the collection of specific traits of a character can be copyrightable, original, individual components of a character's identity may also be protected by copyright. In *New Line Cinema v. Russ Berrie*, the court found that the glove worn by Freddy Krueger in the *Nightmare on Elm Street* films was protectable by copyright on its own.[59] The court in that case opined that where the component part of a character protected by copyright so helps to identify the character, that part, even when separated from the rest of the character, remains protected by copyright.[60] Recently, a court held that the Batmobile was a copyrighted

---

[56] *Id.* at 1296–97.

[57] *Id.* at 1296; *see also* Toho Co. v. William Morrow & Co. 33 F. Supp. 2d 1206, 1216 (C.D. Cal. 1998) ("Toho's Godzilla is a well-defined character with highly delineated consistent traits. Therefore, Toho has demonstrated prima facie ownership of copyrights in the Godzilla character apart from any film.").

[58] *See, e.g., Metro-Goldwyn-Meyer*, 900 F. Supp. at 1296; *see also William Morrow & Co.*, 33 F. Supp. 2d at 1216 ("While Godzilla may have shifted from evil to good, there remains an underlying set of attributes that remain in every film.").

[59] 161 F. Supp. 2d 293, 302 (S.D.N.Y. 2001).

[60] *Id.*

character.[61] In *DC Comics v. Towle*, the court rejected the defendant's argument that the Batmobile is not protectable by copyright because it is a useful item—a car—holding on alternative bases that: (1) the Batmobile is a copyrighted character because it displays "a series of readily identifiable and distinguishing traits . . . [it is] recognizable because it contains bat-like motifs, such as a bat-faced grill or bat-shaped tailfins in the rear of the car, and it is almost always jet black;"[62] and (2) the separately identifiable creative elements incorporated into the Batmobile that are capable of existing independently from the utilitarian aspects of the car are protectable as pictorial, graphic and sculptural works.[63] The original, consistent features of the design of the car are what make it recognizable as a character.

C. Stock Characters Are Not Copyrightable

Characters lacking originality, however, will not be protected by copyright. Stock characters, archetypes, and characters lacking unique expression, cannot be monopolized under copyright law.[64] *Suntrust Bank v.*

---

[61] DC Comics v. Towle, 989 F. Supp. 2d 948 (C.D. Cal. 2013).

[62] *Id.* at 967.

[63] *Id.* at 968.

[64] *See e.g.*, DiTocco v. Riordan, 815 F. Supp. 2d 655, 668 (S.D.N.Y. 2011) ("Young male heroes who must cope with missing parents and display their strength in battles with otherworldly forces are commonplace."). For further examples of characters which are not protected, see Walker v. Time Life Films, Inc., 784 F.2d 44, 50 (2d Cir. 1986) (holding that *scènes à faire*, which have been described as "scenes that necessarily result from the choice of a setting or situation" are not copyrightable.); Hoehling v. Universal City Studios, Inc., 618 F.2d 972, 979 (2d Cir. 1980) (providing more examples of *scènes à faire* such as "incidents, characters or settings which are as a practical matter indispensable, or at least standard, in the treatment of a given topic") (internal quotation omitted); Reyher v. Children's Television Workshop, 533 F.2d 87, 91 (2d Cir. 1976) (holding that "thematic concepts . . . which necessarily must follow from certain similar plot situations" are not copyrightable).

Houghton Mifflin Co. described the "spectrum" of copyright protection for characters.[65] On one end are *scènes à faire*:[66] "stock scenes and hackneyed character types," which are not protectable because they contain no unique aspects.[67] However, as characters become more idiosyncratic, they eventually cross the line into "expression" and are protected by copyright.[68] A character that in its early stages was merely a stock character can be fleshed out enough to bring it into "copyright land."[69] Once the character embodies an "original arrangement of incidents and literary expressions," and does not merely describe a type of character, the character may be protected by copyright.[70] In *Detective Comics v. Bruns*, the court acknowledged that copyright does not extend to "archetypal" elements such as the idea or premise of a "Superman" who is a blessing to mankind. But while the underlying premise for the "benevolent Hercules" type character is not protectable, other elements, such as

---

[65] 268 F.3d 1257 (11th Cir. 2001).

[66] French translation for "scenes of action." *See also* BLACK'S LAW DICTIONARY (9th ed. 2009) ("Standard or general themes that are common to a wide variety of works and therefore not copyrightable.").

[67] *Suntrust Bank*, 268 F.3d at 1266.

[68] *Id.* (internal quotation omitted); *see also* Sid & Marty Krofft Prod., Inc. v. McDonald's Corp., 562 F.2d 1157, 1165 (9th Cir. 1977) (Explaining that there is no infringement if only the ideas from a work are copied because ideas receive no copyright protection. "To constitute infringement the copying must reach the point of 'unlawful appropriation,' or the copying of the protected expression itself.").

[69] Gaiman v. McFarlane, 360 F.3d 644, 659 (7th Cir. 2004).

[70] Detective Comics v. Bruns Publ'ns, 111 F.2d 432, 433–34 (2d Cir. 1940); *see Gaiman*, 360 F.3d at 659 (discussing the court's analysis in the *Detective Comics* case). The author's verbal description of a comic book character is an uncopyrightable stock character. *Id.* at 661. However, once the character is "drawn and named and given speech, he be[comes] sufficiently delineated to be copyrightable." *Id.*

incredible feats, characterizations (such as employment and secret identities), and unique antics are.[71]

IV. PROTECTION OF CHARACTERS THROUGH TRADEMARK RIGHTS

A. Trademark Rights Are Separate from Copyrights

Because trademark and copyright principles apply to and protect different aspects of a creative work and are not mutually dependent, trademark rights in a character may be owned and enforced even if the trademark owner does not own the copyright in the character.[72] For example, in *Tri-star Pictures, Inc. v. Del Taco, Inc.*, even though the plaintiff did not own any copyrights in the "Zorro" character, it was not barred from bringing a trademark infringement claim when the defendant sought to use Zorro-related indicia to promote its restaurant chain.[73] Trademark law offers character owners protections independent of copyright law, which can be exercised by the owner of a character notwithstanding that any copyright in the character may have expired.[74]

B. Character Elements Must Act as Source Identifiers

Just as copyright law does not protect all elements of a character, not all character elements are protectable by trademark law. Only those elements of a character that assist the public in associating the character with a

---

[71] *See id.* at 433–34.

[72] *See, e.g.*, Silverman v. CBS, Inc., 870 F.2d 40 (2d Cir. 1989); Fleischer Studios, Inc. v. A.V.E.L.A., Inc., 772 F. Supp. 2d 1135, 1153–54 (C.D. Cal. 2008), *aff'd*, 654 F.3d 958 (9th Cir. 2011); Tri-star Pictures, Inc. v. Del Taco, Inc., 1999 WL 33260839 (C.D. Cal. 1999).

[73] *See Tri-star*, 1999 WL 33260839, at *2–4.

[74] *Id.* at *3–4. *See generally* Sony Pictures Entm't, Inc. v. Fireworks Entm't Grp., Inc., 137 F. Supp. 2d 1177 (C.D. Cal. 2001).

specific source may receive trademark protection.[75] A
character's name may be a protectable component of a
character under trademark law.[76] In *Wyatt Earp
Enterprises, Inc. v. Sackman, Inc.*, the court held that the
plaintiff had established secondary meaning and hence
trademark rights in the "Wyatt Earp" name even though
Wyatt Earp was a real person of historic significance.[77]
The court recognized that the commercial value of the
character's name was attributable almost entirely to a
television program produced by the plaintiff along with
the plaintiff's extensive licensing program, which
"battered [the name] into the public consciousness."[78]
The secondary meaning in the Wyatt Earp name
generated by the plaintiff's use of the name allowed the
plaintiff to stop the licensee from selling and promoting
Wyatt Earp costumes after its license had expired.[79] The
court found that defendant's use of the Wyatt Earp
name on children's play costumes would very likely
cause the consuming public to believe that the costumes
came from the plaintiff because of the goodwill
contributed to the Wyatt Earp name through the
plaintiff's radio and television shows.[80]

---

[75] DC Comics, Inc. v. Filmation Assocs., 486 F. Supp. 1273, 1277
(S.D.N.Y. 1980) ("[W]here the product sold by plaintiff is
'entertainment' in one form or another, then not only the advertising
of the product but also an ingredient of the product itself can amount
to a trademark protectable under § 43(a) because the ingredient can
come to symbolize the plaintiff or its product in the public mind.").

[76] *E.g.* Conan Properties, Inc. v. Conans Pizza, Inc., 752 Fed.2d 145
(5th Cir. 1985); Am. Broad. Co. Merch., Inc. v. Button World Mfg., Inc.,
1966 WL 7657 (N.Y. Sup. Ct. 1966); Wyatt Earp Enters., Inc. v.
Sackman, Inc., 157 F. Supp. 621 (S.D.N.Y. 1958).

[77] *Wyatt Earp*, 157 F. Supp. at 623–625.

[78] *Id.* at 624.

[79] *Id.* at 627.

[80] *Id.* at 625.

In a case construing the related doctrine of unfair competition, the court in *Lone Ranger, Inc. v. Cox* enjoined the defendants from using any language that could be construed by the public as suggesting a connection between defendant's circus and the "Lone Ranger" name.[81] The court held that the Lone Ranger name was the trade name under which plaintiff producers' radio program was distributed.[82] Plaintiff had engendered good will in the Lone Ranger name, and by using the title "the Original Lone Ranger" for a performer in its circus—an obvious attempt to trade off plaintiff's good will in the Lone Ranger name—the defendants had fraudulently appropriated that good will.[83]

Costumes worn by characters can also qualify for trademark protection,[84] and the unauthorized use of a character's costume can falsely suggest a connection between the unauthorized user and the character owner.[85] The issue in *Dallas Cowboys Cheerleaders v. Pussycat Cinemas* was whether the plaintiff owned a trademark in the unique costumes worn by its cheerleaders.[86] The court found that plaintiff's "combination of the white boots, white shorts, blue blouse, and white star-studded vest and belt is an

---

[81] Lone Ranger, Inc. v. Cox, 124 F.2d 650, 653 (4th Cir. 1942).

[82] *Id.*

[83] *See id.; see also Button World Mfg.* 1966 WL 7657 at *1 (enjoining defendant from "using the very name which plaintiffs have popularized and which is associated in the public mind with their broadcasting programs.").

[84] Dallas Cowboys Cheerleaders, Inc. v. Pussycat Cinema, Ltd., 604 F.2d 200, 204 (2d Cir. 1979).

[85] *See* Brown v. It's Entm't, Inc., 34 F. Supp. 2d 854, 859 (E.D.N.Y. 1999) (granting preliminary injunction against defendant renting infringing "Arthur the Aardvark" costume); Warner Bros. Inc. v. Rooding, 1989 WL 76149 at *3-*4 (N.D. Ill. 1989).

[86] *Dallas Cowboys*, 604 F.2d at 203–04.

arbitrary design which makes the otherwise functional uniform trademarkable."[87] In *Warner Bros. Inc. v. Rooding*, the court enjoined the owner of a movie theater from jumping out of a helicopter wearing a Batman costume on the day of the release of the Batman movie.[88] The timing and advertising for the stunt demonstrated to the court defendant's obvious intention to exploit plaintiff's trademarks "in the form of a Batman costume."[89] In *Brown v. It's Entertainment, Inc.*, the plaintiff owners of the "Arthur the Aardvark" character sought to enjoin the defendant's unauthorized commercial use of an unlicensed "Arthur" costume.[90] The court found "Arthur," a stylized Aardvark with the persona of a schoolboy, to be an inherently distinctive, and as the evidence showed, a famous trademark.[91]

Other indicia, such as a prop, well-known saying, or slogan, of a character can be protected by trademark if it is so connected to the character so as to identify the character's source.[92] Bugs Bunny's "What's up, doc?"[93] and "E.T. phone home"[94] are trademarks. In *Lone Ranger v. Cox*, the court found defendant's use of the familiar call of plaintiff's character—"Hi Ho Silver!"—in its circus served to accentuate defendant's deceptive use of the

---

[87] *Id.* at 204.

[88] *Rooding*, 1989 WL 76149 at *3; *see also id.* at *4 (explaining how the injunction applied only to the defendant's commercial use of the costume, explicitly permitting him to wear it for "a walk down the beach . . . [h]anding out free candy at orphanages . . . .").

[89] *Id.* at *3.

[90] Brown v. It's Entertainment, Inc., 34 F. Supp. 2d 854 (E.D.N.Y 1999).

[91] *Id.* at 858–59.

[92] *See supra* note 75 (discussing protectability of an "ingredient" of an entertainment product).

[93] WHAT'S UP, DOC?, Registration No. 75,844,359.

[94] Universal City Studios, Inc. v. Kamar Indus., Inc., 217 U.S.P.Q. 1162 (S.D. Tex. 1982).

Lone Ranger character.[95] Holding that the familiar coloring and symbols on the "General Lee" had attainted secondary meaning, the court in *Warner Bros. v. Gay Toys* concluded that defendant's unauthorized toy cars were likely to confuse consumers into believing that the infringing cars originated with the creators of the *Dukes of Hazzard*.[96]

C. Distinctive Visual Representations Are Protectable by Trademark Law.

Visual representations of characters are also protectable under trademark law. For example, defendant's chain of pizza restaurants named "Conans Pizza," and whose "menus, signs, promotional materials, and general décor featured a barbarian-like man who closely resembled" plaintiff's "Conan the Barbarian" character was found to have infringed the image of the trademarked character.[97] At trial, the jury found it likely that "the pervasive, inescapable aura of Conan the Barbarian" present at the restaurants could lead consumers to conclude that the restaurants were associated with the plaintiff owners of the "Conan the Barbarian" character."[98] In *DC Comics v. Filmation*, the court compared defendant's "Manta," "Moray," and "Superstretch" characters to plaintiff's "Aquaman" and "Plastic Man" characters and found that the similarity of the physical appearances and costumes of the defendant's characters were likely to cause confusion among consumers as to whether such characters were

---

[95] Lone Ranger, Inc. v. Cox, 124 F.2d 650, 652 (4th Cir. 1942).

[96] Warner Bros., Inc. v. Gay Toys, Inc., 724 F.2d 327, 333 (2d Cir. 1983).

[97] Conan Properties, Inc. v. Conans Pizza, Inc., 752 F.2d 145, 148 (5th Cir. 1985); *id.* at 155 (holding that plaintiff owns protectable rights in the Conan the Barbarian name and character).

[98] *Id.* at 150.

associated with plaintiff, thereby demonstrating trademark infringement and unfair competition.[99]

D. General Traits Are Not Protected by Trademark

While a competitor's use of an existing character's distinctive elements may cause confusion as to the source of the competing character, the use of similar, common character traits will not. The owner of a character will not be able to use trademark law to claim exclusive rights in the general traits and abilities of its character, just as it cannot use copyright law to claim exclusive rights in the stock elements contained in the character.[100] Because there are infinite potential manifestations of personality traits and physical abilities in a character, each can never be consistent enough to serve as a single source identifier, and therefore cannot be protected by trademark law.[101] For example, in *American Greetings Corp. v. Easter Unlimited, Inc.*, the court found that in selling its stuffed bears with messages displayed on their chests, the defendant may have capitalized on the enhanced demand for stuffed bears arising from the 75th anniversary of the teddy bear, but it had not infringed on any trademark rights plaintiffs held in their "Care Bears" stuffed bears which also bore symbols on their chests.[102]

V. PROTECTION OF CHARACTERS THROUGH RIGHTS OF PUBLICITY

Separate from, and in addition to, copyrights and trademark rights, the character persona adopted by an

---

[99] *See* DC Comics, Inc. v. Filmation Assocs., 486 F. Supp. 1273 (S.D.N.Y. 1980).

[100] *Id.* at 1277.

[101] *Id.*

[102] Am. Greetings Corp. v. Easter Unlimited, Inc., 579 F. Supp. 607, 617 (S.D.N.Y. 1983).

actor or other celebrity may be protectable by rights of publicity.[103] The right of publicity gives a celebrity portraying a character or other famous persona the right to control the exploitation of her "identity."[104] The "identity" of a character or other persona may be a name, image, signature, general appearance, or even voice. In *Wendt v. Host Int'l, Inc.*, the Ninth Circuit rejected the district court's ruling that plaintiffs' rights of publicity were not violated because no reasonable jury could find that three dimensional robots resembling television characters played by plaintiffs looked enough like plaintiffs to violate their rights of publicity.[105] The appeals court held that it was the physical likenesses of the actors that had value to the defendant, and regardless of plaintiff's lack of copyright ownership in the "Norm" and "Cliff" characters they played on television, a reasonable trier of fact could conclude that defendant's robots appropriated the actors' likenesses.[106] Accordingly, the use of likenesses of actors who portray copyrighted characters on television may violate their rights of publicity and constitute false endorsements if the resemblance is to the actors themselves, and not just characteristics

---

[103] Although the case law typically involves the rights of publicity of famous people, non-celebrities hold this property right as well.

[104] *See* Carson v. Here's Johnny Portable Toilets, Inc., 698 F.2d 831, 835 (6th Cir. 1983). Note that most state laws provide rights of publicity for living persons only. Some states do provide post-mortem rights of publicity. New York does not recognize a post-mortem right of publicity, but California provides seventy years post-mortem right of publicity that is descendible and transferable. *Compare* N.Y. CIV. RIGHTS LAW §§ 50–51 (Consol. 2000) *with* CAL. CIV. CODE § 3344.1 (f)–(h) (2012).

[105] Wendt v. Host Int'l, Inc., 125 F.3d 806, 810 (9th Cir. 1997).

[106] *Id.* at 811 (stating actors do not lose the right to control the commercial exploitation of their identities simply by portraying fictional characters).

unique to the copyrighted characters that they played.[107]

A celebrity's identity can also include a signature saying, [108] his name or nickname,[109] or his car.[110] These identity elements can be misappropriated by a commercial user even without the use of the celebrity's likeness.[111] An actor's claim that his right of publicity has been violated by the commercialization, without his consent, of the character he portrays will only lie if the accused character evokes the persona of the actor.[112] Where it is not an actual person's identity being exploited, but only the character he portrays, it is likely there will be no violation of a right of publicity.[113]

VI. LIMITATIONS ON EXCLUSIVE USE

Even if a person or entity owns copyrights and trademarks in a character, there are limitations on that person or entity's exclusive use of the character. Not all uses of existing characters, copyrightable elements, or

---

[107] *Id.* at 812.

[108] *See Carson v. Here's Johnny*, 698 F.2d at 832, 836 ("Here's Johnny").

[109] *See* Ali v. Playgirl, Inc., 447 F. Supp. 723, 726–27 (S.D.N.Y. 1978) ("the Greatest").

[110] *See* Motschenbacher v. R.J. Reynolds Tobacco Co., 498 F.2d 821, 822, 827 (9th Cir. 1974) (image of famous race car driver's car with a solid red body and a distinctive narrow white pinstripe on the leading edge).

[111] *See infra* notes 142–44.

[112] *See* Landham v. Lewis Galoob Toys, Inc., 227 F.3d 619, 624–25 (6th Cir. 2000).

[113] *See id.* at 625; *accord* Burck v. Mars, Inc., 571 F. Supp. 2d 446, 454 (S.D.N.Y. 2008) (holding that while an M&M dressed as a naked cowboy in Times Square evokes the character of the Naked Cowboy portrayed by Burck it does not evoke Burck himself, and therefore does not violate New York's right of publicity law). *Contra* White v. Samsung Elecs. Am., Inc., 971 F.2d 1395, 1399 (9th Cir. 1992) (holding a robot that looks like Vanna White violated her rights of publicity).

character indicia infringe on any party's exclusive rights. Not only will the copyrightable elements of characters all eventually enter the public domain after a limited time, but all characters, even while still eligible for copyright protection or entitled to trademark protection or protectable under one's right of publicity, may be used in new works in certain circumstances without violating the rights of the character rights holder. These exceptions to an owner's monopoly over a character, discussed below, ensure a proper balance between the exclusive rights of character owners and the rights of the public and new creators to use existing characters.

A. Non-infringing Uses—Copyright

It is typically the challenge of an infringement action that determines whether a character is protected by copyright, and, if so, whether copyright in that character has been infringed.[114] The court may examine the similarities between the specific aspects of the characters in dispute,[115] or between the totality of the characters' look and feel,[116] or it may engage in combination of the foregoing.[117] Because stock character

---

[114] See 1–2 NIMMER, supra note 42, at § 2.12 (explaining that the copyrightability of characters is "more properly framed as relating to the degree of substantial similarity required to constitute infringement rather than in terms of copyrightability per se"). But see Klinger v. Conan Doyle Estate Ltd., 988 F. Supp. 2d 879, 889 (N.D. Ill. 2013) aff'd, 755 F.3d 496 (7th Cir. 2013) (seeking declaratory judgment); Silverman v. CBS, Inc., 632 F. Supp. 1344 (S.D.N.Y. 1986), vacated by 870 F.2d 40 (2d. Cir. 1989) (seeking declaratory judgment).

[115] See Nichols v. Universal Pictures Corp., 45 F.2d 119 (2d Cir. 1930) (abstraction/filtration test).

[116] See Sid & Marty Krofft, 562 F.2d 1157 at 1164 (extrinsic/intrinsic test).

[117] See Hogan v. DC Comics, 48 F. Supp. 2d 298 at 309–10.

traits are not copyrightable,[118] some courts will distill the
generic, unprotectable elements from a character
before making a comparison to an allegedly infringing
character.[119]

Under the "abstraction/filtration" test, even if a
character is original, its unique features must outweigh
its stock characteristics to withstand the scrutiny of a
comparison of protectable elements in an infringement
action.[120] Before the court compares the substantial
similarity between two characters, it must first remove
from each character all unprotectable ideas and themes,
so that it can compare only the protectable components
of each character.[121] Even if one party's character
contains original stylistic choices, those characteristics
must be enhanced significantly to warrant copyright
protection after the unprotectable elements have been
filtered.[122] In *Mattel v. MGA*, the court analyzed the

---

[118] Walker v. Viacom Intern. Inc., 2008 WL 2050964, at *9 (N.D.
Cal. 2008) ("the similarities between the two characters are limited to
the stock elements used to humanize a sponge").

[119] This method employs the "abstraction/filtration" test famously
set forth by Judge Hand in *Nichols*:
"Upon any work, and especially upon a play, a great number
of patterns of increasing generality will fit equally well, as
more and more of the incident is left out. The last may
perhaps be no more than the most general statement of what
the play is about, and at times might consist only of its title;
but there is a point in this series of abstractions where they
are no longer protected, since otherwise the playwright could
prevent the use of his ideas . . . ."
Nichols, 45 F.2d at 121 (internal quotation omitted).

[120] *See id.* (discussing abstraction/filtration test).

[121] *See* Blehm v. Jacobs, 702 F.3d 1193, 1200 (10th Cir. 2012); Mattel
Inc. v. MGA Entm't, Inc., 616 F.3d 904, 916 (9th Cir. 2010); Original
Appalachian Artworks, Inc. v. Toy Loft, Inc., 684 F.2d 821, 829 (11th
Cir. 1982).

[122] *Blehm*, 702 F.3d at 1200–01(stick figures engaging in
commonplace activities); Scholastic, Inc. v. Spiers, 28 F. Supp. 2d 862,
868 (S.D.N.Y. 1998) (skeleton wearing sneakers and a cap).

substantial similarity between defendants' Bratz dolls, and the doll sketches and sculptures owned by plaintiff.[123] The appeals court held that the district court's filtration of unprotectable elements was insufficient, and that it had erred by actually comparing similarities between non-protectable ideas.[124] Upon further filtering of themes and ideas, the appeals court held that no reasonable trier of fact could find the characters substantially similar if they were only looking at the protectable expression.[125]

In determining whether one character infringes the copyright of another, some courts not only look at the specific traits of each character, but also consider the overall look and feel and the total expression of character elements such as background story, personality attributes, and interaction with other characters.[126] In *Sid & Marty Krofft Television Productions v. McDonalds Corp.*, the defendant attempted to dissect each trait—clothing, colors, mannerism, speech—

---

[123] *Mattel*, 616 F.3d 904.

[124] *Id.* at 916 ("[A plaintiff] can't claim a monopoly over fashion dolls with a bratty look or attitude, or dolls sporting trendy clothing— these are unprotectable ideas."); *see also* Ideal Toy Corp. v. Kenner Prods. Div. of Gen. Mills Fun Grp. Inc., 443 F. Supp. 291, 304 (S.D.N.Y. 1977) ("The defendants have no more right to a monopoly in the theme of a black-robed, helmeted, evil figure in outer-space conflict with a humanoid and a smaller non-humanoid robot than Shakespeare would have had in the theme of a 'riotous knight who kept wassail to the discomfort of the household' . . . .") (quoting *Nichols*, 45 F.2d at 121).

[125] *See Mattel*, 616 F.3d at 917.

[126] This method employs the "extrinsic/intrinsic test" set forth in *Sid & Marty Krofft Television Productions v. McDonald's Corp.*, 562 F.2d 1157, 1164 (9th Cir. 1977) ("The test for similarity of *ideas* is still a factual one, to be decided by the trier of fact. . . . We shall call this the 'extrinsic test.' . . . The test to be applied in determining whether there is substantial similarity in *expressions* shall be labeled an intrinsic one depending on the response of the ordinary reasonable person.") (emphasis added).

comprising its character, and compare it to a
corresponding trait in the plaintiff's character, to
conclude that because each individual trait was not
exactly copied by its character, there was no
infringement.[127] The court rejected this argument,
taking the position that the characters must be
compared with respect to the overall look and feel in
the context of the works in which they appear.[128] In a
case comparing the "Superman" character to a character
appearing in the episodic television show, *The Greatest
American Hero*, the *Warner Bros., Inc. v. American
Broadcasting Cos.* court articulated its rationale for
comparing the overall look and feel of the characters by
distinguishing the analysis of literary characters from
visual characters.[129] Unlike a literary work, it reasoned, a
graphic or three-dimensional work "is created to be
perceived as an entirety."[130] What the character thinks,
feels, says, and does, and the descriptions conveyed by
the author through the comments of other characters in
the work episodically, fill out a viewer's understanding
of the character.[131] Noting that "[s]tirring one's memory
of a copyrighted character is not the same as appearing
to be substantially similar to that character," defendant's
"Hinkley" character, in the context of the television
show in which he appeared, was so different from

---

[127] *Id.* at 1166–67 (rebuking defendant's analysis with "[w]e do not
believe that the ordinary reasonable person, let alone a child, viewing
these works will even notice that Pufnstuf is wearing a cummerbund
while Mayor McCheese is wearing a diplomat's sash.").

[128] *See id.* at 1167. *But see* Am. Greetings Corp. v. Easter Unlimited,
Inc., 579 F. Supp. 607, 614 (S.D.N.Y. 1983) (holding that defendant's
bears do not appropriate the look and feel of plaintiff's bears).

[129] *See* Warner Bros., Inc. v. Am. Broad. Cos., 720 F.2d 231, 239–45
(2d Cir. 1983).

[130] *Id.* at 241.

[131] *Id.* at 241–42.

Superman that no infringement could be found.[132] In *Hogan v. DC Comics*, the court agreed with the defendant's position that "the works must share a similarity of expression, such as similarities of treatment, details, scenes, events and characterization, or a similarity in their 'total concept and feel.'"[133] The court found that even though the main characters in both works had the same name, the similarities between these characters were mostly unprotectable ideas, such as their half-human/half-vampire genealogy, their struggles with good and evil, and their "Generation X" appearance.[134] Furthermore, the total concept and feel of the characters was not substantially similar, as they had very different interactions and personalities.[135] A character owner cannot stop all uses of traits that merely remind the public of the proprietary character; only those instances where the traits used are substantially similar to the protectable features of the proprietary character.

B. Non-infringing Uses—Trademark

Trademark infringement involves the use of mark in a way that is likely to confuse consumers as to the source or origin of a product.[136] Accordingly, where there is no substantial similarity between an allegedly infringing character and a plaintiff's character from a

---

[132] *Id.* at 243 ("The total perception of the Hinkley character is not substantially similar to that of Superman. On the contrary, it is profoundly different.").

[133] Hogan v. DC Comics, 48 F. Supp. 2d 298, 309 (S.D.N.Y. 1999) (citations omitted).

[134] *Id.* at 310–12.

[135] *Id.* at 312–13.

[136] *See, e.g.*, Conan Props., Inc. v. Conans Pizza, 752 F.2d 145, 148 (5th Cir. 1985); Warner Bros., Inc. v. Am. Broad. Cos., 654 F.2d 204, 211 (2d. Cir. 1981); Wyatt Earp Enters., Inc. v. Sackman, Inc., 157 F. Supp. 621, 626 (S.D.N.Y. 1958).

copyright perspective, it is likely that potential confusion under trademark law also will not be found.[137] In addition, trademarks can be used by others if the marks are not being used as a source identifier. In the long-running case of *Fleischer Studios, Inc. v. A.V.E.L.A., Inc.*, the court ultimately held that the use of the "Betty Boop" name in connection with the sale of merchandise incorporating public domain images of that character did not constitute trademark infringement because the defendants' use was a non-trademark use.[138] Both the Ninth Circuit and the district court on remand held that the use of the name by the defendants was an aesthetically functional use, meaning that consumers bought the Betty Boop merchandise because of the decorative function of the "Betty Boop" name.[139] The district court reasoned that because the name was adapted from public domain posters in a way that made it a "decorative component and part of the aesthetic design of the defendant's goods," the purpose of the use of the name was to look aesthetically pleasing to potential customers, not to identify a source.[140] On remand, the district court also held in the alternative

---

[137] Warner Bros. v. American Broadcasting Companies, 720 F.2d 231, 246 (2d Cir. 1983) (noting "[o]ur discussion of the differences in 'total concept and feel' of the central characters of Superman and Hinkley applies to the issue of likelihood of confusion as well as to copyright infringement."); American Greetings Corp. v. Easter Unlimited, Inc., 579 F. Supp. 607 (S.D.N.Y. 1983); *see also* Harvey Cartoons v. Columbia Pictures Inc., 645 F. Supp. 1564 (S.D.N.Y. 1986) (finding look and feel of plaintiff's "Ghastly Trio" not infringed by defendant's "Ghostbusters" logo).

[138] Fleischer Studios v. A.V.E.L.A., 925 F. Supp. 2d 1067, 1074 (C.D. Cal. 2012) ("Fleischer II").

[139] Fleischer Studios v. A.V.E.L.A., 636 F.3d 1115 (9th Cir, 2011) ("Fleischer I"); *Fleischer II* at 1067.

[140] *Fleischer II*, 925 F. Supp. 2d at 1074. While Fleischer I was withdrawn and superseded by Fleischer Studios v. A.V.E.L.A., 654 F.3d 958 (9th Cir. 2011) on remand, the district court in Fleischer II held defendants' use of the word mark was aesthetically functional.

that the defendants' use of the "Betty Boop" name on their products was fair use, because it was not being used to identify the source of the goods, but merely to name the character.[141] The court reasoned that the manner in which the defendants used the words was descriptive and therefore "otherwise than as a mark" pursuant to the Lanham Act.[142]

To retain trademark rights in a character or its indicia, the owner of the trademark must continue to use that trademark in commerce. A character owner may therefore lose its exclusive trademark rights in a character or any of that character's indicia if it abandons the mark.[143] Pursuant to the Lanham Act, three years of non-use of a trademark with "intent not to resume" use is prima facie evidence of trademark abandonment.[144] The burden is on the alleged mark owner to produce evidence that it used the mark during that time period, or that it intends to resume use.[145] In *Crash Dummy Movie v. Mattel Inc*, the court found that Mattel had met its burden of demonstrating its intent to use its "Crash Dummies" mark, despite three years of non-use, by providing evidence of discussions with a prospective distributor, ongoing research and development into future toys using the mark, and evidence of shipments of sample toys for research and development purposes.[146] In contrast, the former owners of the "Amos 'n' Andy" mark were unable to overcome the presumption of abandonment when they had not used

---

[141] *Fleischer II*, 925 F. Supp. 2d at 1076.

[142] *Id.* (quoting 15 U.S.C. § 1115(b)(4)).

[143] *See* Crash Dummy Movie, LLC v. Mattel, Inc., 601 F.3d 1387 (Fed. Cir. 2010); Silverman v. CBS, 870 F.2d 40 (2d Cir. 1989).

[144] 15 U.S.C. § 1127 (2012) ("Nonuse [of a trademark] for 3 consecutive years shall be prima facie evidence of abandonment.").

[145] *Id.*

[146] *Crash Dummy Movie*, 601 F.3d at 1391.

the mark for over twenty years, and could not show any intent to revive its use.[147]

It is important to keep in mind, however, that regardless of whether confusion is likely, the owner of trademark elements of a character can separately maintain an action for trademark dilution. Trademark dilution can occur where a latter party's use of a character or character indicia is the same or so similar to a famous mark already in use by another party that its use would dilute or weaken the distinctive value of the senior user's mark.[148] For example, in the "Arthur the Aardvark" costume case, the plaintiff was entitled to the injunction because if the defendants used their confusingly similar "Arthur" costume in connection with "unwholesome causes, . . . the image sought by the plaintiffs for Arthur will be difficult to control and might easily become blurred or tarnished, resulting in a loss of credibility, public affection, and consumer interest.[149] In *Dallas Cowboys Cheerleaders, Inc. v. Pussycat Cinemas, Ltd.*, the appeals court upheld the district court's injunction against defendant's use of the plaintiff's trademarked cheerleader outfit on actors in its "sexually depraved" film on the basis that such use tarnishes the Dallas Cowboys Cheerleaders brand.[150]

C. Copyright Fair Use

The fair use doctrine, codified in the Copyright Act of 1976, significantly limits character owners' exclusive

---

[147] *Silverman*, 870 F.2d at 48.

[148] 15 U.S.C. § 1125(C) (2012); *see* Mattel, Inc. v. MCA Records, Inc., 296 F.3d 894 (9th Cir. 2002).

[149] *See* Brown v. It's Entm't, Inc., 34 F. Supp. 2d 854, 860 (E.D.N.Y. 1999).

[150] Dallas Cowboys Cheerleaders, Inc. v. Pussycat Cinemas, Ltd., 604 F.2d 200, 206 (2d Cir. 1979)

rights.[151] A new creator's use of another's character in a new work will not constitute infringement if the use falls within the parameters of fair use. Fair use protects free speech by permitting use of another's copyrighted work for "purposes such as criticism, comment, news reporting, teaching . . . , scholarship, or research."[152] Courts engage in a four-part inquiry to determine whether an unauthorized use of another's copyrighted work is a "fair use" and therefore not an infringement.[153] In recent years, some courts have put less emphasis on the four-factor fair use analysis and focused instead on whether the unauthorized use amounts to a "transformative" use—that is, a use that gives new message or meaning to the work used.[154]

A common scenario in which the court analyzes whether the defendant's use of the plaintiff's character is fair use occurs when the defendant claims it used plaintiff's character for the purpose of parodying the character or the work in which it appeared.[155] If a defendant successfully parodies a character, the "purpose and character of the use" is transformative

---

[151] *See* 17 U.S.C. § 107 (1992); Suntrust Bank v. Houghton Mifflin Co., 268 F.3d 1257, 1262–63 (11th Cir. 2001).

[152] 17 U.S.C. § 107 (1992).

[153] *See* Campbell v. Acuff-Rose Music, Inc., 510 U.S. 569, 577 (1994); Salinger v. Colting, 641 F. Supp. 2d 250, 255 (S.D.N.Y. 2009), *vacated*, 607 F.3d 68, 73-74 (2d Cir. 2010); *Suntrust Bank*, 268 F.3d at 1268.

[154] *See, e.g.*, Seltzer v. Green Day, Inc., 725 F.3d 1170, 1175–76 (9th Cir. 2013); Cariou v. Prince, 714 F.3d 694, 705–06 (2d Cir. 2013); Monge v. Maya Magazines, Inc., 688 F.3d 1164, 1171–74 (9th Cir. 2012).

[155] 17 U.S.C. § 107; *see, e.g.*, *Salinger*, 641 F. Supp. 2d at 256; *Suntrust Bank*, 268 F.3d at 1268; Walt Disney Prods. v. Air Pirates, 581 F.2d 751, 756 (9th Cir. 1978); *see also* Lyons P'ship v. Giannoulas, 179 F.3d 384, 388 (5th Cir. 1999) (holding defendant's use of plaintiff's "Barney the Dinosaur" character as a victim to its sports mascot was parody).

and weighs heavily in favor of fair use.[156] In the parody
context, one issue is whether the defendant copied
more than needed to "conjure up the original."[157] The
more famous the character is, the less that is needed.[158]
Moreover, with visually represented characters, such as
those in comic books, very little is needed for an
effective parody.[159] Accordingly, in *Walt Disney Prods. v.
Air Pirates,* defendant's near exact replications of
"Mickey Mouse" and "Donald Duck" constituted too
much of a taking to warrant a fair use finding.[160]

In *Salinger v. Colting,* the defendant argued that his
appropriation of plaintiff's Holden Caufield character
was fair use because his book was a parody of *The
Catcher in the Rye.*[161] The court reasoned that merely
rehashing the themes of plaintiff's book with an aged

---

[156] *See, e.g., Salinger,* 641 F. Supp. 2d at 256; Mattel, Inc. v. Walking
Mountain Prods., 353 F.3d 792, 800–01 (9th Cir. 2003); *Suntrust Bank,*
268 F.3d at 1269.

[157] *Walt Disney Prods.,* 581 F.2d at 757.

[158] *See id.* (recognizing that very little of the Mickey Mouse or
Donald Duck characters need be used in the parodic work in order to
put those characters in the viewer's mind).

[159] *See id.; see also* Lucasfilm Ltd. v. Media Mkt. Grp., Ltd., 182 F.
Supp. 2d 897, 900–01 (N.D. Cal. 2002) (denying preliminary
injunction against defendant's pornographic film parodying Star
Wars).

[160] *Walt Disney Prods.,* 581 F.2d at 757; *see also* Walt Disney Prods. v.
Air Pirates, 345 F. Supp. 108, 115 (N.D. Cal. 1972) ("It can scarcely be
maintained that there is no other means available to defendants to
convey the message they have, nor is it even clear that other means
are not available within the chosen genre of comics and cartoons.").

[161] *See Salinger,* 641 F. Supp. 2d at 258 (S.D.N.Y. 2009), *vacated,* 607
F.3d at 73 (2d Cir. 2010). The court did note that while a work need
not be labeled a parody to be treated as one, a defendant cannot "post
hoc" seek to characterize his potentially infringing work as a parody
to avoid liability. *Id.* at 260 (citing Campbell v. Acuff-Rose, 510 U.S.
569, 600 (1994)). There was evidence in this case that prior to the
commencement of the infringement action against him, the
defendant author had characterized his book as a sequel or tribute to
The Catcher in the Rye. Salinger, 641 F. Supp. 2d at 260 n.3.

version of the book's protagonist was insufficient to
demonstrate that the defendant had any intention to
comment on or criticize that book or that character.[162]
Recognizing that a parodist must appropriate some
amount of the existing work in order to comment upon
it, the court warned: "If . . . the commentary has no
critical bearing on the substance or style of the original
composition, which the alleged infringer merely uses to
get attention or to avoid the drudgery in working up
something fresh, the claim to fairness in borrowing
from another's work diminishes accordingly (if it does
not vanish). . . ."[163] In *United Feature v. Koons*, the court
held that Jeff Koons' appropriation of plaintiff's "Odie"
character was infringing.[164] There the court reasoned
that defendant's sculpture of "Odie" (from "Garfield")
was not an effective parody because Koons admittedly
selected the "Odie" character arbitrarily, and not with
the purpose of commenting on the character itself—
demonstrating that at best, the work was a "parody of
society at large . . ."[165] Moreover, because the defendant
copied plaintiff's "Odie" character in its entirety and
nearly identically, and he was found to have no
motivation in creating the Odie sculpture other than to
sell it, the court rejected Koons' fair use defense.[166]

In contrast to *Salinger v. Colting*, the court in *Suntrust
Bank v. Houghton Mifflin Co.* held that the author of a
book entitled *The Wind Done Gone* made fair use of the
classic novel, *Gone with the Wind*.[167] The defendant,

---

[162] *Id.* at 260.

[163] *Id.* at 257 (quoting *Campbell*, 510 U.S. at 581).

[164] United Feature Syndicate v. Koons, 817 F. Supp. 370, 384–85
(S.D.N.Y. 1993).

[165] *Id.* at 383–84.

[166] *See id.* at 384.

[167] Suntrust Bank v. Houghton Mifflin Co., 628 F.3d 1257 (11th Cir.
2001).

publisher of *The Wind Done Gone*, argued that it should
not be enjoined from publishing the book because the
book was a fair use parody criticizing slavery, the Civil
War-era south, and the characters in *Gone with the
Wind*.[168] The court analyzed the manner in which the
author of *The Wind Done Gone* used the characters from
Gone with the Wind and concluded that she made fair use
of those characters.[169] Applying the four factors to the
facts at bar, the court found: (1) the use was commercial
in the sense that it was written for-profit, but because it
was highly transformative, factor one weighed in favor
of fair use;[170] (2) *Gone with the Wind* was entitled to "the
greatest degree of copyright protection" as an original
work of fiction;[171] (3) the defendant took a substantial
portion of plaintiff's characters but that alone was not
dispositive;[172] and (4) the parodic nature of the
defendant's work indicated that it would not act as a
substitute for the plaintiff's work.[173] For these reasons
the court held that *The Wind Done Gone* did not infringe
Gone with the Wind.

Another fair use of a proprietary character was
found in the case of *Mattel v. Walking Mountain*.[174] There,
the defendant photographer created and photographed
scenes comprised of "carefully positioned, nude, and
sometimes frazzled looking Barbies in often ridiculous

---

[168] *Id.*

[169] *Id.* at 1267–76 (11th Cir. 2001). *But see* Toho Co., Ltd. v. William
Morrow & Co., Inc., 33 F. Supp. 2d 1206, 1216–18 (C.D. Cal. 1998)
(applying the four factor test and concluding defendant's use of stills
of plaintiff's copyrighted Godzilla films in his compendium not fair
use).

[170] *Suntrust Bank*, 268 F.3d at 1269–71.

[171] *Id.* at 1271.

[172] *Id.* at 1272–74.

[173] *Id.* at 1275–76.

[174] Mattel, Inc. v. Walking Mountain Prods., 353 F.3d 792, 806 (9th
Cir. 2003).

and apparently dangerous situations."[175] Mattel sued him for, *inter alia*, copyright infringement. The photographer argued that the purpose of his photographs was to criticize society's objectification of women, which was exemplified by the popularity of the Barbie doll.[176] After addressing each of the fair use factors, the court concluded that the defendant's use of the Barbie character was fair use because: "(1) his use was parody meant to criticize Barbie, (2) he only copied what was necessary for his purpose, and (3) his photographs could not affect the market for Mattel's products. . . ."[177] Even the use of famous proprietary characters in their entirety will be permissible where the use is fair pursuant to the Copyright Act.

D. Literary Works in the Public Domain

But characters will not remain proprietary forever. Characters, like all copyrighted works, will be entitled to copyright protection only for the applicable term of copyright. Once the copyright in the work in which a character appears expires—whether it be a book, a play, a radio program, a movie or otherwise—that character, as depicted in that work, enters the public domain. The extent to which later published works featuring the same character include further protectable development of the character will determine whether and to what extent the owner retains exclusive right to use the character. Where a character appears in a series of works over time, inevitably, at some point, the earliest of the works will enter the public domain while others remain protected by copyright. In this situation, a character can exist in two or more incarnations, some of which may enter the public domain, while others

---

[175] *Id.* at 802.
[176] *See id.* at 796.
[177] *Id.* at 800.

remain protected. Courts have held that where an author has used a character in a series of works, and any of those have entered the public domain, anyone can use the story and character elements from the works that have entered the public domain.[178]

In a case involving characters appearing in a radio series, *Silverman v. CBS*, the plaintiff sought a declaratory judgment that the "Amos 'n' Andy" characters were in the public domain so he could use them in his original musical.[179] The court had to consider the many appearances of "Amos 'n' Andy" over time, first via radio programs, and later on television.[180] Because the facts showed that the pre-1948 radio scripts—in which the characters first appeared and were sufficiently delineated—had entered the public domain, the court found that the "Amos 'n' Andy" characters as they appeared in those pre-1948 scripts were in the public domain.[181] However, CBS still owned the increments of original expression that appeared in the later, derivative works, even if some of that original expression further developed the

---

[178] Klinger v. Conan Doyle Estate, Ltd., 988 F. Supp. 2d 879, 889 (N.D. Ill. 2013), *aff'd*, 755 F.3d 496 (7th Cir. 2013); *see* Silverman v. CBS Inc., 870 F.2d 40 (2d Cir. 1989); Pannonia Farms, Inc. v. USA Cable, No. 03 Civ. 7841 (NRB), 2004 WL 1276842 (S.D.N.Y. June 8, 2004), *aff'd in part*, 426 F.3d 650 (2d Cir. 2005); *see also* Siegel v. Warner Bros Entm't, Inc., 690 F. Supp. 2d 1048, 1059 ("Subsequent works in a series (or sequels) are in a sense derivative works, while the characters which appear throughout the series are a part of the underlying [initial] work upon which the later works are based . . . . So copyright in a particular work in a series will not protect the character as contained in such series if the work in the series in which the character first appeared has entered the public domain[; instead,] protection for the character extends only to those . . . elements added in [the sequel].") (quoting 1 Nimmer, *supra* note 42, at § 2.12 at 2–178.31 to –178.32).

[179] *Silverman*, 870 F.2d at 42 (2d Cir. 1989).

[180] *See id.* at 43.

[181] *Id.* at 50.

characters.[182] It was this later-created expression that Silverman was precluded from using.[183] Silverman was therefore allowed to use the "Amos 'n' Andy" characters, so long as they didn't display any traits first appearing after 1948.[184]

Klinger v. Conan Doyle Estate was another declaratory judgment action by a plaintiff who desired to use characters purportedly owned by the defendants in his original work.[185] Sherlock Holmes and John Watson appeared in four novels and fifty-six stories, only the last ten of which remained protected by copyright at the time of the litigation.[186] The author's estate argued that because the characters were developed throughout the entire canon, including the last ten stories still protected by copyright, the characters remained protected by the estate's copyrights in those last ten stories.[187] Both the district court and the appeals court rejected that argument, holding that the characters were delineated upon their first appearance in the first novel, and that all subsequent novels and stories containing the characters were derivative works.[188] Applying the "increments of expression" doctrine to the derivative works, the Seventh Circuit did find, however, that even though the characters themselves were in the public domain, the estate still owned the original expression

---

[182] *See id.*

[183] *Id.*

[184] *Id.*

[185] *See* Klinger v. Conan Doyle Estate, Ltd., 988 F. Supp. 2d 879, 882 (N.D. Ill. 2013).

[186] *See id.* at 892.

[187] *Id.* at 888.

[188] *See* Klinger v. Conan Doyle Estate, Ltd., 755 F.3d 496, 503 (7th Cir. 2014) ("From the outset of the series of Arthur Conan Doyle stories and novels that began in 1887 Holmes and Watson were distinctive characters and therefore copyrightable.").

added to the characters in those last ten stories,
precluding Klinger's use of those elements.[189]

Thus, new creators can take characters from the
public domain, add new creative elements to those
characters, and in effect bring their versions of those
characters to copyright life—as Universal Pictures did
with Mary Shelley's "Frankenstein" and Bram Stoker's
"Dracula," and Disney did with the Brothers' Grimm
"Snow White," "Cinderella," and "Rapunzel." [190] The
new creative elements will be protected by copyright as
long as they do not infringe upon any creative elements
that remain protected by copyright by a prior user.[191]

E. Visual Images in the Public Domain

Another situation in which a character owner's
exclusive rights may be tempered arises where a work
that contains visual images of that character has entered
the public domain. In *Warner Brothers v. X one X
Productions*, the plaintiffs challenged the defendant's
right to create and sell merchandise derived from
publicity shots and posters from the *The Wizard of Oz*
and *Gone with the Wind* films.[192] The defendant argued
that because its merchandise used only public domain
images, as opposed to stills from the actual films, it was
not infringing on the plaintiff's copyrights in the

---

[189] *Id.* at 501.

[190] *See* M.H. Segan Ltd. Partnership v. Hasbro, Inc., 924 F. Supp.
512 (S.D.N.Y. 1996) (accepting as true that MCA/Universal
Merchandising, Inc. owns the copyright in the visual image of the
Frankenstein character); *see also Sleeping Beauty, The Little Mermaid,
Aladdin,* and *Pinocchio.*

[191] Warner Bros. Entm't, Inc. v. X One X Prods., 644 F.3d 584, 586
(8th Cir. 2011). ("[T]his freedom to make new works based on public
domain materials ends where the resulting derivative work comes
into conflict with a valid copyright.").

[192] *Id.* at 584.

films.[193] The posters and still images were in the public
domain because they were published without
complying with then-required copyright formalities
such as including copyright notice or filing copyright
renewals.[194] Analyzing the attributes of the characters in
the public domain publicity materials, and those
embodied by the films, the court reasoned that because
the publicity materials "reveal[ed] nothing of each film
character's signature traits or mannerisms,"[195] and
because "the characters' visual appearances in the
publicity materials for *The Wizard of Oz* do not present
the requisite consistency to establish any 'copyrightable
elements' of the film characters' visual appearances,"
even if those images were in the public domain, the
characters in the films were not.[196] Therefore, the
defendant was only permitted to faithfully reproduce
the public domain images on merchandise because
those particular images, in contrast to the characters
depicted in those images, were in the public domain.
The defendant was precluded from extracting the
images of the characters from the public domain works
in which they appeared and creating new composite
works featuring the characters and their famous

---

[193] *See id.* at 596.

[194] *See id.* at 597–98.

[195] *Id.* at 599.

[196] *Id.* at 602 ("[A]lthough the derivative work may enter the
public domain, the matter contained therein which derives from a
work still covered by statutory copyright is not dedicated to the
public. The established doctrine prevents unauthorized copying or
other infringing use of the underlying work or any part of that work
contained in the derivative product so long as the underlying work
itself remains copyrighted.") (quoting Russell v. Price, 612 F.2d 1123,
1128 (9th Cir. 1979)); *see also* Fleischer Studios, Inc. v. A.V.E.L.A., 772 F.
Supp. 2d 1135, 1148 (C.D. Cal. 2008) ("[E]ven if the poster did fall into
the public domain as a result of the lack of a copyright notice, the
original Betty Boop character that is a component part of the pre–
July–1931 cartoon films did not.").

maxims (such as "There's no place like home"), because
such new composite works would "evoke the film
character in a way the individual items of public
domain material did not," even if each composite work
was "composed entirely of faithful extracts from public
domain materials."[197] The combination of the images
and aphorisms, the court held, added the increments of
expression required to infringe upon the more
developed film characters.[198]

In contrast to the above-cited cases in which the
seminal works embodying the character remained
protected by copyright, the purported owners of the
"Fatso" the ghost character (a friend of "Casper the
Friendly Ghost") were unable to sustain a copyright
infringement claim against the producers of the
Ghostbusters film for use of a ghost image in their
marketing, because the early "Casper" cartoons in which
"Fatso" appeared had entered the public domain.[199]
Because "Fatso" appeared in later "Casper" episodes
identical to the way he appeared in public domain
episodes, he had entered the public domain when those
early episodes did.[200]

The fact that the copyright in a visual image of
character has fallen into the public domain does not
mean that the character, or elements of the character,
may not still function as a trademark.[201] For instance,
the plaintiff in *Frederick Warne & Co. v. Book Sales, Inc.*
conceded that the pictures on the covers of the books

---

[197] *Warner Bros.*, 644 F.3d at 602–03.

[198] *Id.* at 600.

[199] Harvey Cartoons v. Columbia Pictures Indus., Inc., 645 F. Supp.
1564, 1570 (S.D.N.Y. 1986).

[200] *See id.*

[201] *See, e.g.*, Tri-star Pictures, Inc. v. Del Taco, Inc., 1999 WL
33260839 (C.D. Cal. Aug. 31, 1999); Frederick Warne & Co. v. Book
Sales, Inc., 481 F. Supp. 1191, 1196 (S.D.N.Y. 1979).

that were the subject of the litigation were in the public
domain, but argued that those same illustrations had
acquired secondary meaning and functioned as
trademarks.[202] Noting that copyright law and trademark
law were not mutually exclusive means to protect a
character, the court in *Warne* held that even if the
illustrations had fallen into the public domain, an
illustration could be protected by trademark law "so
long as it is shown to have acquired independent
trademark significance, identifying in some way the
source or sponsorship of the goods."[203] It is on this same
basis that the producer of the 1998 *The Mask of Zorro*
movie was able to assert its trademark rights in the
Zorro character to prevent a restaurant chain from
adopting Zorro indicia in an advertising campaign.[204]

F. The First Amendment

Free speech rights will allow the use of another's
trademark in the title of a creative work where the mark
is used for creative expression and not primarily for a
commercial purpose.[205] In a case whose rule has been
adopted by the Ninth Circuit and applied to character
cases, the Second Circuit in *Rogers v. Grimaldi* held there
was no Lanham Act violation for false designation of
origin where the defendant filmmaker used the famous
plaintiff's name in the title of his film, *Ginger and*

---

[202] *See Frederick*, 481 F. Supp. at 1193.

[203] *Id.* at 1196. In this case, however, plaintiff had not provided
sufficient evidence of this claim to be granted summary judgment of
the issue. *Id.* at 1198.

[204] *See Tri-star*, at *3.

[205] Rogers v. Grimaldi, 875 F.2d 994, 997 (2d Cir. 1989). *See also*
Silverman, 870 F.2d at 48; Toho Co., Ltd. v. William Morrow & Co. 33
F. Supp. 2d 1206, 1212 (C.D. Cal. 1998) (finding defendant's use of
"Godzilla" as the title of his books about the character likely to
confuse consumers as to source of book).

Fred.[206] With respect to this type of use of a mark or persona, the defendant's freedom of expression outweighed the plaintiff's concern that the title would mislead consumers.[207] Adopting the Second Circuit's "Rogers test" in *Mattel v. MCA*, Judge Kozinski of the Ninth Circuit upheld the district court's ruling that the band Aqua's song "Barbie Girl" did not infringe Mattel's trademark rights in the Barbie name.[208] Cautioning that "the trademark owner does not have the right to control public discourse whenever the public imbues his mark with a meaning beyond its source-identifying function,"[209] the court held that using the Barbie trademark in a song making fun of the values Barbie represents was artistically relevant and did not suggest that the song was sponsored by Mattel.[210] When Mattel returned to the same court shortly thereafter in *Mattel v. Walking Mountain* for the same First Amendment reasons, the court easily found that the defendant's use of the Barbie name in the titles of his photographs depicting Barbies was artistic expression accurately describing the subject of the photos and not suggesting that Mattel was in any way connected to the photographs.[211]

Similarly, claims for violations of rights of publicity may be rejected on First Amendment grounds. For

---

[206] *See Rogers*, 875 F.2d at 997–1002.

[207] *See id.* at 1001. *See also* Mattel, Inc. v. MCA Records, Inc., 296 F.3d 894, 900 (9th Cir. 2002) ("Limited to this core purpose—avoiding confusion in the marketplace—a trademark owner's property rights play well with the First Amendment.").

[208] 296 F.3d at 909 ("I'm a Barbie girl, in my Barbie world; Life in plastic, it's fantastic.").

[209] *Id.* at 900.

[210] *Id.* at 902.

[211] 353 F.3d. 792, 807 (9th Cir. 2003).

example, the "transformative test" articulated in *Comedy III Productions v. Gary Saderup*, sets forth the rule that where a depiction of a celebrity is significantly transformed by the addition of increments of expression to his mere likeness, no violation of his right to publicity will occur, and the user's First Amendment rights will be maintained.[212] In that case, the court averred that whether the use of celebrities' likenesses (in this case, the "Three Stooges" on t-shirts) violates their rights of publicity or is protected First Amendment expression depends upon "whether the celebrities' likenesses are used as one of the 'raw materials' from which an original work is synthesized, or whether the depiction or imitation of the celebrity is the very sum and substance of the work in question."[213] The analysis thus turns on whether a product containing a celebrity's likeness is so transformed that it has become primarily the defendant's own expression rather than the celebrity's likeness.

Accordingly, the court in *Edgar Winter v. DC Comics* held that use of celebrities' likenesses as some of the raw materials comprising a comic book story does not violate the celebrities' rights of publicity where the depictions are transformative—that is, where the depictions contain significant expressive content other than the celebrities' mere likenesses.[214] The expressive content in that case included use of the likenesses in a

---

[212] 21 P.3d 797, 810 (Cal. 2001); *see* No Doubt v. Activision Publishing, Inc., 98 U.S.P.Q.2d 1728, 1740 (Cal. Ct. App. 2011) (holding Avatars representing the band No Doubt in Activision's game did not meet the transformative-use test because the avatars were simply "precise computer-generated reproductions of the band members" which did not "meld with the other elements of the game to become . . . Activision's own artistic expression.").

[213] *Comedy III Prods.*, 21 P.3d at 809.

[214] 69 P.3d 473, 479 (Cal. 2003).

larger story, which itself was quite expressive, as well as distortion, lampooning, parody, and caricature.[215]

Rejecting the "transformative test," the court in *Doe v. MacFarlane* adopted a "predominant use test" when balancing a celebrity's right of publicity against freedom of speech rights.[216] Notwithstanding the expressiveness of the use of the identity, if a product is sold that predominantly exploits the commercial value of an individual's identity, that product should be held to violate the right of publicity and not be protected by the First Amendment, even if there is some "expressive" content in it that might qualify as "speech."[217] If, on the other hand, the predominant purpose of the product is to make an expressive comment on or about a celebrity, the expressive additions could be given greater weight.[218] In *Doe v. MacFarlane*, the court held that the use of the name "Tony Twist," a former professional hockey player, as the name of a mobster in a comic book series violated the player's right of publicity because the evidence demonstrated that the predominant use of Twist's name was to sell comic books and appeal to hockey fans.[219]

VII. CONCLUSION

Trademark, copyright, and rights of publicity laws encourage authors to conceive and develop original fictional characters and offer them to the public to enjoy in various forms of media and merchandise. The

---

[215] *See id.*

[216] 207 S.W.3d 52, 56 (Mo. Ct. App. 2006).

[217] *Id.* at 57 (quoting Doe v. TCI Cablevision, 110 S.W.3d 363, 374 (Mo. 2003)).

[218] *Id.*

[219] *See id.* at 61.

laws also protect the public and other authors by denying the creators and owners of original characters the ability to maintain monopolies over their characters by limiting the scope of exclusive protection available to characters.

Understanding what makes characters protectable will provide an author the opportunity to conceive and develop characters in a way that will enhance their protectability. Fully fleshing out one's characters by including distinctive tangible and intangible traits—including physical appearance; clothing or (if applicable) costume; personality traits; powers; habits; manner of speech; origin and background story; interaction and relationships with other characters; and settings in which the character exists—will all increase the scope of protection afforded to such character under copyright whether in literary or visual imagery or both.

Giving a character a distinctive and memorable name and using that name in or as a series title and otherwise for the branding of publications, media productions, and merchandise will help the character creator establish trademark rights in the character name. This also applies to symbols, emblems, slogans, and visual imagery of or elements associated with the character. To establish and maintain trademark rights in elements associated with one's character, it is important to use those elements in a consistent manner. Character creators seeking to further their rights in their characters may secure trademark registrations and domain names based on their characters' names, and terms or slogans associated with their characters. But while trademark law rewards the entity that expended the time and money to develop a character so that the consuming public identifies it with that entity, those exclusive rights are subject to limitations. Character marks must be consistently used in commerce, and trademark rights cannot be used to prevent others from using characters that have fallen into the public domain, so long as the latter users of such characters use them in a manner that will not confuse the public as to the source of the latter users' works.

Notwithstanding the effort devoted to creating a protectable character, authors and their successors in interest should understand, however, that eventually the copyright in an original character will expire, thereby dedicating even a highly delineated and unique character to the public after some period of time. A character owner can keep a character fresh and alive by adding updates to keep the character current with the time, adding new traits, modifying the character's appearance, and introducing new supporting characters and elements. So, while the earliest versions of a character may enter the public domain, the original character owner or successor thereto can maintain itself in the public eye as the source of the official version of character.

Allowing creators and their assignees to exploit their characters through copyright, trademark, and right of publicity on an exclusive basis—subject to certain limited exceptions—encourages authors, artists, and performers to add to the culture that benefits all of society. By giving character owners confidence that others cannot unfairly trade off their original work and the good will they have generated in connection with their characters, character owners will be encouraged to spend time and money developing the public's favorite characters. If so incentivized, the owners will invest in producing more entertainment products containing those characters for the public to enjoy. Exclusive rights in characters also benefit the public in that encouraging owners to produce more character entertainment products ensures that the owners will maintain the quality of the entertainment product, continuing to meet consumers' high expectations for the products.

The exceptions to exclusive use discussed above put reasonable limitations on a character owner's monopoly over a piece of our collective culture. Trademark law will only protect a character for so long as the owner is using the mark in commerce. Therefore, in order to maintain such exclusivity, owners must provide the public with entertainment products containing those characters. If an owner does abandon its trademark rights in a character, then any member of the public has a right to use whatever previously trademark-protected elements of the character they desire to keep the character alive. When the copyright in a character expires, any member of the public has the right to create original works using that character. If such a second comer desires to establish exclusive rights in a new version of the character, the second comer must add original creativity to the public domain character. This, in turn, will benefit the public by advancing the number and variety of works generated for public enjoyment. In addition, the First Amendment keeps character owners from extending their monopolies unconstitutionally by restricting owners from controlling public discourse, even when their proprietary characters are used. A robust public discourse is also encouraged by the allowance for use of protected characters for purposes such as parody and criticism. In these ways, the law endeavors to balance the exclusivity that owners deserve for adding desirable characters to our shared culture, with the societal goals of encouraging the dissemination of creative works and public discourse by using culturally relevant characters in new works.

RESALE ROYALTIES FOR VISUAL ARTISTS: PROMOTING EQUITY AND EXPRESSION

ALMA ROBINSON†

† Alma Robinson is an attorney and the Executive Director for the California Lawyers for the Arts. She has previously been a lecturer at Stanford University and a journalist at the *Washington Star*. The author would like to thank Sarah A. Howes, Editor-in-Chief of the *Cybaris®, an Intellectual Property Law Review* and Kirsten T. Gonder, a third-year student at the UC Berkeley School of Law, for their assistance in preparing information for this article.

I. INTRODUCTION

California Lawyers for the Arts (CLA) has historically supported the concept of resale royalties as a matter of fairness for visual artists and has continued to make its position known through *amicus* briefs in the current litigation challenging the validity of the California Resale Royalty Act before the U.S. Court of Appeals.[1]

CLA is a statewide nonprofit organization founded in 1974 to provide legal support, education, and advocacy for artists and arts organizations.[2] CLA's membership includes artists of all disciplines, attorneys, and other allied professionals who support our goals of empowerment for artists as vital contributors to our shared democratic ideals.

Through United States copyright protection, statutory frameworks, and industry practices, artists (such as musical, literary, and performance artists) benefit economically from future resales of their works, derivative copies, and adaptations.[3] Singularly, visual

---

[1] *See* Tracy Zwick, *Battle Heats Up Over Resale Royalties for Artists*, ART AM. (May 07, 2013), http://www.artinamericamagazine.com/news-features/news/battle-heats-up-over-resale-royalties-for-artists/. *See generally* Brief of Amici Curiae California Lawyers for the Arts et al. in Support of *En Banc* Rehearing, Estate of Graham v. Sotheby's, Inc., 860 F. Supp. 2d. 1117 (C.D. Cal. 2012) (Nos. 12-56067, 12-56068, 12-56077) 2014 WL 4802407.

[2] *See* CAL. LAWS. FOR ARTS, http://www.calawyersforthearts.org (last visited Nov. 26, 2014) ("California Lawyers for the Arts empowers the creative community by providing education, representation and dispute resolution."); *Members Brochure*, CAL. LAWS. FOR ARTS, http://www.calawyersforthearts.org/Resources/Documents/CLA%20 Membership%20Brochure.pdf (last visited Nov. 26, 2014).

[3] *See* 17 U.S.C. § 106 (2012); *see also* Stephanie B. Turner, *The Artist's Resale Royalty Right: Overcoming the Information Problem*, 19 UCLA ENT. L. REV. 329, 344 (2012) ("Under most countries' copyright law, a book author, for example, reaps continuous benefits from the sale of his books; he generally receives royalties each time his book is sold, so

artists[4] have not had a national framework for reaping such rewards;[5] and for artists working in this genre, most resales involve a single work of art that changes hands after an initial sale—not sales of copies or derivatives.[6]

II. RESALE ROYALTIES

The resale royalty, or *"droit de suite,"*[7] provides the visual artist with an economic incentive to continue to

---

that 'when his book is popular, he is enriched.' In contrast, a world with no resale royalty right, '[t]he sale of [an artist's] painting or sculpture is a single, final event for him; the copyright mechanism offers him no technique for obtaining the comforts of continuing financial stake in the future sales of his art work.' ") (citing Monroe E. Price, *Government Policy and Economic Security for Artists: The Case of the Droit de Suite*, 77 YALE L.J. 1333, 1343 (1968)).

[4] "Visual Art" is defined in the Copyright Act, 17 U.S.C. § 101, as:
  (1) a painting, drawing, print, or sculpture, existing in a single copy, in a limited edition of 200 copies or fewer that are signed and consecutively numbered by the author, or, in the case of a sculpture, in multiple cast, carved, or fabricated sculptures of 200 or fewer that are consecutively numbered by the author and bear the signature or other identifying mark of the author; or
  (2) a still photographic image produced for exhibition purposes only, existing in a single copy that is signed by the author, or in a limited edition of 200 copies or fewer that are signed and consecutively numbered by the author.

[5] *See* Edward J. Damich, *Moral Rights Protection and Resale Royalties for Visual Art in the United States: Development and Current Status*, 12 CARDOZO ARTS & ENT. L.J. 387, 405 (1994) (explaining that there is no federal resale royalty statute).

[6] *See* U.S. COPYRIGHT OFFICE, RESALE ROYALTIES: AN UPDATED ANALYSIS 1–2 (2013) [hereinafter AN UPDATED ANALYSIS], *available at* http://www.copyright.gov/docs/resaleroyalty/usco-resaleroyalty.pdf.

[7] "The phrase *droit de suite* comes from French real property law. An owner or creditor has a 'right of following' (literal translation) to pursue the current holder of the property, even a bona fide one, to satisfy claims against it." Michael B. Reddy, *The Droit De Suite: Why American Fine Artists Should Have the Right to a Resale Royalty*, 15 LOY. L.A. ENT. L. REV. 509, 509 n.5 (1995).

work in a demanding, and often financially challenging as well as lonely, profession. Through the possibility of participating in the financial rewards of secondary sales, visual artists would have external incentives to continue to work in what may be the loneliest environment of all—working alone in a studio without the benefits of teamwork and comradery that many other art disciplines provide through group efforts and support.[8] Musicians, for example, often benefit from strong union support and lobbying organizations that represent their interests before legislative bodies.[9]

In a 2012 survey of CLA members, 84% of the respondents said that the California resale royalty is an important incentive for them to continue their work, even though most have not received such payments.[10] If an artwork gains value because of the growing reputation of its creator, artists have an important financial incentive to create new art. Other considerations are fairness—when compared to other art disciplines—and recognition of their contributions to the vitality of the secondary art market.

III. THE NEED FOR FEDERAL RESALE ROYALTY PROTECTION IN THE UNITED STATES

Artists look forward to fair compensation for the effort involved in increasing their reputation as well as the value of their artwork in the commercial marketplace. Artists who have realized resale royalties are able to re-invest in their work, knowing that their

---

[8] *Id.* at 512 (advocating that a resale royalty right would provide an economic incentive to create new works).

[9] *See, e.g.,* About American Federation of Musicians, AFM.ORG, http://www.afm.org/about (last visited Dec. 30, 2014).

[10] *See* Survey, California Lawyers for the Arts, California Resale Royalty Act (on file with author).

efforts are paying them future dividends, similar to those in other professions.[11] And when the resale royalty provides for payments for a number of years after the death of an artist, artists are assured that a financial legacy is left for their heirs or estates. Considering the growing trend of artist-endowed foundations, there could also be a public benefit in instances where the artist has established a foundation as part of his or her estate.[12]

Furthermore, as the art market continues to expand globally through international art fairs and Internet commerce, American artists are prevented from receiving lucrative resale royalties under article 14 of the Berne Convention from sales in other countries, which artists from more than seventy countries are currently receiving.[13] Under the Berne Convention, the resale royalty will not be administered on behalf of artists whose country of origin does not provide such royalties.[14]

Over the past twenty years, the stature of visual artists in the United States has been eroded as a result of two additional phenomena. First, the lack of funding by the National Endowment for the Arts (NEA) for

---

[11] Jennifer J. Wirsching, Comment, *The Time is Now: The Need for Federal Resale Royalty Legislation in Light of the European Union Directive*, 35 SW. U. L. REV. 431, 445–46 (2006).

[12] CHRISTINE J. VINCENT, THE ASPEN INSTITUTE, THE ARTIST AS PHILANTHROPIST: STRENGTHENING THE NEXT GENERATION OF ARTIST-ENDOWED FOUNDATIONS—STUDY REPORT SUPPLEMENT EXECUTIVE SUMMARY 2, 6, 7 (2013), *available at* http://www.aspeninstitute.org/policy-work/nonprofit-philanthropy/artist-endowed-foundations.

[13] AN UPDATED ANALYSIS, *supra* note 6, at 2, 8.

[14] Berne Convention for the Protection of Literary and Artistic Works, art. 14(*ter*), Sept. 9, 1886, S. Treaty Doc. No. 99-27 (1986), 828 U.N.T.S. 222, *available at* http://www.wipo.int/treaties/en/text.jsp?file_id=283698 (revised in Paris on July 24, 1971, and amended in 1979); *Id.* at 435–36.

individual visual artists sends a strong signal that these artists are not worthy of national recognition and support at the highest level of federal government patronage.[15] This lack of support for visual artists was the result of a political compromise worked out in the 1990s in order to save the NEA from elimination after providing grants for venues that showed controversial art projects. [16] It could be time to re-examine this solution. Second, the lack of support for arts in public education has also degraded the public standing of visual artists.[17]

By not investing in visual literacy and skills among the general public, a likely result is that artists are marginalized as either frivolous and/or elite in popular culture, and in any case, not worthy of public support.[18] Providing a resale royalty for visual artists would be one means of helping to elevate their status through a statutory framework that requires the private

---

[15] NICK RABKIN & E. C. HEDBERG, NORC AT THE UNIVERSITY OF CHICAGO, ARTS EDUCATION IN AMERICA: WHAT THE DECLINES MEAN FOR ARTS PARTICIPATION 42 (2011), *available at* http://arts.gov/sites/default/files/2008-SPPA-ArtsLearning.pdf ("The early disinclination to consider the arts as serious academic subjects continues to this day. The arts are widely assumed to be expressive and affective, not cognitive or academic.").

[16] For discussion and analysis of the compromise reached, see Kimberly A. Schmaltz, Note, *National Endowment for the Arts v. Finley: Viewpoint Discrimination Masked as the Government's Foray Into the Realm of Art Patron*, 26 N. KY. L. REV. 337 (1999).

[17] RABKIN *supra* note 15, at 42; *see* U.S. DEPARTMENT OF EDUCATION, ARTS EDUCATION IN PUBLIC ELEMENTARY AND SECONDARY SCHOOLS: 1999-2000 AND 2009-2010 28–39 (2012), http://nces.ed.gov/pubs2012/2012014rev.pdf (last visited Nov. 26, 2014) (providing a review of arts funding and availability in public schools throughout the country over the past decade).

[18] Elliot W. Eisner, *Why the Arts are Marginalized in Our Schools: One More Time*, ON COMMON GROUND (1995), *available at* http://www.yale.edu/ynhti/pubs/A18/eisner.html ("[T]eachers know little about the arts and often trivialize them in their classrooms. . . .[Parents] want their children engaged in more substantive experiences in school.").

marketplace to provide resale royalties.

IV. THE CALIFORNIA RESALE ROYALTY ACT

Uniquely in the United States, the California legislature enacted the California Resale Royalty Act in 1976—an act that is now under review in federal court in *Estate of Graham v. Sotheby's, Inc.*[19] If the Act is ultimately found to be unconstitutional because of restraints on interstate commerce, this would provide another rationale for enactment of a federal resale royalty.[20]

In 2012, Judge Jacqueline Nguyen of the U.S. district court ruled in favor of the defending auction houses in response to a motion to dismiss the artists' and estates' complaint alleging failure to pay royalties, citing the Dormant Commerce Clause of the U.S. Constitution.[21] The plaintiffs have appealed and await the decision of the Ninth Circuit Court of Appeals.

A. Resale Royalty Rights

There are several elements to review when considering the efficacy of various resale royalty laws: the percentage of the royalty, the domicile of the artist and the seller, the nature of the artwork, the administrative structure, and whether the royalty is applied after the death of the artist.

California Civil Code section 986, the California Resale Royalty Act (CRRA), provides that an artist is entitled to a resale royalty of 5% if the work is resold for more than the seller paid for it[22] and for a gross resale

---

[19] 860 F. Supp. 2d 1117, 1124 (C.D. Cal. 2012).
[20] Toni Mione, *Resale Royalties for Visual Artists: The United States Taking Cues from Europe*, 21 CARDOZO J. INT'L & COMP. L. 461, 497–500 (2013).
[21] *Graham*, 860 F. Supp. 2d at 1124.
[22] CAL. CIV. CODE § 986(a) (West 2014).

price of at least $1,000. [23] This royalty can only be waived in a written agreement for a higher royalty. [24] The work must be an original work of visual art (defined as a painting, drawing, sculpture or original work of glass); [25] and the royalty applies if the seller resides in California or the sale takes place in California. [26] The artist must be a U.S. citizen or a California resident for at least two years, [27] and the work of art must be sold during the artist's lifetime or within twenty years of the artist's death. [28] If the seller cannot locate the artist, the royalty is to be paid to the California Arts Council, [29] which holds the funds in trust for the artist for at least seven years—after which the funds are paid to the Council's Art in Public Buildings Program. [30]

The California legislature, mindful of its role as a national innovator in legislative history, sought to right an imbalance between the economic rights of visual artists and other artists who benefit more from copyright law; to foster a vibrant arts community in California; to set an example for the rest of the nation; to bring California law into line with the best practices of other jurisdictions, including the European Union (EU); [31] and to provide a legacy for the heirs and estates

---

[23] *Id.* § 986(b)(2).

[24] *Id.* § 986(a).

[25] *Id.* § 986(c)(2) (defining "Fine art" as referred to by the statute as "an original painting, sculpture, or drawing, or an original work of art in glass").

[26] *Id.* § 986(a).

[27] *Id.* § 986(c)(1) (defining an "artist" as a person "who, at the time of resale, is a citizen of the United States, or a resident of the state who has resided in the state for a minimum of two years").

[28] *Id.* § 986(a)(7).

[29] *Id.* § 986(a)(2).

[30] *Id.* § 986(a)(5).

[31] *See* Sharon J. Emley, *The Resale Royalties Act: Paintings, Preemption and Profit*, 8 GOLDEN GATE U. L. REV. 239, 239–243 (1978).

of artists including sales that are transacted within twenty years of the artist's death.

B. Procedural History of the CRRA

CLA has worked vigorously to defend the CRRA. In an early test case, involving preemption of federal copyright law, CLA submitted an *amicus* brief supporting the law. In *Morseburg v. Baylon*, the Ninth Circuit decided that the CRRA was not preempted by the 1909 Copyright Act.[32]

In 2011, Attorney Eric George filed a lawsuit against several auction houses (on behalf of artists Chuck Close and Laddie John Dill, the Sam Francis Foundation, and the estate of Robert Graham) claiming unpaid resale royalties under the CRRA.[33] In 2012, the U.S. District Court for the Central District of California ruled for the defendants (Christies, Sotheby's, and eBay) on a motion to dismiss.[34] The court found that the CRRA violated the Dormant Commerce Clause of the U.S. Constitution and was therefore invalid.[35] While the Commerce Clause grants Congress the right to regulate interstate commerce, the Dormant Commerce Clause is a doctrine that prohibits states from passing laws that interfere with interstate commerce. Judge Nguyen also concluded that the law was not severable and could not be applied to in-state sales only.[36] Plaintiffs appealed to

---

[32] Morseburg v. Balyon, 621 F.2d 972, 977 (9th Cir. 1980).

[33] *See* Class Action Complaint, Estate of Graham v. Sotheby's, Inc., 860 F. Supp. 2d 1117 (C.D. Cal. 2012) (No. CV11-8604-JHN (FFMx)) 2011 WL 4947397.

[34] *See* Estate of Graham v. Sotheby's, Inc., 860 F. Supp. 2d. 1117 (C.D. Cal. 2012).

[35] *Id.* at 1125.

[36] *Id.* 1125–26 (explaining the extraterritorial reach of the CRRA, Judge Nguyen noted that "were the CRRA to apply *only* to sales occurring *in* California, the art market surely would have fled the state to avoid paying the 5% royalty").

the Ninth Circuit, which heard oral arguments in early 2014.

CLA continued to defend the CRRA and filed an amicus brief in *Graham*, arguing that the Dormant Commerce Clause cannot be used to invalidate a statute without a solid factual basis that the CRRA discriminated against interstate commerce. [37] In responding to the motion to dismiss, Judge Nguyen did not require the auction houses to show how their compliance with CRRA was a substantial burden on interstate commerce. [38] Rather, her conclusion was based on a hypothetical situation: it was conceivable that the CRRA could affect transactions wholly outside of California.[39] CLA argued in its amicus brief that the CRRA does not discriminate as it was not designed to favor in-state over out-of-state interests or actors, and that there was no proof that the CRRA harmed the art market.[40]

While the parties were awaiting a decision, the court of appeals asked for briefs on whether it should hear the case en banc, citing recent cases that it felt were in conflict on the issue of the Dormant Commerce Clause: *Association des Eleveurs de Canards et d'Oies du Quebec v. Harris*, and *Rocky Mountain Farmers Union v. Corey.* [41] Predictably, the defendants argued that such a re-

---

[37] Brief of Amici Curiae California Lawyers for the Arts et al. in Support of Plaintiffs-Appellants and Reversal at 4, Estate of Graham v. Sotheby's, Inc., 860 F. Supp. 2d. 1117 (C.D. Cal. 2012) (Nos. 12–56067, 12–56068, 12–56077) 2013 WL 1095231.

[38] *Id.* at 23–24.

[39] *Estate of Graham*, 860 F. Supp. 2d. at 1124.

[40] *See* Brief of Amici Curiae California Lawyers for the Arts in Support of Plaintiffs-Appellants and Reversal, *supra* note 37, at 20–24.

[41] Association des Eleveurs de Canards et d'Oies du Quebec v. Harris, 729 F.3d 937 (9th Cir. 2013); Rocky Mountain Farmers Union v. Corey, 730 F.3d 1070 (9th Cir. 2013).

hearing was not needed,[42] while CLA and the plaintiffs filed briefs in support of the en banc hearing.[43] In October 2014, the Court decided to hear the case en banc in December, 2014.[44] Prior to the en banc hearing, the California Attorney General intervened as an amicus and submitted a brief urging the court to reverse the district court decision.[45]

V. THE JUSTIFICATION FOR FEDERAL RESALE RIGHTS

Regardless of the outcome of this case, the purported conflict with federal constitutional principles protecting interstate commerce provides a strong argument for a federal resale royalty act.

In 1992, the Copyright Office wrote a report that did not recommend enactment of the royalty, expressing concern that it might depress primary sales, but held open the possibility of harmonizing the *droit de suite* with the European community "if the [European] [C]ommunity decide[d] to extend the royalty to all its member [S]tates."[46]

---

[42] Supplemental Brief of Appellee Sotheby's, Inc., Sam Francis Foundation v. Sotheby's, Inc., Nos. 12–56067, 12–56068, 12–56077, 2014 WL 4802411 (9th Cir. Sept. 19, 2014).

[43] Brief of Amici Curiae California Lawyers for the Arts et al. in Support of En Banc Rehearing, Sam Francis Foundation v. Sotheby's, Inc., Nos. 12–56067, 12–56068, 12–56077, 2014 WL 4802407 (9th Cir. Sept. 19, 2014).

[44] Estate of Graham v. Sotheby's, Inc., 860 F. Supp. 2d. 1117 (C.D. Cal. 2012), *reh'g granted* Sam Francis Foundation v. Sotheby's, Inc., Nos. 12–56067, 12–56068, 12–56077, 2014 WL 5486475 (9th Cir. Oct. 30, 2014).

[45] Brief for the State of California as Amicus Curiae Supporting Appellants and Reversal, Sam Francis Foundation v. Sotheby's, Inc., Nos. 12–56067, 12–56068, 12–56077, 2014 WL 4802407 (9th Cir. Sept. 19, 2014).

[46] U.S. COPYRIGHT OFFICE, DROIT DE SUITE: THE ARTIST'S RESALE ROYALTY   16   (1992),   *available*   *at* http://www.copyright.gov/history/droit_de_suite.pdf.

Until this right is available in the United States, U.S. artists whose work is sold in countries that administer resale royalties are unable to enjoy this additional income stream.[47] While the Berne Convention formally adopted the *droit de suite* legislation at the 1948 Brussels revision conference, several countries opposed it.[48] As a consequence, the resale right was ultimately made optional and reciprocal. Article 14*ter* of the Berne Convention, *"Droit de Suite" in Works of Art and Manuscripts* (then-titled Article 14*bis*), provides that:

> (1) The author, or after his death the persons or institutions authorized by national legislation, shall, with respect to original works of art and original manuscripts of writers and composers, enjoy the inalienable right to an interest in any sale of the work subsequent to the first transfer by the author of the work.

> (2) The protection provided by the preceding paragraph may be claimed in a country of the Union only if legislation in the country to which the author belongs so permits, and to the extent permitted by the country where this protection is claimed.

> (3) The procedure for collection and the amounts shall be matters for determination by national legislation.

As the result of this lack of reciprocity, it is

---

[47] Kimberly Lee, *Resale Rights for American Artists: the A.R.T. Act of 2014*, WASH. LAWS. FOR ARTS, (May 8, 2014) http://thewla.org/resale-rights-for-american-artists-the-a-r-t-act-of-2014/ ("Because the United States has not adopted droit de suite, an American artist cannot receive royalties if his artwork were resold in a droit de suite country.").

[48] AN UPDATED ANALYSIS, *supra* note 6, at 4–5.

estimated that U.S. artists are losing millions of dollars annually.[49]

In 2001, the EU issued a Directive with guidelines for all member countries to implement the resale royalty right.[50] Since then, there has been no reported evidence that adopting countries, either in the EU or not, have experienced adverse consequences to their art markets. Instead, it was reported by the U.S. Copyright Office in its 2013 report that the market share of the countries that had enacted the royalty had grown over the eight-year period since the directive was issued.[51] By 2013, more than seventy countries had enacted some version of the Resale Royalty Act for visual artists.[52]

A. The Recommendation of the U.S. Copyright Office

After receiving comments from a number of stakeholders, the U.S. Copyright office updated its 1992 report, *Droit de Suite: The Artist's Resale Royalty*, in 2013, recommending that the United States enact a federal law. [53] Meanwhile, legislation was introduced in Congress to provide such a royalty.[54]

The Copyright Office recommended that the royalty should:

---

[49] Berne Convention for the Protection of Literary and Artistic Works, Sept. 9, 1886, S. Treaty Doc. No. 99-27 (1986), 828 U.N.T.S. 222, *available at* http://www.wipo.int/treaties/en/text.jsp?file_id=283698 (revised in Paris on July 24, 1971, and amended in 1979).

[50] Council Directive 2001/84, art. 4, 2001 O.J. (L 272) 35 (EC), *available   at* http://www.wipo.int/edocs/lexdocs/laws/en/eu/eu087en.pdf [hereinafter 2001 Council Directive].

[51] *See* AN UPDATED ANALYSIS, *supra* note 6, at 16.

[52] *Id.* at 2, 8, 118 app. E.

[53] *Id.*

[54] American Royalties Too Act of 2014, H.R. 4103, 113th Cong. (2014).

- Apply to sales of visual art by auction houses, galleries, private dealers, and other persons or entities engaged in the business of selling visual art;
- include a relatively low threshold value to ensure that the royalty benefits as many artists as possible;
- establish a royalty rate of 3 to 5 percent of the work's gross resale price (i.e., a range generally in line with royalty rates in several other countries) for those works that have increased in value;
- include a cap on the royalty payment available from each sale;
- apply prospectively to the resale of works acquired after the law takes effect;
- provide for collective management by private collecting societies, with general oversight by the U.S. Copyright Office;
- require copyright registration as a prerequisite to royalties;
- limit remedies to a specified monetary payment rather than actual or statutory damages;
- at least initially, apply only for a term of the life of the artist; and
- require a Copyright Office Study of the effect of the royalty on artists and the art market within a reasonable time after enactment.[55]

---

[55] AN UPDATED ANALYSIS, *supra* note 6, at 3–4, 14, 74, 79 ("most participants in the Office's review process felt that an appropriate threshold should fall within the $1,000 to $5,000." The report further

By enacting a U.S. version of the *droit de suite*, American artists would be able to participate in the worldwide statutory resale royalties now available in seventy countries. Similarly, artists in those seventy countries would be able to claim resale royalties in the U.S. market, releasing millions of dollars into the bank accounts of foreign royalties administrators and the artists they represent. The Copyright Office recommended that this should be explicit in U.S. legislation or in the legislative history.[56]

B. Congressional Support

Shortly after the Copyright Office issued its report in 2013, the American Royalties Too Act of 2014 (ART) was introduced in the Senate by U.S. Senators Tammy Baldwin and Ed Markey, along with a companion bill which was introduced in the House by Representative Jerrold Nadler.[57] The proposed act would apply only to visual artworks sold for at least $5,000 at an auction, limiting the effectiveness of the law by potentially driving some sales away from the auction market.[58] The royalty would be limited to the lesser of 5% of the purchase price or $35,000.[59] The administrator of the auction would collect and pay the royalties to a collecting society.[60] The collecting society would then transmit the net proceeds after reasonable

---

notes that Directive 2001/84/EC "caps the royalty to be paid at €12,500 (approximately $17,000 USD), regardless of the resale price." Additionally, the "Office agrees, that a resale royalty system should be collectively managed by private collecting societies, whose functions would be similar to those of SoundExchange in the music context.").

[56] *Id.* at 2, 8.
[57] S. 2045, 113th Cong. (2014), *available at* https://www.congress.gov/bill/113th-congress/senate-bill/2045.
[58] *Id.* § 3.
[59] *Id.*
[60] *Id.*

administrative expenses to the artist or their successor.[61]

In contrast to the recommendations of the Copyright Office,[62] the ART would extend the royalty after the artist's death, providing income for the artist's heirs and estate.[63]

C. Effect of "Droit de Suite" in France

In further support of federal resale rights in the U.S., *Droit de Suite* is now provided in more than seventy countries throughout the world, [64] including France, which was the first to adopt such legislation. The droit de suite was first legislated in France in 1920 in response to the sale of a painting of French peasants, which Jean-Francois Millet had painted in 1858.[65] While the owner made a huge profit for the sale in 1889, the artist's his family lived in poverty. [66] Currently, the French law provides a resale royalty that is based on an incremental scale of 0.25% to 4% of the price, e.g.:

(a) 4% for the portion of the sale price up to €50,000;

(b) 3% for the portion of the sale price from €50,000.01 to €200,000;

(c) 1% for the portion of the sale price from €200,000.01 to €350,000;

---

[61] *Id.* § 3(b)(3)

[62] AN UPDATED ANALYSIS, *supra* note 6, at 4.

[63] S. 2045 § 3(b)(6)(B)

[64] AN UPDATED ANALYSIS, *supra* note 6, at 2, 4, 8.

[65] Tiernan Morgan & Lauren Purje, *An Illustrated Guide to Artist Resale Royalties (aka 'Droit de Suite')*, HYPERALLERGIC (Oct. 24, 2014), http://hyperallergic.com/153681/an-illustrated-guide-to-artist-resale-royalties-aka-droit-de-suite/.

[66] *See* Alexander Bussey, *The Incompatibility of Droit de Suite with Common Law Theories of Copyright*, FORDHAM INTELL. PROP. MEDIA & ENT. L.J. 1063, 1068 (2013).

(d) 0.5% for the portion of the sale from
€350,000.01 to €500,000;

(e) 0.25% for the portion of the sale price
exceeding €500,000.[67]

In 2013, Société des Auteurs Dans les Arts
Graphiques et Plastiques (ADAGP), the French
collecting society for visual artists, distributed royalties
to 1840 artists and their estates—44% were living
artists.[68] The French law extends the resale royalty to
seventy years after the artist's death.[69] ADAGP collected
over €12.5 million in resale royalties: €8.3 million from
sales in France and the rest from foreign markets.[70]

It is time for the United States to join the
community of nations on this issue. American artists,
too, and their families and estates, should be able to
enjoy the legacies of resale royalties.

---

[67] 2001 Council Directive, *supra* note 60, at 35.

[68] E-mail from Fabienne Gonzalez, Société des Auteurs Dans les
Arts Graphiques et Plastiques, to author (January 15, 2015, 13:42 CST)
(on file with author).

[69] *See* Council Directive 93/98, art. 1, § 1, 1993 O.J. (L 290) (EC),
*available   at   http://eur-lex.europa.eu/legal-
content/EN/TXT/?qid=1416675593286&uri=CELEX:31993L0098.

[70] E-mail from Fabienne Gonzalez, Société des Auteurs Dans les
Arts Graphiques et Plastiques, to author (January 15, 2015, 13:42 CST)
(on file with author).

FAIR USE AND APPROPRIATION ART

NIELS SCHAUMANN†

† Niels Schaumann is the President and Dean, California Western School of Law. The author would like to gratefully acknowledge the capable research assistance of Marlena Balderas and Marko Radisavljevic. Any errors that remain are, of course, mine.

I. INTRODUCTION

In 1997, I wrote an article[1] on the treatment of appropriation artists[2] under the Copyright Act of 1976 (the Act).[3] The thrust of the article was that copyright law was suppressing appropriation art. [4] This was happening because the Act did not recognize the circumstances of the late twentieth century, when a significant chunk of the aesthetic vocabulary of the day was privately owned. [5] Many artists were targeting popular culture, but that was becoming difficult to do when most of that culture was owned by litigious cultural landlords who stood ready to bring copyright infringement actions against anyone using their "property." The article predicted that appropriation artists would "abandon their art" if some solution was not devised.[6] The article provided one such solution[7] in the form of a narrowly tailored copyright privilege extending to the creation of "works of visual art" as defined in the Copyright Act—works of painting or sculpture that are created in single copies or editions of not more than 200.[8]

My earlier article was written seventeen years ago. In this article, I will revisit the circumstances of

---

[1] Niels B. Schaumann, *An Artist's Privilege*, 15 CARDOZO ARTS & ENT. L.J. 249 (1997).

[2] "Appropriation in art and art history refers to the practice of artists using pre-existing objects or images in their art with little transformation of the original." *Appropriation*, TATE, http://www.tate.org.uk/learn/online-resources/glossary/a/appropriation (last visited Nov. 2, 2014).

[3] *See* Act for the General Revision of the Copyright Law (Copyright Act of 1976), ch. 17, Pub. L. No. 94-553, 90 Stat. 2541 (codified as amended at 17 U.S.C. §§ 101–810 (2012)).

[4] Schaumann, *supra* note 1, at 249–51.

[5] *Id.* at 252–54.

[6] *Id.* at 273.

[7] *See id.* at 274–80.

[8] 17 U.S.C. § 101 (defining "work of visual art").

appropriation subject artists to see how the law has evolved and whether they are freer to create than they were in the late 1990s. In particular, although the Supreme Court in 1994 clearly sent a signal that "transformation" of the copied work would be important in fair use cases,[9] this idea had not been applied to appropriation art cases. How, then, has "transformation" affected appropriation art? Does appropriation art still pose a challenge to copyright law?

Although I will build on my earlier article, I will not assume familiarity with it. This article stands on its own. Whereas *An Artist's Privilege* investigated a number of different alternatives to the treatment of appropriation art under the Copyright Act, the current article looks only at the changes in the fair use doctrine and discusses whether those changes would suffice to make a privilege like the one suggested in the earlier article unnecessary.

Part I provides some background regarding aesthetic vocabulary in the arts, and traces the use of appropriated images in the twentieth- and twenty-first centuries. Part II discusses the general application of copyright law to appropriation art. Part III examines the current status of the fair use cases that address appropriation art and concludes that the fair use results are better than before, largely because of the ascendancy of "transformativeness" as an important fair use factor. It also concludes, however, that fair use remains insufficient to protect appropriation art. Finally, Part IV re-proposes a solution—an exception to copyright, limited to fine art—grounded in the public benefit of dissemination of knowledge and the lack of damage to the original author's economic interest resulting from appropriation art.

---

[9] Campbell v. Acuff-Rose Music, Inc., 510 U.S. 569, 572 (1994).

II. AESTHETIC VOCABULARY

Aesthetic vocabulary changes with the times. Voluptuous female nudes are no longer a common subject of painters; neither are religious allegories. Art today is more openly critical of the culture in which it arises, and it does so in many cases by referring explicitly to that culture. This section will briefly review the history of appropriation as an artistic technique.[10] The art historian will no doubt see this as woefully inadequate, but for legal purposes it will suffice.

Beginning in the early twentieth century, artists began to take objects from their surroundings for incorporation into works of art, for example the collages of Picasso and Braques.[11] These collages were followed by the use of industrially-manufactured objects that were complete, stood alone, and were identified as art. Marcel Duchamp's "ready-mades" famously included a piece titled "Fountain," consisting of a men's urinal atop a pedestal, signed "R. Mutt 1917."[12]

The use of objects from the environment was continued by the Surrealists. Meret Oppenheim's *Object* is a cup, saucer, and spoon—covered in the fur of a

---

[10] A similarly brief exposition of this subject can be found on the Tate Gallery web site. TATE, *supra* note 2.

[11] Both artists were responsible for introducing collages, or *papiers collés*, into fine art in 1912. Pablo Picasso used newspaper clippings to create forms. See, for example, *Bottle of Vieux Marc, Glass, Guitar, and Newspaper*, which may be viewed at Tate online. Pablo Picasso, *Bottle of Vieux Marc, Glass, Guitar, and Newspaper*, TATE, http://www.tate.org.uk/art/artworks/picasso-bottle-of-vieux-marc-glass-guitar-and-newspaper-t00414 (last visited Nov. 2, 2014).

[12] Shelley Esaak, *Special Exhibition Gallery: Dada at MoMA—New York*, ABOUT EDUCATION (2014), *available at* http://arthistory.about.com/od/dada/ig/DadaatMoMANewYork/dada _newyork_07.htm (last visited Nov. 2, 2014)(showing an original photograph of the work taken by Alfred Stieglitz).

Chinese gazelle. [13] Soon, however, artists began to appropriate the works of other artists as subject matter, rather than pre-existing utilitarian objects. In 1938, Joseph Cornell—who had become infatuated with the actress Rose Hobart—purchased a print of the B-movie *East of Borneo* featuring the actress, removed all the sections of the film in which she did not appear, and projected what was left at silent-film speed through a blue-tinted lens with a new soundtrack from a record album he had purchased. He called this work *Rose Hobart*.[14]

Twenty years later, more film works were appropriated. The year 1958 saw two works that consisted of appropriated images: *A Movie*, by Bruce Connor,[15] and the film *Cowboy and Indian*, by Raphael Montanez Ortiz.[16] Connor's film used found footage and pre-recorded sounds to present a meditation on sex, war, and the nature of the film medium.[17] Ortiz cut apart footage from a Western film, threw the cut-up pieces in a bag, and then randomly pulled out pieces of

---

[13] An image of this work, and its gallery label text, are available at the Museum of Modern Art website. Meret Oppenheim, *Object*, MUSEUM OF MODERN   ART, http://www.moma.org/collection/object.php?object_id=80997 (last visited Nov. 2, 2014).

[14] Vivian Sobchak, Nostalgia for a Digital Object: Regrets on the Quickening of QuickTime, Nordicom Review 29, 37 (2004), available at http://www.nordicom.gu.se/sites/default/files/kapitel-pdf/134_029-038.pdf. The film Rose Hobart is available on YouTube. Joseph Cornell, Rose   Hobart,   YouTube   (July   15,   2012) https://www.youtube.com/watch?v=pQxtZlQlTDA.

[15] David Conner Haney, *Documentary, Postmodernism, and La Mémoire des anges*,   OFFSCREEN   (July   2011) http://offscreen.com/view/documentary_postmodernism.

[16] Rocío Aranda-Alvarado, *Unmaking: The Work of Raphael Montañez Ortiz*,   JERSEY   CITY   MUSEUM,   (Feb.-Aug.   2007), http://centropr.hunter.cuny.edu/sites/default/files/Interview%20with%20Ortiz.pdf.

[17] Haney, *supra* note 15.

the film and spliced the parts together to create a new work.[18]

In the 1960s, the Pop Art movement began to appropriate images from popular culture. Roy Lichtenstein's *Look Mickey*,[19] painted in 1961, takes an image from a Little Golden Book featuring Donald Duck.[20] Later, Lichtenstein painted images in his comic-book style based on paintings by Picasso.[21] Picasso, too, appropriated: in 1957, he painted his *Las Meninas* series—a suite of fifty-eight paintings reinterpreting *Las Meninas* by Diego Velazquez.[22]

The 1960s also brought Pop Art icon Andy Warhol, whose silkscreened images of flowers on the walls of Leo Castelli's gallery generated what might be the first

---

[18] Aranda-Alvarado, *supra* note 16, at 33.
[19] An image of the painting appears at the National Gallery of Art website. Roy Lichtenstein, *Look Mickey*, NATIONAL GALLERY OF ART, http://www.nga.gov/content/ngaweb/Collection/art-object-page.71479.html (last visited Nov. 3, 2014).
[20] An image of the painting may be viewed in the public domain. CARL BUETTNER, DONALD DUCK LOST AND FOUND (1960), *available at* http://www.nga.gov/content/dam/ngaweb/Education/learning-resources/an-eye-for-art/AnEyeforArt-RoyLichtenstein.pdf.
[21] An image of one of the paintings may be viewed at Christie's website. Roy Lichtenstein, *Woman with Flowered Hat*, CHRISTIE'S http://www.christies.com/lotfinder/paintings/roy-lichtenstein-woman-with-flowered-hat-5684070-details.aspx (last visited Nov. 3, 2014). This painting sold for more than $56 million at Christie's in May 2013. The Picasso original, which sold for more than $95 million in 2006, can be viewed on Wikipedia. Pablo Picasso, *Dora Maar au Chat*, WIKIPEDIA, http://en.wikipedia.org/wiki/Dora_Maar_au_Chat (last visited Nov. 3, 2014).
[22] These paintings may be viewed at BCN.CAT, http://www.bcn.cat/museupicasso/swf/en/lacoleccio/meninas/meninas.html (last visited Nov. 3, 2014); Diego Velazquez, *Las Meninas-Picasso*, LAS MENINAS, http://www.velazquezlasmeninas.com/las-meninas-picasso.html (last visited Nov. 3, 2014).

lawsuit based on artistic appropriation.[23] Even Roy Lichtenstein's appropriation of Disney characters, noted above, did not provoke a lawsuit. The case against Warhol was settled out of court, with Warhol agreeing to a royalty for future uses of Caulfield's work.[24] Warhol also gave Caulfield two of the silkscreened flower pieces.[25]

At the same time, Elaine Sturtevant was copying the works of other artists, meticulously reproducing the technique and results obtained by others. It is frequently difficult to spot a Sturtevant; her works are superb repetitions of the works of others.[26] When questioned intensively about his own technique, Warhol reportedly said, "I don't know. Ask Elaine."[27] Sturtevant herself summed up her purpose by saying, "I create vertigo."[28] Although she was creating since the

---

[23] Warhol was sued by Patricia Caulfield, whose copyrighted photograph of four poppies Warhol found in an issue of Modern Photography. Warhol enlarged the image and had it professionally silkscreened onto canvases that were then painted in bright, often unrealistic colors by Warhol's friends and associates at his studio, "the Factory." The resulting series of approximately 1,000 works, entitled Flowers, were shown in the Leo Castelli gallery and eventually licensed as posters. Caulfield discovered Warhol's unauthorized use when she came across the posters in a New York City bookstore. One of Warhol's biographers claims that Caulfield was not concerned about the infringement to her work, but rather that she "had been prompted to sue him when she heard that Andy was 'rich.'" Emily Meyers, *Art on Ice: The Chilling Effect of Copyright on Artistic Expression*, 30 COLUM. J.L. & ARTS 219, 225–26 (2007).

[24] *Id.* at 226.

[25] *Id.*

[26] *See* Andrew Russeth, *Sturtevant, Uncompromising Progenitor of Appropriation Art, Has Died*, N. Y. OBSERVER (May 7, 2014, 9:43 PM), http://observer.com/2014/05/sturtevant-uncompromising-progenitor-of-appropriation-has-died/.

[27] Margalit Fox, *Elaine Sturtevant, Who Borrowed Others' Work Artfully, Is Dead at 89*, N.Y. TIMES, May 16, 2014, *available at* http://www.nytimes.com/2014/05/17/arts/design/elaine-sturtevant-appropriation-artist-is-dead-at-89.html.

[28] *Id.*

1960s, Sturtevant, unlike Warhol, was not sued for copying others' works, although she reportedly annoyed Claes Oldenburg severely when she copied his *Store*.[29]

By 1975, Richard Prince was re-photographing images taken from cigarette advertisements,[30] the beginning of a career of appropriation that by 2012 had extended to a complete appropriation of the novel *The Catcher in the Rye*, identical in every way to the original first edition, except that the author's name had been changed from J.D. Salinger to Richard Prince.[31] Along the way, Prince created the works shown in his *Canal Zone* exhibition, which prompted a lawsuit from photographer Patrick Cariou, thirty-five of whose photographs were used in Prince's exhibition.[32]

The 1980s saw the adoption of the term "appropriation art" in the art world.[33] Sherrie Levine photographed the work of other photographers (while

---

[29] Christopher Bagley, *Sturtevant: Repeat Offender*, W (May 8, 2014, 8:12 PM), http://www.wmagazine.com/people/2014/05/sturtevant-moma-retrospective/photos/.

[30] One example from 1989 can be seen at the Metropolitan Museum of Art. THOMAS P. CAMPBELL, THE METROPOLITAN MUSEUM ART GUIDE 448 (Michael Sittenfeld & Robert Weisberg ed., 2012), *available at* http://books.google.com/books?id=3C4AFXFLmZEC (last visited Nov. 2, 2014); Richard Prince, *Untitled (Cowboy)*, METMUSEUM, http://www.metmuseum.org/toah/works-of-art/2000.272 (last visited Nov. 2, 2014).

[31] Kenneth Goldsmith, *Richard Prince's Latest Act of Appropriation: The Catcher in the Rye*, POETRY FOUNDATION (Apr. 19, 2012), http://www.poetryfoundation.org/harriet/2012/04/richard-princes-latest-act-of-appropriation-the-catcher-in-the-rye/.

[32] *See* Cariou v. Prince, 714 F.3d 694, 698 (2d Cir. 2013), *cert. denied*, 134 S. Ct. 618, (2013).

[33] *See* TATE, *supra* note 2; Sven Lütticken, *The Feathers of the Eagle*, 36 NEW LEFT REV. 109, 109 (2005), *available at* http://dspace.ubvu.vu.nl/bitstream/handle/1871/21431/182536.pdf?sequence =2.

scrupulously identifying the originals and distinguishing them from her own work).[34] Jeff Koons took images from popular culture, recreating them in sculpture, painting, and collage.[35] He was sued for copyright infringement three times in the late 1980s, and lost each case.[36] In 2006, Koons finally won a case, based on his "transformation" of the appropriated work.[37]

The foregoing short history demonstrates that the practice of appropriating objects and images from the world surrounding the artist has a distinguished and lengthy pedigree. So common is appropriation in the art world that a 2010 exhibition at the New Museum in New York, entitled *Free*, was built "partly around the very idea of the borrowing culture."[38] Nevertheless, beginning in 1965 with the lawsuit against Andy Warhol,[39] copyright infringement cases against artists who reuse images have proliferated.

---

[34] *See* Schaumann, *supra* note 1, at 250; *see also* John Carlin, *Culture Vultures: Artistic Appropriate and Intellectual Property Law Review*, 13 COLUM.-VLA J.L. & ARTS 103, 103–04 (1988); Gerald Marzorati, *Art in the (Re)making*, ARTNEWS, May 1986, at 90, 97. "Copying such images, whether or not for artistic purposes, is likely to result in litigation." Schaumann, *supra* note 1, at 254; *see, e.g.*, Rogers v. Koons, 960 F.2d 301 (2d Cir. 1992); United Feature Syndicate, Inc. v. Koons, 817 F. Supp. 370 (S.D.N.Y 1993); Campbell v. Koons, No. 91 Civ. 6055(RO), 1993 WL 97381, at *1 (S.D.N.Y. Apr. 1, 1993).

[35] *See* Schaumann, *supra* note 1, at 251; *Rogers*, 960 F.2d at 304–306.

[36] *See, e.g.*, *Rogers*, 960 F.2d at 301; *United Feature Syndicate, Inc*, 817 F. Supp. at 370; *Campbell*, 1993 WL 97381, at *1.

[37] Blanch v. Koons, 467 F.3d 244, 246 (2d Cir. 2006) (affirming the district court's grant of summary judgment to the defendants on the ground that Koons's appropriation of Blanch's photograph was fair use).

[38] Randy Kennedy, *Apropos Appropriation*, N.Y. TIMES, Jan. 1, 2012, at AR1, *available at* http://www.nytimes.com/2012/01/01/arts/design/richard-prince-lawsuit-focuses-on-limits-of-appropriation.html?pagewanted=all.

[39] *See supra* notes 23–25.

III. COPYRIGHT LAW AND APPROPRIATION ART

It is the nature of appropriation art that the subject matter is copied. [40] When that subject matter is a copyrighted work, the artist commits at least one infringement under the Copyright Act, and likely more. [41] This is not something exclusive to the 1976 Act, as the (pre-1976) lawsuit against Andy Warhol noted above makes clear. However, after the Act became effective on January 1, 1978, a new copyright regime took hold. The 1976 Act attempted, as nearly as possible, to fully allocate the right to engage in *every feasible use of a copyrighted work* to the owner. [42] Under this scheme, exceptions were narrowly drawn to serve the interests of existing users. [43] There were few gray areas, and the only way in which a user might legally use a copyrighted work without permission was under the fair use doctrine, codified for the first time in section 107 of the new Act. [44]

Just a few years after the new Act became effective, artists were continuing and extending the tradition of copying from pre-existing works. By the 1980s, the term "appropriation art" came into use and while the art was visually similar to the earlier varieties of copied art, the context and culture were different. The innocence and playfulness of the earlier copying seemed no longer to exist: appropriation art had become edgy, self-

---

[40] TATE, *supra* note 2.

[41] At a minimum, they violate the Act's prohibition against unlawful copying. 17 U.S.C. § 106(1). In addition, many appropriation art cases include the use of a work as part of the later artist's work, as well as the public display of the work, implicating 17 U.S.C. §§ 106(2) and 106(5). *See generally* Schaumann, *supra* note 1, at 254–56 nn.19–24.

[42] *See* JESSICA LITMAN, DIGITAL COPYRIGHT 37 (Prometheus Books, 2006).

[43] Id.

[44] 17 U.S.C. § 107.

conscious, and it seemed (sometimes, at least) knowingly to infringe copyright. Consider the Jeff Koons's 1988 *Banality* show: the title of the show identifies the subjects as banal, which is to say, lacking utterly in originality. Copyright, of course, protects only original works of authorship. Yet, the artist's copies of the banal works of others were held to infringe copyright.[45] Koons's infringing works were different from Roy Lichtenstein's *Look Mickey*, which retains a genuine innocence despite copying Disney characters. When Koons copied cartoon characters, they were implicated in sexual activities.[46] The controversy this generated was hardly accidental: Koons's *Made In Heaven* show, following immediately in the footsteps of the *Banality* show, contained many works that graphically depict Koons and his then-wife, porn star Ilona Staller, having sex.[47]

Sherrie Levine was another conspicuously transgressive artist who became known in the 1980s. Her 1980 show, *After Walker Evans*, featured works she created by re-photographing catalog images out of a Walker Evans exhibition catalog. She exhibited these photographs as her own art.[48] While Jeff Koons was

---

[45] *See* Rogers v. Koons, 960 F.2d 301, 310 (2d Cir. 1992); United Feature Syndicate, Inc. v. Koons, 817 F. Supp. 370, 379 (S.D.N.Y. 1993); Campbell v. Koons, 91 CIV. 6055 (RO), 1993 WL 97381 (S.D.N.Y., Apr. 1, 1993).

[46] See, for example, the artist's description of his work entitled "Pink Panther," as quoted in a 1992 Taschen Books retrospective of Koons's work: "Pink Panther is about masturbation." ECKHARD SCHNEIDER ET AL., JEFF KOONS 113 (Angelika Muthesius ed.) (1992).

[47] *See id.* at 124–61; *see also* Tom Leonard, *Porn star La Cicciolina sues ex-husband Jeff Koons for child support*, THE TELEGRAPH, Mar. 27, 2008 *available at* http://www.telegraph.co.uk/news/uknews/1583034/Porn-star-La-Cicciolina-sues-ex-husband-Jeff-Koons-for-child-support.html. Although the *Made in Heaven* works were controversial, they were not alleged to appropriate from other images or to infringe copyright.

[48] *See Biography: Sherry Levine*, ARTNET, http://www.artnet.com/artists/sherrie-levine/biography (last visited Oct. 28,

sued several times, Levine was merely threatened with a lawsuit. Eventually, the Walker Evans estate simply bought Levine's works and declined to exhibit them.[49]

When I wrote my 1997 article, Koons and Levine were the two artists I chose to represent appropriation art. Since then, however, appropriation has become more, not less, common. Many other artists are copying in order to make their artistic statements. The Wikipedia entry for "appropriation art" includes a list of "notable" artists using appropriation techniques; the list contains a hundred names.[50]

The fact that there are a hundred or more artists who practice appropriation can mean different things to different readers. Some might take it as a sign that copyright law is irrelevant to the actions of artists, who don't care about copyright if their chosen means of expressions leads them toward infringement. Others might say the fact that only a hundred artists have been brave enough to face litigation (out of all the artists in the world) is evidence that copyright has chilled artistic expression.

2014). However, the title of the show indicates the provenance of the images. Her practice of signifying appropriated subjects by using the word "After" in the title has continued throughout her career. Some of her other artworks based on appropriation include *After Miro*; *Equivalents: After Stieglitz 1-18*; *After August Sander*; and others. *See Artworks: Sherry Levine*, ARTNET, (last visited Nov. 1, 2014). Levine's work questions traditional concepts of originality: where is originality, in a photograph (by Levine) of a photograph (by the catalog photographer) of a photograph of people posing (by Walker Evans)? In other words, each of the photographers created an image of something that already existed, either in nature or in someone else's photograph. Why are some of these images "original" and others not?

[49] See id.

[50]   *Appropriation*   *(art)*,   WIKIPEDIA, http://en.wikipedia.org/wiki/Appropriation (art) (last visited Nov. 1, 2014).

While the actions of artists may be ambiguous, the purpose of copyright is not. It is stated in the Constitution: "To promote the progress of Science . . . ."[51] The term "Progress of Science" is used in its eighteenth-century sense, meaning the dissemination or spread of knowledge.[52] Copyright accomplishes this purpose "by securing for limited Times to Authors . . . the exclusive Right to their . . . Writings . . . ."[53] Restated, then, copyright exists to further the dissemination of knowledge, and it does so by providing authors with exclusive rights in their original works of authorship. Note, however, that the primary purpose (to disseminate knowledge) can easily be at odds with the secondary purpose (to secure rights to authors). The conflict arises because securing rights to authors limits dissemination; the requirement of obtaining (and often paying for) the right to do something with the author's work implies that such rights will be exercised less often than if no permission or payment were required.

In the absence of any provision expressly exempting art from copyright law, how is the tension between the primary and secondary purposes of copyright to be resolved in the case of appropriation art? The usual crucible in which such outcomes are forged is litigation under the fair use doctrine. In a fair use case, a user asserts the right to use a work without seeking

---

[51] U.S. CONST. art. I, § 8, cl. 8.

[52] *See, e.g.*, Golan v. Holder, 132 S. Ct. 873, 888 (2012) ("The 'Progress of Science,'petitioners acknowledge, refers broadly to 'the creation and spread of knowledge and learning.'"); *see also* Eldred v. Ashcroft, 537 U.S. 186, 212 n.18 (2003) (citing Am. Geophysical Union v. Texaco Inc., 802 F. Supp. 1, 27 (S.D.N.Y. 1992)), *aff'd*, 60 F.3d 913 (C.A.2 1994) ("Accordingly, 'copyright law *celebrates* the profit motive, recognizing that the incentive to profit from the exploitation of copyrights will redound to the public benefit by resulting in the proliferation of knowledge . . . . The profit motive is the engine that ensures the progress of science.'").

[53] U.S. CONST. art. I, § 8, cl. 8.

permission or paying a fee; the copyright owner claims
that such a use is infringement. The user's case asserts
the primacy of the dissemination of knowledge or the
"Progress of Science," while the copyright owner
emphasizes the "exclusive Rights" granted by copyright.
Fair use cases determine, on the facts before the court,
which purpose shall prevail.

Fair use is thus a potentially powerful antidote to the
rights that belong to the copyright owner. Fair use is
appropriation artists' best hope for escaping liability. It
is no surprise, then, that most of the scholarly
discussion over the application of copyright law to
appropriation art has focused on the application of the
fair use doctrine. Indeed, of the various approaches that
might be used, fair use is the only one that has been
applied by courts.[54]

The next part of this article will consider the rise of
transformativeness in the law of fair use to see if the
trend in the cases since 1997 is less oppressive to art
than it was previously. If so, then perhaps the
difficulties besetting appropriation artists have been
mitigated.

IV. FAIR USE AND APPROPRIATION ART

The law of fair use was first codified in the United
States when the Copyright Act of 1976 was passed.
Section 107 lays out the defense:

> Notwithstanding   the   provisions   of
> sections 106 and 106A, the fair use of a
> copyrighted work, including such use by

---

[54] My 1997 article described some other possibilities, some of which
had been suggested by contemporary commentators, including
compulsory license and the unlikely expedient of abandoning copyright
altogether. See Schaumann, *supra* note 1, at 271–75.

reproduction in copies or phonorecords
or by any other means specified by that
section, for purposes such as criticism,
comment, news reporting, teaching
(including multiple copies for classroom
use), scholarship, or research, is not an
infringement of copyright. In
determining whether the use made of a
work in any particular case is a fair use
the factors to be considered shall
include—

(1) the purpose and character of the use,
    including whether such use is of a
    commercial nature or is for nonprofit
    educational purposes;

(2) the nature of the copyrighted work;

(3) the amount and substantiality of the
    portion used in relation to the
    copyrighted work as a whole; and

(4) the effect of the use upon the potential
    market for or value of the copyrighted
    work.[55]

Although the four factors listed are non-exclusive,
each must be included in the fair use analysis.[56] In the
case law interpreting section 107, two factors stand out
as the most important: the purpose and character of the
use (factor one),[57] and the market impact of the use on

---

[55] Copyright Act of 1976, ch. 17, Pub. L. No. 94-553, 90 Stat. 2541
(codified as amended at 17 U.S.C. §§ 101–810 (2012)).

[56] Id. ("[T]he factors to be considered *shall include* . . . .") (emphasis
added). In other words, consideration of the factors stated in section 107 is
mandatory ("shall"); also, the factors are non-exclusive ("include").

[57] See, e.g., Campbell v. Acuff-Rose Music, Inc., 510 U.S. 569, 589 (1994);
Sony Corp. v. Universal City Studios, Inc., 464 U.S. 417, 496 (1984)
(Blackmun, J., dissenting); see also Benjamin Kaplan, An Unhurried View
of Copyright 68 (Columbia University Press 1967); Pierre Leval, *Toward a
Fair Use Standard*, 103 Harv. L. Rev. 1105, 1111 (1990).

the market for the copied work (factor four).[58] A heavy
market impact (for example, the defendant selling her
works in direct competition with the plaintiff) tends to
weigh against fair use; light or no impact, in favor of fair
use.[59]

A. Purpose and Character of the Use

The first of the key factors—the "purpose and
character" of the use—has evolved over the Act's first
thirty-six years.[60] The Act states that in determining
"purpose and character," a court must address "whether
such use is of a commercial nature or is for nonprofit
educational purposes." [61] Predictably, then, the early
cases focused on whether the use was commercial or
not.[62]

But the purpose and character of the use can
obviously be more complicated than simply whether
the use is commercial or not. In 1990, then-District
Judge Pierre N. Leval wrote an article in the Harvard
Law Review that dynamited the notion that the purpose

---

[58] *See, e.g., Campbell v. Acuff-Rose*, 510 U.S. at 590–94; Harper & Row
Publishers, Inc. v. Nation Enters., 471 U.S. 539, 566 (1985) ("This . . . factor is
undoubtedly the single most important element of fair use."); Salinger v.
Random House, Inc., 811 F.2d 90, 99 (2d Cir. 1997); Leval, *supra* note 57.

[59] Harper & Row Publishers, Inc., 471 U.S. at 603.

[60] *See* An Act for the General Revision of the Copyright Law, Pub. L.
No. 94-553, 90 Stat. 2541 (1976). The Copyright Act of 1976 became effective
in 1978, 36 years before this article was written. *See* 17 U.S.C.A. § 107(1) (West,
Westlaw through 2014).

[61] 17 U.S.C.A. § 107(1).

[62] *See Harper & Row Publishers., Inc.*, 471 U.S. at 562 ("The fact that a
publication was commercial as opposed to nonprofit is a separate factor
that tends to weigh against a finding of fair use."); *Sony Corp.*, 464 U.S. at 451
("[E]very commercial use . . . is presumptively . . . unfair"). Ten years after
Sony, however, the Court in *Campbell v. Acuff-Rose* noted that "the mere fact
that a use is educational and not for profit does not insulate it from a
finding of infringement, any more than the commercial character of a use
bars a finding of fairness." 510 U.S. at 584.

and character of the use was mostly about commerciality.[63] Leval's seminal article argued instead that analysis of the purpose and character of the use should focus on whether the use was transformative. By transforming the prior work, the later artist adds something creative, which justifies the copying.[64]

Judge Leval's article laid the foundation for the analysis of transformation in fair use. But it was the Supreme Court's explicit approval in *Campbell*[65] that transformed Leval's idea into law.[66] The *Campbell* court described the purpose of analysis under the first fair use factor as determining "whether the new work merely 'supersede[s] the objects' of the original creation,"[67] or whether the use "adds something new, with a different purpose or different character, altering the first with new expression, meaning, or message . . . in other words, whether and to what extent the new work is 'transformative.'"[68] After *Campbell*, transformation was at the heart of fair use.

How does a court determine whether a use is transformative? One obvious approach is to assess the changes made to the original work by the secondary

---

[63] Leval, *supra* note 57, at 1116 n.53 (citing 17 U.S.C. § 107(1) (1982))("The interpretation of the first factor is complicated by the mention in the statute of a distinction based on 'whether such use is of a commercial nature or is for nonprofit educational purposes.' One should not exaggerate the importance of this distinction.").

[64] *See id.* at 1111.

[65] Campbell v. Acuff-Rose Music, Inc., 510 U.S. 569, 572 (1994) ("I believe the answer to the question of justification [of fair use] turns primarily on whether, and to what extent, the challenged use is transformative. The use must be product and must employ the quoted matter in a different manner or for a different purpose from the original.").

[66] *Id.* at 579.

[67] *Id.* (quoting Folsom v. Marsh, 9 F. Cas. 342, 348 (C.C.D. Mass. 1841) (No. 4,901)).

[68] *Id.* (citing Leval, *supra* note 57, at 1111).

user.[69] But courts have also considered the context in which the original work appears in the secondary work.[70] More broadly, the "composition, presentation, scale, color palette, and media" of the secondary work, as well as its "expressive nature"[71] (compared with the original) could be seen as transformative.

Most broadly, each author's purpose in creating work is important to determining transformation, and thus, fair use. [72] Even if the second work is not transformative, the use may be fair if the author's purpose is transformative. Thus, the creation of images much smaller than the originals ("thumbnails") used for internet navigation, but not otherwise transformative, has been found to be a fair use of the original works.[73]

Transformation has also influenced the way in which courts approach other aspects of the defendant's use. For example, transformation can mitigate the negative impact of a commercial use.[74] On the other hand, lack of transformation may have the opposite effect, increasing the weight given to such evidence.[75]

---

[69] *E.g.*, Blanch v. Koons, 467 F.3d 244, 253 (2d Cir. 2006); Kienitz v. Sconnie Nation LLC, 965 F. Supp. 2d 1042, 1051 (W.D. Wis. 2013), *aff'd on other grounds*, 766 F.3d 756 (7th Cir. 2014).

[70] Mattel Inc. v. Walking Mountain Prods., 353 F.3d 792, 801 (9th Cir. 2003).

[71] Cariou v. Prince, 714 F.3d 694, 706 (2d Cir. 2013), cert. denied, 134 S. Ct. 618, (2013).

[72] *Blanch* , 467 F.3d at 253; Bill Graham Archives v. Dorling Kindersley Ltd., 448 F.3d 605, 706 (2d Cir. 2006); Warner Bros. v. RDR Books, 575 F. Supp. 513, 539 (S.D.N.Y. 2008).

[73] *See* Perfect 10, Inc. v. Amazon.com, Inc., 508 F.3d 1146, 1168 (9th Cir. 2007); Kelly v. Arriba Soft Corp., 336 F.3d 811, 822 (9th Cir. 2003).

[74] *See* Suntrust Bank v. Houghton Mifflin Co., 268 F.3d 1257, 1271 (11th Cir. 2001).

[75] *See* On Davis v. The Gap, Inc., 246 F.3d 152, 175 (2d Cir. 2001).

Important as it is, however, transformation has not superseded the other fair use factors.[76] It is just one aspect, albeit the most important aspect, of the first factor (the "purpose and character of the use").[77] The "purpose and character of the use" also depends on whether the use is commercial or for nonprofit educational purposes, in bad faith, or parody.[78] Parody holds a privileged status among kinds of use because permission to create parodies is rarely given, and they are frequently created for profit, hence commercial.[79] Before the rise of transformativeness, defendants often claimed that their work was a parody in an attempt to escape sanctions in a copyright case.[80] Thus, in the first infringement lawsuits against Jeff Koons, which took place before transformation was widely acknowledged as an important element, Koons claimed that his work was parody, as that was the clearest route to winning a fair use case for the defendant.[81] For Koons, the parody

---

[76] *See id.* at 174 (2d Cir. 2001) (quoting Campbell v. Acuff-Rose Music, Inc., 510 U.S. 569, 579 (1994)) (internal quotation marks omitted) ("Although such transformative use is not absolutely necessary for a finding of fair use, the goal of copyright, to promote science and the arts, is generally furthered by the creation of transformative works.").

[77] *See id.* (quoting 17 U.S.C. § 107(1)) ("The heart of the fair use inquiry is into the first specified statutory factor identified as 'the purpose and character of the use.'").

[78] Rogers v. Koons, 960 F.2d 301, 309 (2d Cir. 1992).

[79] *See Campbell v. Acuff-Rose*, 510 U.S. at 596–600 (Kennedy, J., concurring). Justice Kennedy's concurrence in the opinion emphasized that a legitimate parody must target or comment on the original work, using humor. *Id.* at 597. It is not enough that the work use the original to comment on things other than the original, for example society at large or the genre of art to which the original belongs. *Id.* at 599. Kennedy characterized such broader works as "satire," rather than "parody," and found them less deserving of fair use because the need to copy is less than it is when creating a parody. *Id.* at 597.

[80] *See, e.g.*, Hoehling v. Universal City Studios, Inc., 618 F.2d 972 (2d Cir. 1980).

[81] *See generally* Rogers v. Koons, 751 F. Supp. 474 (1990).

defense was conspicuously unsuccessful.[82] Nevertheless, parody is still mentioned in appropriation art cases, usually in conjunction with transformation.[83]

B. Nature of the Copyrighted Work

The second factor under section 107 is the nature of the copyrighted (that is, the copied)[84] work.[85] Courts generally consider whether the copied work is a work of imagination or the arts (which cuts against fair use), or whether it is more fact-based (which tends to cut in favor of fair use).[86] Imaginative and artistic works are closer to the core of intended copyright protection than fact-based works, with the consequence that fair use is more difficult to establish when the former works are copied.[87]

Many works of appropriation art copy expressive works, which are close to the core of copyright protection. We might expect that courts would weigh that factor against fair use in appropriation art cases, and so they did, before *Campbell*.[88] As transformation has become a crucial concept in fair use, however, the

---

[82] *See Rogers*, 960 F.2d at 310; United Feature Syndicate, Inc. v. Koons, 817 F.Supp. 370, 379 (S.D.N.Y. 1993); Campbell v. Koons, 91 CIV. 6055 (RO)), 1993 WL 97381 (S.D.N.Y. Apr. 1, 1993).

[83] This was the case in *Campbell v. Acuff-Rose*. 510 U.S. at 599; *see also* Mattel Inc. v. Walking Mountain Productions, 353 F.3d 792, 803 (9th Cir. 2003); Kienitz v. Sconnie Nation LLC, 965 F. Supp. 2d 1042, 1052 (W.D. Wis. 2013), *aff'd*, 766 F.3d 756 (7th Cir. 2014).

[84] The Act uses the term "the copyrighted work" to refer to the work from which the user copied. The work to which the user copied is simply referred to as the "use." If the use is fair, then both works are copyrighted.

[85] 17 U.S.C. § 107(2) (2012).

[86] See, e.g., Campbell v. Acuff-Rose, 510 U.S. 569.

[87] *Id.* at 586 (Souter, J., majority opinion). The distinction is of less use in a parody case, as parodies seem inevitably to "copy publicly known, expressive works." *Id.*

[88] *See* Rogers v. Koons, 960 F.2d 301, 308 (2d Cir. 1992); United Feature Syndicate, Inc. v. Koons 817 F. Supp. 370, 380 (S.D.N.Y. 1993).

significance of the second factor—the nature of the copyrighted work—seemed to decline. The Second Circuit has held that when the use is transformative, the second factor will not be given much weight.[89] The Ninth Circuit has taken this a step further and held that "the more transformative the new work, the less will be the significance of other factors."[90] The Second Circuit's recent appropriation art case, *Cariou v. Prince*, is in accord.[91]

C. Amount and Substantiality of the Portion Used

The third statutory fair use factor—the amount and substantiality of the portion used in relation to the copyrighted work as a whole—disfavors extensive copying and favors uses that appropriate relatively little from their sources. No court has ever attempted a bright-line rule about how much can be taken. It is clear, though, that "how much" depends on "what for"— that is, how much may be taken depends on the use to be made of the materials (which is factor one).[92] The artist is not limited to taking only what is necessary.[93] The Supreme Court has found that copying an entire work was fair use when the use consisted of videotaping broadcast television programs for home, non-

---

[89] Cariou v. Prince, 714 F.3d 694, 708 (2d Cir. 2013), *cert. denied*, 134 S. Ct. 618 (2013); On Davis v. The Gap, Inc., 246 F.3d 152, 175 (2d Cir. 2001) (finding that even under the best of circumstances, the second factor was "rarely determinative.").

[90] Seltzer v. Green Day, Inc., 725 F.3d 1170, 1176 (9th Cir. 2013) (quoting *Campbell v. Acuff-Rose*, 510 U.S. at 579); *see also Campbell v. Acuff-Rose*, 510 U.S. at 586 (A similar de-emphasis of this factor has happened in parody cases, in which the second factor is not weighed heavily because "parodies almost invariably copy publicly known, expressive works.").

[91] 714 F.3d 694, 708 (2d Cir. 2013), *cert. denied*, 134 S. Ct. 618 (2013) (quoting *Campbell v. Acuff-Rose*, 510 U.S. at 579).

[92] See Campbell v. Acuff-Rose, 510 U.S. at 589.

[93] *Id.* at 588.

commercial use,[94] but all other things being equal, the more that is copied, the less likely a finding of fair use.[95]

Like the other factors, the third factor seems to have diminished in importance with the ascendancy of "transformation" in fair use analysis. [96] The inquiry regarding "transformation" may have completely subsumed this factor, much as it appears to have subsumed the second factor. That is, if the use is highly transformative, the fact that a lot was copied from the original work will not deter a finding of fair use; in fact, sufficient transformation has led some courts to conclude that this factor weighed in favor of fair use— even when the whole underlying work has been copied.[97]

D. Effect of the Use Upon the Potential Market

In 1985, the Supreme Court stated that this factor was "undoubtedly the single most important element of fair use."[98] It requires courts to consider not only the extent of market harm caused by the particular actions of the alleged infringer, but also "whether unrestricted and widespread conduct of the sort engaged in by the

---

[94] Sony Corp. of Am. v. Universal City Studios, Inc., 464 U.S. 417, 496 (1984).

[95] See Harper & Row Publishers, Inc. v. Nation Enters., 471 U.S. 539, 564 (1985); On Davis v. The Gap, Inc., 246 F.3d 152, 175 (2d Cir. 2001); Rogers v. Koons, 960 F.2d 301, 311 (2d Cir. 1992); United Feature Syndicate, Inc. v. Koons, 817 F. Supp. 370, 381 (S.D.N.Y. 1993). But see Blanch v. Koons, 467 F.3d 244, 246, 259 (2d Cir. 2006) (copying entire work does not rule out fair use).

[96] The Second and Ninth Circuits have said the importance of the other factors declines when transformation is found. See supra text accompanying notes 86-93.

[97] Cariou v. Prince, 714 F.3d 694 (2d Cir. 2013), cert. denied, 134 S. Ct. 618 (2013); Bill Graham Archives v. Dorling Kindersley Ltd., 448 F.3d 605 (2d Cir. 2006); Mattell, Inc. v. Walking Mountain Prods., 353 F.3d 792 (9th Cir. 2003).

[98] Harper & Row Publishers, Inc.., 471 U.S. at 566.

defendant . . . would result in a substantially adverse impact on the potential market" for the original.[99] The kind of market harm cognizable under this factor is the harm caused by the new work's substitution for the old work in the market. [100] It is not the *suppression* of demand for the original work that matters, it is *usurpation* of the demand for the original work.[101]

Impact on the market for derivative works may also be considered. Courts have not been very consistent in the analysis of derivative works in this regard.[102] Some courts, taking their cue from the cases before them, simply state that it is obviously possible that someone else might seek to do the very thing done by the defendant but in exchange for payment of a license fee.[103] This kind of judicial speculation inevitably leads to the conclusion that the fourth factor cuts against fair use—one can always imagine the defendant paying for her use. However, when there is evidence of a market for derivative works—similar to the one created by the defendant—and that market would be adversely affected if the derivative use were to become widespread, then a market impact can be shown.[104]

---

[99] Campbell v. Acuff-Rose, 510 U.S. 569, 590 (1994) (quoting 3 M. NIMMER & D. NIMMER, NIMMER ON COPYRIGHT §13.05 (1993)).

[100] *Id.* at 570–71.

[101] *Id.* (finding that most parodies easily pass muster because it is a rare parody that can substitute for the original in the marketplace). *But see* Benny v. Loew's, Inc., 239 F.2d 532 (9th Cir. 1956) (stating a concern that a parody of the movie *Gas Light* might adversely impact the market for the movie—although this case preceded the 1976 Act, and therefore did not consider the factors provided therein).

[102] 1 Howard B. Abrams, The Law of Copyright § 5:171 (2014).

[103] *See, e.g.*, Rogers v. Koons, 960 F.2d 301, 312 (2d Cir. 1992).

[104] *Compare* United Feature Syndicate, Inc. v. Koons, 817 F. Supp. 370 (S.D.N.Y. 1993) (market for sculptures in the shape of a cartoon dog plausible) *with* Mattel Inc. v. Walking Mountain Prods., 353 F.3d 792 (9th Cir. 2003) (market for "adult-oriented artistic photographs of Barbie" doll not plausible).

In today's market for appropriation art, impact on the plaintiff's market is usually negligible. Although one could always speculate that a third party might offer a fee in exchange for the right to create a derivative work like the defendant's, in the absence of such a market or plans to create such a market, a court should ignore such speculation. Moreover, as a practical matter, the plaintiff's and the defendant's works are often not sold in the same market.[105] Hence, the defendant's work cannot substitute for the plaintiff's. When the audiences, the purchasers, and the prices are different for the two works, it is unlikely that there would be a market impact on the plaintiff.[106] But, because one can imagine copying that does not match this description, analysis of the market impact of the copying continues to be important in appropriation art cases.[107]

V. MODEST PROPOSAL

The fair use landscape has been transformed by transformation. The rise of transformation analysis, based on Judge Leval's article, is nothing short of remarkable. It has affected fair use in nearly every context in which fair use can be found. [108] When

---

[105] *See e.g.*, Harper & Row Publishers, Inc. v. Nation Enters., 471 U.S. 539 (1985); Campbell v. Acuff-Rose Music, Inc., 510 U.S. 569 (1994).

[106] *See* Cariou v. Prince, 714 F.3d 694, 708–09 (2d Cir. 2013), *cert. denied*, 134 S. Ct. 618 (2013).

[107] For example, someone might copy a piece of popular, mass-produced art, and sell a large number of copies at about the same price as the original. In such a case, the fact that the copies might be called "art" should not shield the user from a claim of infringement. The appropriation art cases to date, however, involve what we might think of as "gallery art" and do not involve mass production of copies.

[108] Not every fair use case addresses transformation. A study of fair use judicial opinions up to 2005 found that, after *Campbell*, more than 41% of district court opinions, and nearly 19% of circuit court opinions, did not mention transformation. *See* Barton Beebe, *An Empirical Study of U.S.*

transformation is found, the outcome is nearly always a finding of fair use.[109]

We would expect, then, that appropriation art has benefited from the addition of transformation to the fair use analysis. Indeed, it has: the appropriation art cases won by the defendant (i.e., the artist) since *Campbell* were won because of the defendant's "transformation" of the underlying work.[110] That must be seen as progress: Pre-*Campbell*, no appropriation artist had won a case, while post-*Campbell* there have to date been three wins for appropriation art.[111]

Even with transformation, however, fair use is no panacea for appropriation artists. To be sure, most appropriation art strives to be transformative. It seeks to evoke a different response in the viewer than did the original. But, judges can be unpredictable; they might not find the work to be transformative, or even insert some other limit—for example that the degree of copying exceeded the judge's notion of what is necessary for the artist's purpose, even if the use is transformative.[112]

Copyright Fair Use Opinions, 1978-2005, 156 U. PA. L. REV. 549, 604–05 (2008). Nearly 37% of the 68 post-*Campbell* opinions finding fair use did not mention transformation. *See id.* at 605. The analyzed cases are current only through 2005, however, and it is possible that the cases since then have increasingly taken up the idea of transformation.

[109] *See* Beebe, *supra* note 108, at 606.

[110] *See Cariou,* 714 F.3d at 710; Blanch v. Koons, 467 F.3d 244, 253, 256–57, 259 (2d Cir. 2006); *Mattel,* 353 F.3d at 806, 811.

[111] *See, e.g., Cariou,* 714 F.3d 694; *Blanch,* 467 F.3d 244; *Mattel,* 353 F.3d 792.

[112] *E.g.,* Warner Bros. Entm't Inc. v. RDR Books, 575 F. Supp. 2d 513, 544 (S.D.N.Y. 2008) ("A finding of verbatim copying in excess of what is reasonably necessary diminishes a finding of a transformative use."). The idea that a judge, lacking any training, experience, or other qualification, would second-guess what was "necessary" to achieve the artist's purpose is dismaying, and disregards Justice Holmes' famous admonishment that "[i]t

Worse yet for the artist, fair use is an affirmative defense,[113] which can be established only by litigating the question of infringement. It is usually litigated after the plaintiff has made at least a prima facie case of infringement because if infringement cannot be established, there is no need for an affirmative defense. [114] From an academic perspective, this may seem to pose no problem. After all, judicial opinions are an important component of the law that we study. But, a practitioner should immediately see the problem: copyright litigation is expensive.[115] Telling artists that they have the right to make fair use of others' works as long as they are willing to litigate the matter is telling them that they have all the rights they can afford to buy. To allocate the right to create art according to the financial resources of the artist is extravagantly protective of existing work at the expense of new work.

The public interest, too, is damaged by applying copyright law to suppress appropriation art. [116] Copyright's primary purpose is to increase access to copyrighted works.[117] Secondarily, it creates incentives for authors to create.[118] If an author's incentives are not damaged by a use, then, all other things being equal, copyright should not prohibit the use. [119] Yet, the

---

would be a dangerous undertaking for persons trained only to the law to constitute themselves final judges of the worth of pictorial illustrations, outside of the narrowest and most obvious limits." Bleistein v. Donaldson Lithographing Co., 188 U.S. 239, 251 (1903).

[113] 17 U.S.C. § 107 (2012).

[114] *See, e.g.,* Celotex Corp. v. Catrett, 477 U.S. 317 (1986).

[115] Professor Litman refers to it as "hideously expensive." JESSICA LITMAN, DIGITAL COPYRIGHT 183 (Prometheus Books 2001).

[116] *See* Schaumann, *supra* note 1, at 263–65.

[117] *Id.* at 263.

[118] *Id.* at 260.

[119] *Id.* at 264

mechanism for balancing those interests, fair use, is so costly that for artists it is inadequate.

A solution exists that would allow a court to limit the damage to the public interest without damaging the authors' incentive. It is both workable and practical. Of course, it would be opposed, but even the opponents would find it hard to argue that it would cause harm.[120]

Courts could accomplish this by recognizing that a use that fits the definition of a "work of visual art," as defined in the Copyright Act,[121] is highly likely to be a fair use. The court would evaluate transformativeness, but also should look at harm to the market. In this regard, it is hard to imagine a work of visual art

---

[120] One fear might be that such a proposal could lead to an industry of so-called "artists" making "appropriation art" based on high-value existing works, selling the copies as if they were the originals. In other words, favoring appropriation art might promote widespread art fraud. But, the art world is already familiar with the problem of fraud, and it is a criminal matter. Any connection between copyright rules and art fraud is pure speculation. For their part, copyright owners might prefer that all uses of their works, whether harmful or not, be left to their discretion. But the question is not which rule copyright owners would favor; rather, it is which rule is most in the public interest.

[121] A "work of visual art" is (1) a painting, drawing, print, or sculpture, existing in a single copy, in a limited edition of 200 copies or fewer that are signed and consecutively numbered by the author, or, in the case of a sculpture, in multiple cast, carved, or fabricated sculptures of 200 or fewer that are consecutively numbered by the author and bear the signature or other identifying mark of the author; or (2) a still photographic image produced for exhibition purposes only, existing in a single copy that is signed by the author, or in a limited edition of 200 copies or fewer that are signed and consecutively numbered by the author. A work of visual art does not include—(A)(i) any poster, map, globe, chart, technical drawing, diagram, model, applied art, motion picture or other audiovisual work, book, magazine, newspaper, periodical, data base, electronic information service, electronic publication, or similar publication; (ii) any merchandising item or advertising, promotional, descriptive, covering, or packaging material or container; (iii) any portion or part of any item described in clause (i) or (ii); (B) any work made for hire; or (C) any work not subject to copyright protection under this title. 17 U.S.C. § 101 (2012).

harming the market for more commercialized works
because "works of visual art" can exist only in two
hundred or fewer copies, signed and consecutively
numbered. The market for such works is relatively
small, and it consists of purchasers who are generally
sophisticated and knowledgeable about what they are
purchasing. Buyers in this market are familiar with the
practice of selling copies of works; they are called
"reproductions." There are generally at least two
differences between a reproduction and a work of
appropriation art: First, appropriation art itself is
attributed to an artist, different from the artist who
created the original work, whereas reproductions are
uncredited. Second, the intention of the appropriation
artist is different from that of the creator of the original
work, while reproductions seek to simulate the presence
of the original work. Attribution is enough to take care
of most of the potential problems that copying might
create. For example, Sherri Levine's photographs of
photographs taken by Edward Weston would not
compete in the art market with the Weston originals:
Levine's practice of naming those works *After Edward
Weston* and signing her works would take care of that.

VI. CONCLUSION

Appropriation art is a legitimate and long-standing
art form practiced by many twentieth- and twenty-first
century artists. Copyright law, which is intended to
promote access to creative works, has struggled to come
to grips with appropriation art because this kind of art
uses preexisting works as its subject material; it
comments on culture using the icons of culture.
Because appropriation art copies without the
permission of the copyright holder, copyright law tends
to sweep it into the category of infringement. However,
unlike most copying, appropriation art does not raise

the problems of unauthorized exploitation and usurpation of the market for the original.

A relatively easy solution is available. Courts should recognize the legitimacy of appropriation art as an artistic practice and take account of the lack of danger to existing art markets posed by appropriation artists, as long as the copying takes the form of a "work of visual art" as defined in the Copyright Act. The common characteristics of such works, described in this definition, are enough to assure that no significant harm can result from the practice. That lack of harm together with the primary purpose of copyright—to increase access to creative works—are enough to suggest that appropriation artists should win all or nearly all the infringement cases brought against them.

THE EMPEROR'S NEW DIGITAL CLOTHES: THE ILLUSION OF COPYRIGHT RIGHTS IN SOCIAL MEDIA

Mihajlo Babovic†

---

†Mihajlo Babovic is a student at William Mitchell College of Law expected to graduate in the spring of 2015. Babovic's primary area of interest is accommodating media and IP laws to address new technologies and digital interactions. He has been active on Facebook since 2005, following a brief stint on MySpace, and has amassed nearly 1,000 friends. Babovic can also be found on Twitter and LinkedIn. He can be reached by email at mihajlo.babovic@wmitchell.edu.

I. INTRODUCTION

Increasingly, life takes place in a digital world. In 2012, Internet users across the US, UK, and Australia spent 27% of their time online participating on social media websites. [1] More than ever before, social interactions are governed by emerging technology—yet our copyright system has been slow to react, allowing companies, which offer the services that users love, to take advantage of those same users. Plain and simple, a large portion of the content posted on social websites is copyrightable. [2] But, through Terms of Service agreements, users license away every single exclusive right that copyright laws grant them.[3] For this, they receive nothing. Artful contract writing allows these agreements to satisfy the law, continuing a trend where users give away their valuable content in exchange for social network access.[4] A remedy does not yet exist, at least so far as a court would recognize, that would allow users to nullify these oppressive agreements. These agreements change the incentive structure underlying copyright law and should be constitutionally prohibited.[5]

---

[1] *Experian Marketing Services Reveals 27 Percent of Time Spent Online is on Social Networking in 2012*, EXPERIAN (Apr. 16, 2013), http://press.experian.com/United-States/Press-Release/experian-marketing-services-reveals-27-percent-of-time-spent-online-is-on-social-networking.aspx.

[2] *See infra* Part I.

[3] *See infra* Part II.A.1.a–d.

[4] *See infra* Part III.

[5] *See infra* Part IV.

II. WHAT CONSTITUTES A SOCIAL MEDIA WEBSITE AND IS CONTENT POSTED TO THESE WEBSITES COPYRIGHTABLE?

Social media usage has grown exponentially since the turn of the century, and as of January 2014, 74% of Internet users above the age of 18 use some form of social networking website.[6] While users of these sites can likely envision exactly what constitutes a "social networking" or "social media" website, defining the term in a legal sense presents more difficulty. I propose a definition of social media: Internet-based applications and tools that allow users and communities to share, co-create, discuss, and modify information and user-generated content (UGC).[7] This concept is different from that of social networking, which describes websites that "facilitate the connection of users via online technologies."[8] The distinction is a fine one, and certain websites would certainly fall into both social

---

[6] *Social Networking Fact Sheet*, PEW RESEARCH INTERNET PROJECT, http://www.pewinternet.org/fact-sheets/social-networking-fact-sheet/ (last visited Oct. 24, 2014) (82% of internet users aged 30–49 and 89% of users aged 18–29 utilize at least one social networking website).

[7] Andreas M. Kaplan & Michael Haenlein, *Users of the World, Unite! The Challenges and Opportunities of Social Media*, 53 BUS. HORIZONS 59, 61 (2010) (defining social media as "a group of Internet-based applications . . . that allow the creation and exchange of User Generated Content" creating interactive platforms through which this content can be shared and modified); *see also Social Media*, WIKIPEDIA, http://en.wikipedia.org/wiki/Social_media (last modified Oct. 21, 2014).

[8] Steven A. Cook, Hiroaki Ogata & Mark G. Elwell, *Meta-Documentation: The Dissemination of the Tacit Knowledge Inherently Attached to Organisational Documents*, PROCEEDINGS OF THE 21ST INTERNATIONAL CONFERENCE ON COMPUTERS IN EDUCATION, 2 (2013), *available at* http://icce2013bali.org/datacenter/mainconferenceproceedingsforindividualdownloa d/c4/C4-s-164.pdf ("Social Network Services (SNS) . . . have been defined as a network of users who are typically connected offline . . . [but studies have demonstrated] that SNS is also used as a way for users to venture out and make contact with users outside their immediate circle of offline friends/acquaintances.").

media and social networking categories—the important difference being a question of what the focus of user interaction is, that is, whether the focus is UGC (social media), as opposed to creating and maintaining social connections (social networking).[9] So, much like the relation of squares to rectangles, social networking websites will always include UGC, but a social media site will not always include the type of community categorized as a social networking website. This article will specifically discuss four social media websites: Facebook, Twitter, LinkedIn, and YouTube. Before that discussion, however, the above provided definition of social media admittedly requires further qualification; most notably, what is UGC? Is this content copyrightable? And, if so, who owns the copyright?

A. What is User-Generated Content?

Following the conclusion that social media websites are online communities where users can interact with, post, and modify UGC, we must determine precise boundaries for what might be considered "user-generated" content.[10] One author suggested that a "user," in regards to social media, might be synonymous with an "amateur,"[11] but such a statement is simply not true—to be a user simply requires an online avatar, whether famous or not, that can represent either an

---

[9] See id. (explaining that users are drawn to Social Network Services for benefits such as friendship and advice giving/receiving, and eventually form connections of trust).

[10] See generally Len Glickman & Jessica Fingerhut, User-Generated Content, 30 NOV. ENT. & SPORTS L. 3 (2012) (explaining that "there is no widely accepted definition of user-generated content," and generally describing UGC as "material uploaded on the Internet by website users").

[11] See Steven Hetcher, User-Generated Content and the Future of Copyright: Part One—Investiture of Ownership, 10 VAND. J. ENT. & TECH. L. 863, 871 (2008).

individual or an organization.[12] The word "generate" is a verb used to describe the process of producing something, or causing something to be produced.[13] User-generated content, then, means that the individual or organization has created, produced, or developed the content—the phrase in itself would seem to contain an implicit level of creativity.[14]

Content that is user-generated implies that the user had a hand in making or editing the content to a large extent. Ultimately, however, creativity is not the primary distinction between the creation and curation of content—the latter describing the process of gathering, sifting through, selecting, and presenting content. Take for example Pinterest, where users curate content and compile "pins" that "are visual bookmarks for good stuff you find anywhere around the web."[15] Can the assembling of these "pins" be inherently creative? Absolutely, and the law is prepared to reward authors for such work.[16] The contrast between curating and creating, then, must lie in the user's role in producing the content—where "the user is not merely a

---

[12] *Twitter Top 100 Most Followers*, TWITTER COUNTER, http://twittercounter.com/pages/100 (last visited Oct. 24, 2014). This regularly updated list of the 100 most "followed" users on Twitter is comprised of actors, musicians, athletes, politicians, as well as news outlets such as CNN.

[13] *Generate*, MERRIAM-WEBSTER.COM, http://www.merriam-webster.com/dictionary/generate (last visited Oct. 24, 2014) (defining generate as "to produce (something) or cause (something) to be produced").

[14] Sacha Wunsch-Vincent & Graham Vickery, *Participative Web: User-Created Content*, WORKING PARTY ON THE INFORMATION ECONOMY 8 (2007), http://www.oecd.org/sti/38393115.pdf.

[15] *About Pinterest*, PINTEREST, https://about.pinterest.com/en (last visited Oct. 24, 2014).

[16] Fiest Publ'ns, Inc. v. Rural Tel. Serv. Co., 499 U.S. 340, 350–51 (1991) ("A factual compilation is eligible for copyright if it features an original selection or arrangement or facts, but the copyright is limited to the particular selection or arrangement.").

casual part of a new copy of some preexisting content being reproduced."[17] The role of the user in creating the content, or put another way, the extent of his or her original contribution, has important implications as to the copyright protection granted to the work. Before discussing the strength of copyright protections in various UGC, we must first determine what content, if any, is copyrightable.

B. Is User-Generated Content Copyrightable?

In order to receive copyright protection, a work must be both original and fixed in a tangible medium of expression.[18] Case law has held that copying a file to RAM fulfills the fixation requirement because the copy can be "perceived, reproduced, or otherwise communicated," even if for a temporary period of time.[19] Applying this standard to social media content will result in the same outcome, as the work is posted online for the purpose of being perceived and reproduced, and will thus satisfy the constitutional requirement of fixation.[20] A more disputable question arises when UGC is forced to fulfill the requirement of originality. The long applied standard for originality in copyright is "extremely low . . . [requiring only] some creative spark, 'no matter how crude, humble, or

---

[17] Hetcher, *supra* note 11, at 871–872.

[18] 17 U.S.C. § 102(a) (2012); *see* London-Sire Records, Inc. v. Doe 1, 542 F. Supp. 2d 153, 171 (D. Mass. 2008) (holding that a sound recording downloaded via peer-to-peer file sharing was fixed for the purposes of the Copyright Act); Stenograph L.L.C. v. Bossard Assocs., Inc., 144 F.3d 96 (D.C. Cir. 1998) (holding that the installation of software onto a computer constituted created a "fixed" copy).

[19] MAI Sys. Corp. v. Peak Computer, Inc., 991 F.2d 511, 519 (9th Cir. 1993) (quoting 17 U.S.C. § 101 (2012)); *see also* Vault Corp. v. Quaid Software, Ltd., 847 F.2d 255 (5th Cir. 1988).

[20] 17 U.S.C. §102(a) (2013) ("Copyright protection subsists . . . in original works of authorship *fixed in any tangible medium of expression . . . .*") (emphasis added).

obvious' it might be." [21] And, while novelty is not necessary, [22] the work must "owe its origin" [23] to the author, or—in the case of online media—to the posting user. [24] But as a baseline, user-generated content can be copyrightable, and courts have fielded a variety of infringement actions regarding UGC and the websites that host it. [25] While not all UGC posted online will meet this originality threshold, some certainly will. But where are we to draw the dividing line?

1. What UGC is Copyrightable?

Spontaneity and community, two features that make social media so unique and popular, also present the most difficult issues regarding the copyrightability of UGC. A "tweet," an opinionated blog posting, or a Facebook "status update" come directly from the mind of the user and are posted to the internet—this is expression in its most basic sense, and would certainly seem to fulfill the originality and fixation requirements of copyright law. [26] Due to its nature, however, UGC

---

[21] *Feist*, 499 U.S. at 345 (1991) (quoting 1 M. NIMMER, NIMMER on COPYRIGHT § 108[c][1] (1988)).

[22] Baker v. Selden, 101 U.S. 99, 102–103 (1879).

[23] Burrow-Giles Lithographic Co. v. Sarony, 111 U.S. 53, 57–58 (1884).

[24] Alfred Bell & Co. v. Catalda Fine Arts, 191 F.2d 99, 102 (2d Cir. 1951) ("'Original' in reference to a copyrighted work means that the particular work 'owes its origin' to the 'author.' No large measure of novelty is necessary.") (quoting *Baker*, 101 U.S. at 102–103)).

[25] Perfect 10, Inc. v. Giganews, Inc., 993 F. Supp. 2d 1192 (C.D. Cal. 2014) (questioning whether a bulletin board website that hosted infringing photographs could receive immunity under the §512 safe harbor provision); Wolk v. Kodak Imaging Network, Inc., 840 F. Supp. 2d 724 (S.D.N.Y. 2012) (action concerning the application of the §512 safe harbor provision for the website Photobucket); *See* Lenz v. Universal Music Corp., 572 F. Supp. 2d 1150 (N.D. Cal. 2008) (infringement action concerning a video on YouTube).

[26] *Feist*, 499 U.S. at 346 (1991) (a work is original if it is "founded in the creative powers of the mind").

runs into problems when coping with (1) the interaction of originality and length, and (2) the related issues presented when considering the doctrine of merger.

a.   The Preclusion of Copyright Protection Due to Length or the Doctrine of Merger

The social media platform Twitter, where tweets are famously limited to 140 characters, would seem to come under the heaviest scrutiny when discussing the interplay between length and originality. While there is no length requirement for a work to be eligible for copyright protection, courts are averse, for good reason, to grant protection to short phrases.[27] This is not an end-all, but it does raise the bar for copyrightability— for the "smaller the effort the greater must be the creativity in order to claim copyright protection."[28] For a tweet to be copyrightable, then, it would need to contain a patently original arrangement of words, or perhaps the creative fashioning of new (or combined) words.[29] Copyrightability also hinges on the necessity

---

[27] Kitchens of Sara Lee, Inc. v. Nifty Foods Corp., 266 F.2d 541, 544 (2d Cir. 1959) ("[S]logans, and other short phrases or expressions cannot be copyrighted." (quoting Copyright Office Publ'n, No. 46, COPYRIGHT IN COMMERCIAL PRINTS AND LABELS (1958)); see also Ets-Hokin v. Skyy Spirits, Inc., 225 F.3d 1068, 1080–81 (9th Cir. 2000) (explaining that copyright could not be granted to the textual logo on a Skyy vodka bottle without accompanying illustrations or considering the bottle as a whole).

[28] 1 M. Nimmer, NIMMER ON COPYRIGHT § 2.01[B] (1988).

[29] Rich Stim, Copyright Protection for Short Phrases, STANFORD UNIVERSITY   LIBRARIES   (Sept.   9,   2003), http://fairuse.stanford.edu/2003/09/09/copyright_protection_for_sh ort/ ("Whether you can stop someone else from using your literary phrases is dependent upon the uniqueness and value of the phrases as well as the way in which you use them."); see Heim v. Universal Pictures Co., 154 F.2d 480, 488 (2d Cir. 1946) (copying might be demonstrated "by showing that a single brief phrase, contained in both pieces, was so idiosyncratic in its treatment as to preclude coincidence").

that the work represents an expression, rather than an idea, and that the idea is capable of many modes of expression—certainly we would not grant copyright protection to a tweet that simply states, "So excited for the weekend!"

The doctrine of merger focuses on whether a specific idea is capable of various modes of expression, or whether the expression is "ineluctably and inextricably intertwined with the idea."[30] UGC on social media websites—much of which is aimed at expressing one's self[31]—can in many circumstances be so simple or common that the subject matter would be appropriated were we to award a copyright for its expression.[32] Or, take a news service posting breaking stories on social media: could a short description of the story followed by a link to the entire story be copyrightable? It would seem that a summary of a factual story would necessarily be merged with the factual content it

---

[30] Coquico, Inc. v. Rodriguez-Miranda, 562 F.3d 62, 68 (1st Cir. 2009); see Mason v. Montgomery Data, Inc., 967 F.2d 135, 139 (5th Cir. 1992) ("If the court concludes that the idea and its expression are inseparable, then the merger doctrine applies and the expression will not be protected."); Apple Computer, Inc. v. Franklin Computer Corp., 714 F.2d 1240, 1253 (3d Cir. 1983) (stating that the inquiry is whether the idea and its expression have merged, which occurs "when there are no or few other ways of expressing a particular idea").

[31] Sonia Livingstone, *Taking Risky Opportunities in Youthful Content Creation: Teenagers Use of Social Networking Sites of Intimacy, Privacy and Self-Expression*, 10(3) NEW MEDIA & SOC'Y 393, 397 (2008) (explaining that teenagers use Facebook as a medium to express who they are and what they are feeling to others in their online community).

[32] 2 William F. Patry, PATRY ON COPYRIGHT § 4:46 (WestlawNext Database updated Sept. 2014) ("[I]t is necessary to say that subject matter [merged with its expression] would be appropriated by permitting the copyrighting of its expression. We cannot recognize copyright as a game of chess in which the public can be checkmated.").

expresses, making it unfit for copyright.[33] Yet, this certainly does not preclude all UGC from copyright protection—there exist a plethora of sufficiently unique UGC to be found on any social media website.

Another example is a photograph uploaded to a social media website. Our copyright system has long recognized copyright protection for photographs, so long as they are "original conceptions of the author."[34] The fact that the author of a photograph, a user, uploads the photo onto a social media website does not exhaust his or her interest in controlling the distribution of the work—no compensation was paid, meaning that this situation does not implicate the "first sale" doctrine.[35] Similarly, a user who recounts a story via a Facebook status update could claim copyright ownership to that writing, so long as a grant of copyright would not be precluded by the doctrines

---

[33] Kimberley Isbell, *The Rise of the News Aggregator: Legal Implications and Best Practices* BERKMAN CENTER RESEARCH PUBLICATION NO. 2010-10 (Aug. 30, 2010), *available at* SSRN: http://ssrn.com/abstract=1670339.

[34] Burrow-Giles Lithographic Co. v. Sarony, 111 U.S. 53, 58 (1884) ("We entertain no doubt that the constitution is broad enough to cover an act authorizing copyright of photographs, so far as they are representatives of original intellectual conceptions of the author."); *see* Latimer v. Roaring Toyz, Inc., 601 F.3d 1224 (11th Cir. 2010) (analyzing a case of alleged infringement of digital photographs and shows that copyright can indeed be granted to photos that exist only in digital format).

[35] Sebastian Int'l, Inc. v. Consumer Contacts, Ltd., 847 F.2d 1093, 1095 (3d Cir. 1988) ("The copyright statutes have been amended repeatedly in an attempt to balance the authors' interest in the control and exploitation of their writings with society's competing stake in the free flow of ideas, information and commerce. Ultimately, the copyright law regards financial reward to the owner as a secondary consideration." (citing Sony Corp. of Am. v. Universal City Studios, Inc., 464 U.S. 417 (1984)) (citation omitted)).

discussed above. Or, even a joke being told via Twitter[36] can certainly possess the originality required to receive copyright protection in the work. Take for instance original videos, scholarly articles, and blog posts; the examples are plenty, and users clearly have copyright interests in original content uploaded to social media websites. This framework is more complicated, however, when considering compilation works where users have appropriated content from all over the web.

b.   Modifying or Combining Previously Posted Works

In the case of a compilation work where the user has not created any of the compiled material, the compilation only receives limited protection to the extent that the "selection, coordination, or arrangement" of the material is original.[37] So in the case of a Pinterest user's "pins," the user would need to show that an infringer had copied an original element of the compilation—this would certainly not be an easy task.[38] Similarly, a user who modifies a work or object from the public domain would receive thin copyright protection for the new work.[39] This grant of copyright

---

[36] *E.g.*, @Jay_FrickinLynn, TWITTER (May 7, 2014, 5:05 PM), https://twitter.com/Jay_FrickinLynn/status/464164101665476610 ("Stabbing yourself in the gums with a chip is God's way of fat shaming you.").

[37] Fiest Publications, Inc. v. Rural Tel. Serv. Co., 499 U.S. 340, 359 ("[C]opyright protects only the elements that owe their origin to the compiler—the selection, coordination, and arrangement" of material.); *see* 17 U.S.C. § 103(b) (2012) ("The copyright in a compilation . . . extends only to the material contributed by the author of such work, as distinguished from the preexisting material employed in the work, and does not imply any exclusive right in the preexisting material.").

[38] *Fiest*, 499 U.S. at 361 ("[T]he selection and arrangement of facts cannot be so mechanical or routine as to require no creativity whatsoever . . . .").

[39] Satava v. Lowry, 323 F.3d 805, 812 (9th Cir. 2003) (An artist who created a jellyfish sculpture was only granted copyright protection to

would only protect original expressions that the user actually contributed to the underlying idea.[40] In both cases, the ability of the user to safeguard his or her work is extremely limited because of the reduced copyright protection interests therein.

Alternatively, because of the ease of appropriating content illegally online, there are issues with the copyrightability of much posted content—namely, that these works do not "owe [their] origin" to the posting user (the purported author). [41] Under these circumstances, the appropriating user could consider a fair use defense; however, the availability of such a defense is contingent on the user's purpose for reproducing the original.[42] The Copyright Act lists a four-factor analysis for fair use; however, such a determination is "an open-ended and context-sensitive inquiry."[43] Because fair use is fact intensive and many

---

the extent that the artistic choices were not governed by jellyfish physiology. The court explained that this protection is "thin" in that the artist "may prevent others from copying the original features he contributed, but he may not prevent others from copying elements of expression that nature displays for all observers . . . .").

[40] *Id.* at 813 ("An artist may . . . protect the original expression he or she contributes to these ideas. An artist may vary the pose, attitude, gesture, muscle structure, facial expression, coat, or texture of animal.").

[41] Alfred Bell & Co. v. Catalda Fine Arts, 191 F.2d 99, 102 (2d Cir. 1951). This is assuming the user does not attribute the material to its author or home website.

[42] 17 U.S.C. § 107 (2012) (The fair use defense applies so long as the original work was appropriated "for purposes such as criticism, comment, news reporting, teaching (including multiple copies for classroom use), scholarship, or research . . . .").

[43] Blanch v. Koons, 467 F.3d 244, 250–51 (2d Cir. 2006); *see* 17 U.S.C. § 107 (1–4) (listing the factors to determine the existence of fair use: (1) the purpose and character of the use, (2) the nature of the copyrighted work, (3) the amount and substantiality of the portion used in relation to the copyrighted work as a whole, and (4) the effect of the use upon the potential market for or value of the copyrighted work).

social media Terms of Service agreements prohibit illegal posting of material,[44] user appropriation of otherwise copyrighted material is outside the scope of this article's discussion.[45] Additionally, because of their reduced copyright protection interests, curated works (compilations) and those with thin copyright protection also fall somewhat outside of this discussion.

---

[44] Most, if not all, social media websites are immune from liability for infringing material uploaded by its users via the mechanisms outlined in § 512 of the copyright act. This section lists takedown requirements for websites that host user material, which, if followed, allow the site to gain immunity from contributory infringement claims. Because of this, social media sites hold little responsibility regarding user posted material infringing copyrights within their domains. For more information on these requirements see 17 U.S.C. § 512 (2012).

[45] *See Statement of Rights and Responsibilities*, § 5.1, FACEBOOK (last updated Nov. 15, 2013), https://www.facebook.com/legal/terms [hereinafter *Facebook Rights & Responsibilities*] (The user must agree to "not post content or take any action on Facebook that infringes or violates someone else's rights or otherwise violates the law."); *Terms of Service*, § 9, TWITTER (last updated Sept. 8, 2014), https://twitter.com/tos [hereinafter *Twitter Terms of Service*] ("Twitter respects the intellectual property rights of others and expects users of the Services to do the same. We will respond to notices of alleged copyright infringement that comply with applicable law and are properly provided to us."); *User Agreement*, § 11, LINKEDIN (last updated Mar. 16, 2014), https://www.linkedin.com/legal/user-agreement [hereinafter *LinkedIn User Agreement*] ("[T]his Agreement requires that information posted by Members be accurate and not in violation of the intellectual property rights or other rights of third parties."); *Terms of Service*, § 6.F, YOUTUBE (last updated June 9, 2010), https://www.youtube.com/static?template=terms [hereinafter *YouTube Terms of Service*] ("YouTube does not permit copyright infringing activities and infringement of intellectual property rights on this Service, and YouTube will remove all Content if properly notified that such Content infringes on another's intellectual property rights.").

C. Who Owns Copyrightable Content on Social Media Websites?

The Copyright Act states that a "copyright in a work protected under this title vests initially in the author or authors of the work."[46] In many cases, this analysis is very straightforward: a user creates a song, video, or text posting from scratch, and uploads it to the social media site of their choice—thus there is little question as to who owns the copyrighted content.[47] Issues of ownership, however, do arise, sometimes in ways that are unique to social media, and in ways that are not. These questions span topics from collaborative work[48] and works made for hire [49] to infringement and associated penalties.

1. Implications of Joint Authorship in Social Media

A joint work is defined in the Copyright Act as one that is "prepared by two or more authors with the

---

[46] 17 U.S.C. § 201(a) (2012) (also relevant is that "authors of a joint work are coowners of copyright in the work").

[47] Will Clark, *Copyright, Ownership, and Control of User-Generated Content on Social Media Websites* 8, CHI.-KENT COLL. L. REV. (2009), http://www.kentlaw.edu/perritt/courses/seminar/papers%202009%20f all/Jerry%20clark%20final%20Copyright,%20Ownership,%20and%20Co ntrol%20of%20User-Generated%20Content%20on%20Social%20Media%20Websites.pdf (listing examples of a mother posting a picture of her child on Facebook, or an independent band uploading a self-made music video on YouTube).

[48] *See generally* Aalmuhammed v. Lee, 202 F.3d 1227 (9th Cir. 2000) (establishing a framework for determining, the point at which a contributor can be considered an author in joint work, for "that authorship is not the same thing as making a valuable and copyrightable contribution").

[49] *See generally* Cmty. for Creative Non-Violence v. Reid, 490 U.S. 730 (1989) (establishing a balancing test for determining when an author is an employee, as described using common law agency principles, for the purposes of whether a created work is a "work made for hire").

intention that their contributions be merged into inseparable or interdependent parts of a unitary whole."[50] This requires a specific mental state, and in the absence of a contractual agreement, courts will look to whether the contributing artists expected to be viewed as "co-authors."[51] While in some ways social media brings nothing new to the joint authorship table (artists corresponding digitally to co-author a book, a virtual band,[52] etc.), there are ways in which digital interaction differs fundamentally from the real world.

Take, for example, a conversation on Facebook taking place through a single "post" and numerous "comments" on that post (for simplicity's sake, let us assume this is a two-user conversation). Quite obviously, it is unlikely that the users had the intent to create *any* work, let alone a unitary work with any consideration of joint authorship. Such a conclusion is unsurprising; yet, it does not end our analysis. First, the call-and-response nature of online chat interaction lends itself well to an implicit intent to create a joint work. Surely, both users understand that they are contributing only part of the original material in the work, and intend the final chat dialog to be a summation of both users' responses to one another. Objectively, and assuming the users contributed a

---

[50] 17 U.S.C. § 101 (2012).

[51] Childress v. Taylor, 945 F.2d 500, 508 (2d Cir. 1991) (explaining that the inquiry is whether the authors "entertain in their minds the concept of joint authorship, whether or not they understood precisely the legal consequences of that relationship"); *see also* Erickson v. Trinity Theatre, Inc., 13 F.3d 1061, 1069 (7th Cir. 1994) ("Even if two or more persons collaborate with the intent to create a unitary work, the product will be considered a 'joint work' only if the collaborators can be considered 'authors.'").

[52] *See* Cristen Conger, *What is a Virtual Band?*, HOWSTUFFWORKS, http://electronics.howstuffworks.com/virtual-band.htm (last visited Oct. 20, 2014).

relatively equal amount to the original post and various comment responses, there would seem to be intent to create a joint work.[53] While either user would have a difficult time showing subjective intent to create a work (simply because neither user considers their chat to be the creation of a work at all), intent of the parties can also be determined through their actions in creating the work.[54] Such a determination would ultimately be fact intensive, but, as a general matter, two users writing and responding to one another certainly seem to have a mutual intent to create a chat dialog.[55]

Along with intent to create a joint work, each party's contribution must be independently copyrightable.[56] Without a specific chat interaction to analyze, this discussion will remain relatively rudimentary. The originality threshold for copyrightable works is low— assuming that the summation of each user's chat contributions was somewhat significant and creative,

---

[53] Therese M. Brady, *Manifest Intent and Copyrightability: The Destiny of Joint Authorship*, 17 FORDHAM URB. L.J. 257, 269 (1989) ("The authors' objective contributions to a joint work determine ownership.").

[54] *Id.* at 277 ("[T]he court in *Strauss v. Hearst Corp.* followed the common design doctrine by determining the intent of the parties from their actions in creating the work."); *see* Strauss v. Hearst Corp., 1988 WL 18932, *6 ("Here there is no doubt that Strauss and Popular Mechanics intended that 'their contributions be merged into inseparable or interdependent parts of a unitary whole.' In fact, it is hard to imagine a set of facts that is any clearer on that point.").

[55] Thomson v. Larson, 147 F.3d 195, 201–02 (2d Cir. 1998) ("[T]he contribution even of significant language to a work does not automatically suffice to confer co-author status on the contributor . . . a specific finding of mutual intent remains necessary.").

[56] Erickson v. Trinity Theatre, Inc., 13 F.3d 1061, 1071 (7th Cir. 1994) (applying a two-pronged test for joint authorship, requiring: (1) that the parties intended to be joint authors at the time of work creation, and (2) that their contribution were independently copyrightable).

there should be no issue in regards to originality.[57] Once a chat response is posted, it has been fixed in a tangible medium, the second requirement of copyrightability.

So, it would seem that two users could be granted joint authorship protection for a combined chat dialog. But, does the same reasoning apply in a more complicated context where users contribute independently to a much larger whole?

a. The Wikipedia Conundrum

Wikipedia is "a multilingual, web-based, free-content encyclopedia project . . . [that] is written collaboratively by largely anonymous Internet volunteers who write without pay." [58] These circumstances seem most comparable to a film, a large-scale project where the legal question yearning for an answer is whether a particular contributor is an author of the joint work under the purposes of 17 U.S.C. § 101.[59] The court in *Aalmuhammed v. Lee* outlined important factors when looking for joint authorship in absence of a contract:[60] (1) the degree of control exercised over the

---

[57] Nimmer, *supra* note 28, § 2.01[A] ("Originality in the copyright sense means only that the work owes its origin to the author, *i.e.*, is independently created, and not copied from other works.").

[58]   *Wikipedia:*   *About*,   WIKIPEDIA, http://en.wikipedia.org/wiki/Wikipedia:About (last modified Oct. 8, 2014) (Wikipedia allows anybody with Internet access to edit and write new material for its articles, as well as contribute references, images, and other media).

[59] Aalmuhammed v. Lee, 202 F.3d 1227, 1232 (9th Cir. 2000) (holding that authorship is statutorily required for the formation of a joint work, and that "authorship is not the same thing as making a valuable and copyrightable contribution"); *see* 17 U.S.C. § 101 (2012).

[60] It is recognized that Wikipedia contributors must agree to the website's Terms of Use, which is a contract. And while the lack of reference to joint authorship in these terms is telling, there is potential joint authorship between the many contributors of a particular article, and certainly these independent writers have not

work; (2) an objective manifestation of shared intent to
be coauthors; and (3) the share of each contribution in
the work's success cannot be appraised.[61] Because of the
wide range of interactions and contributions that might
arise on Wikipedia, there are some circumstances
where the *Aalmuhammed* test is fulfilled, and many
where it is not.

Consider two specific fact scenarios: First, where a
group of five users write an entire Wikipedia article
about the company that they work for together. Second,
where a few unacquainted users submit content on a
large Wikipedia article (let's say, Spider-Man[62]) that is in
turn edited by another set of users (this is the common
practice on the website).[63] Looking to the first set of
facts and applying the *Aalmuhammed* factors, the
Wikipedia article could be found to be a joint work
(relying on some important assumptions about the
users' conduct). Control, the first factor, looks to
exercising superintendence over the work; in other
words, creating or giving effect to the ideas.[64] To fulfill
this element, the users would need to work on a level

---

signed a contract between one another. *See Terms of Use*, WIKIMEDIA
FOUNDATION,   http://wikimediafoundation.org/wiki/Terms_of_Use
[hereinafter *Wikimedia Terms of Use*] (last modified July 8, 2014).

[61] *See Aalmuhammed*, 202 F.3d at 1234 ("Control in many cases will
be the most important factor.").

[62] *Spider-Man*, WIKIPEDIA (last updated Oct. 20, 2014, 7:48 AM),
http://en.wikipedia.org/wiki/Spider-Man.

[63] Henry Blodget, *Who the Hell Writes Wikipedia, Anyway?*,
BUSINESS   INSIDER   (Jan.   3,   2009,   8:39   AM),
http://www.businessinsider.com/2009/1/who-the-hell-writes-
wikipedia-anyway ("The bulk of the original content on Wikipedia is
contributed by tens of thousands of outsiders, each of whom may not
make many other contributions to the site. The bulk of the *changes* to
the original text, then, are made by a core group of heavy editors who
make thousands of tiny edits.").

[64] *Aalmuhammed*, 202 F.3d at 1234 ("[A]n author 'superintend[s]'
the work by exercising control." (quoting Burrow-Giles v. Sarony, 111
U.S. 53, 61 (1884)).

playing field, where no single writer would tell the others what to write or have the ability to unilaterally veto contributions of the others. [65] Running on this assumption, the users would likely each contribute a comparable amount to the work, and through these efforts could be said to have met the second factor by making an "objective manifestation of intent to be coauthors." [66] And finally, because each user would equally help bring about the ultimate whole, the "audience appeal of the work" would turn on their collective, not individual, contributions. [67] These facts are, admittedly, quite specific and somewhat unrealistic, but they do illustrate that a group of users could contribute to a Wikipedia article, and have an expectation of copyright ownership in it.

The more common occurrence on Wikipedia is one where multiple authors contribute a bulk of the substance, which is in turn edited by a number of other users. Clearly, there is no control by any one user over the work—indeed, any Internet user can make changes to a Wikipedia page.[68] It is this same characteristic that makes it impossible for all contributors to a work to

---

[65] *See id.* at 1234–35. In *Aalmuhammed,* Spike Lee was in control of the creation of a movie because Lee was not bound to accept any recommendations and ultimately chose what was included in the film and what was not.

[66] *Id.* at 1235.

[67] *Id.* at 1234 ("[T]he audience appeal of the work turns on both contributions and 'the share of each in its success cannot be appraised.'" (quoting Edward B. Marks Music Corp. v. Jerry Vogel Music Co., 140 F.2d 266, 267 (2d Cir. 1944))).

[68] *See Wikimedia Terms of Use, supra* note 60 ("We welcome you ('you' or the 'user') as a reader, editor, author, or contributor of the Wikimedia Projects, and we encourage you to join the Wikimedia community."); *see also* Blodget, *supra* note 63 ("What users love about Wikipedia is the ability to make minor contributions (on the fly) to an existing piece of work—they don't want to read or vote on a handful of competing 'articles' and petition a single author to make changes.").

hold any expectation of joint authorship: edits can be
made anonymously and without approval of previous
writers/editors. [69] The ability to appraise each
contribution need not be discussed, for the first two
elements weigh strongly against the determination that
a joint work has been created.[70]

Regardless, Wikipedia states in its Terms of Service
agreement that users who submit copyrightable work
agree to license such work under either (or both) the
Creative Commons Attribution-ShareAlike 3.0
Unported License or the GNU Free Documentation
License.[71] The Creative Commons license allows other
users to share and adapt uploaded content (even
commercially) so long as proper attribution is given,
and additional restrictions are not added to the
content.[72] The GNU license carries very similar terms.[73]
Wikipedia contributors must agree to apply one of
these licenses to their copyrighted work, so it is of little

---

[69] *See Aalmuhammed*, 202 F.3d at 1235 (noting as significant that
none of the parties expressed any intention of co-authorship).
Likewise, a heavy content contributor on Wikipedia could not express
an intention to be considered a co-author with an editor whom he or
she knows nothing about.

[70] *Id.* ("[A]bsence of control is strong evidence of the absence of
co-authorship.").

[71] *Wikimedia Terms of Use, supra* note 60.

[72] *Attribution 3.0 United States*, CREATIVE COMMONS,
https://creativecommons.org/licenses/by/3.0/us/ (last visited Oct. 21,
2014) (defining "Share" as "copy and redistribute the material in any
medium or format" and Adapt as "remix, transform, and build upon
the material."). Also worth noting is that the "licensor cannot revoke
these freedoms as long as you follow the license terms." *Id.*

[73] *GNU Free Documentation License*, GNU OPERATING SYSTEM § 2
(Nov. 3, 2008), http://www.gnu.org/copyleft/fdl.html ("You may copy
and distribute the Document in any medium, either commercially or
noncommercially, provided that this License, the copyright notices,
and the license notice saying this License applies to the Document are
reproduced in all copies, and that you add no other conditions
whatsoever to those of this License.").

consequence whether or not a joint work has been created. However, such issues could arise on other social media platforms and illustrate a complex and unique copyright issue presented by Internet usage in conjunction with authorship.

b. Social Media and Employment

The use of social media within the employment sphere presents unique issues in regards to the ownership of UGC. If an employee uses his or her social media avatar to develop business contacts, court new clients, or post company information, could this not be part of their work on behalf of the employer?[74] The Copyright Act provides for two circumstances in which a work will be one that was made for hire: (1) the work is prepared by an employee in the scope of his or her employment, or (2) the work is specially ordered or commissioned.[75] Of those two mechanisms for creating a work made for hire, the former can create much more substantial issues for employees.

What does it mean for content to be prepared in the scope of employment? Statutory interpretation of this part of the Copyright Act has led to the adoption of common-law agency principles for determining what

---

[74] *See* G. Ross Allen & Francine D. Ward, *Things Aren't Always as They Appear: Who Really Owns Your User Generated Content?*, 3 No. 2 LANDSLIDE 49, 52 (2010) ("A business's social media policy should be sure to address how employees may reference and use business property such as communications, press releases, and trademarks, when mixing such content with the employees' personal property.").

[75] 17 U.S.C. § 101 (2012) ("A 'work made for hire' is . . . a work specially ordered or commissioned for use as a contribution to a collective work . . . if the parties expressly agree in a written instrument signed by them that the work shall be considered a work made for hire.").

constitutes the scope of employment. [76] Looking to
those principles, an employee is acting within the scope
of employment if: (1) it is the kind of work "he is
employed to perform"; (2) "it occurs substantially
within the authorized time and space limits"; and (3) "it
is actuated, at least in part, by a purpose to serve" the
employer.[77] As is evident, these limits go beyond the use
of a company avatar in social media, and could very
easily extend to UGC posted from an employee's
personal account.

III. TERMS OF SERVICE AND THEIR USE IN SOCIAL MEDIA

Terms of Service, also referred to as Terms of Use
or Terms and Conditions, are a series of rules or
conditions one must agree to in order to use a web
service. Earning the name "clickwrap" agreements, such
terms have been upheld by courts so long as users are
given a clear opportunity to read through the
agreement.[78] While each social media site drafts and

---

[76] *See* Cmty. for Creative Non-Violence v. Reid, 490 U.S. 730, 740
(1989) ("[W]e have concluded that Congress intended to describe the
conventional master-servant relationship as understood by common-
law agency doctrine.").

[77] RESTATEMENT (SECOND) OF AGENCY § 228 (1958) (listing a fourth
factor: "if force is intentionally used by the servant against another,
the use of force is not unexpectable by the master").

[78] Hancock v. AT&T Co., 701 F.3d 1248, 1256 (10th Cir. 2012)
("Courts evaluate whether a clickwrap agreement's terms were clearly
presented to the consumer, the consumer had an opportunity to read
the agreement, and the consumer manifested an unambiguous
acceptance of the terms."); *see also* Specht v. Netscape Commc'ns
Corp., 306 F.3d 17, 32–35 (2d Cir. 2002) ("[W]here consumers are
urged to download free software at the immediate click of a button, a
reference to the existence of license terms on a submerged screen is
not sufficient to place consumers on inquiry or constructive notice of
those terms.... [R]easonably conspicuous notice of the existence of
contract terms and unambiguous manifestation of assent to those
terms by consumers are essential if electronic bargaining is to have

implements its own terms, the agreements share many similarities [79] —unsurprising considering how comparable the services offered through the various websites are. So long as the terms of service do not bury specific terms so as to surprise users,[80] the contracts are enforceable. Thus, users are faced with a choice to either accept the terms or refrain from taking part in social media.

A. Licensing the Use of User-Generated Content

A user does not relinquish ownership or rights in copyrightable material merely by agreeing to the terms of service of a particular social media website. For example, a Twitter user grants Twitter "a worldwide, non-exclusive, royalty-free license (with the right to sublicense) to use, copy, reproduce, process, adapt, modify, publish, transmit, display and distribute such Content."[81] The agreement also allows Twitter to share this content with other companies "with no compensation paid" to the user.[82] But even though the user retains ownership of the content, he or she effectively loses the right control the dissemination of

---

integrity and credibility.") (footnote omitted); Serrano v. Cablevision Sys. Corp., 863 F. Supp. 2d 157, 164 (E.D.N.Y. 2012) ("In the context of agreements made over the internet, such "click-wrap" contracts are enforced under New York law as long as the consumer is given a sufficient opportunity to read the end-user license agreement, and assents thereto after being provided with an unambiguous method of accepting or declining the offer.").

[79] *Compare Facebook Rights & Responsibilities, supra* note 45, *with Twitter Terms of Service, supra* note 45, *and LinkedIn User Agreement, supra* note 45, *and YouTube Terms of Service, supra* note 45.

[80] Bragg v. Linden Research, Inc., 487 F. Supp. 2d 593, 606 (E.D.Pa. 2007) (explaining that burying an arbitration provision in a lengthy paragraph under the heading "GENERAL PROVISIONS" caused surprise to the user).

[81] *Twitter Terms of Service, supra* note 45.

[82] *Id.*

the work. Terms of service agreements, in general, license a significant chunk of exclusive rights associated with copyright, and have vague limitations on such a license. However, each should be individually examined to determine exactly what rights a user forfeits by registering an account on the specific website.

What follows is an analysis of the intellectual property license provisions found in the Terms of Service agreements of four social media websites: Facebook, Twitter, LinkedIn, and YouTube. When interpreting contracts, the "fundamental objective . . . is to give effect to the expressed intentions of the parties."[83] The objective intent of the parties governs the interpreted meaning, and when the contractual language is unambiguous, "the instrument alone is taken to express the intent of the parties."[84] If ambiguity does exist as to the terms of a contract, the principal purpose of the parties is given great weight (if ascertainable); the writing is interpreted as a whole; and, unless a different intention is manifested, words are given their prevailing meaning. [85] If the contract

---

[83] Klos v. Lotnicze, 133 F.3d 164, 168 (2d Cir. 1997).

[84] Swaminathan v. Swiss Air Transp. Co., 962 F.2d 387, 389 (5th Cir. 1992) ("When interpreting the meaning of a contract it is the objective, and not the subjective intent of the parties which controls. When a contract is unambiguous, the instrument alone is taken to express the intent of the parties.") (citing Fuller v. Phillips Petroleum Co., 872 F.2d 655 (5th Cir. 1989); Shelton v. Exxon Corp., 921 F.2d 595 (5th Cir. 1991)); see also Royal Ins. Co. of Am. v. Orient Overseas Container Line Ltd., 525 F.3d 409, 421 (6th Cir. 2008) (Where contract language is unambiguous, "a court should not use extrinsic evidence to 'attempt to discern the intent of the parties,' but rather should determine their intent from 'the plain language of the contract.'" (quoting United States v. Donovan, 348 F.3d 509, 512 (6th Cir. 2003))).

[85] RESTATEMENT (SECOND) OF CONTRACTS § 202 (1981); see also Firestone Tire & Rubber Co. v. United States, 444 F.2d 547, 551 (Ct. Cl. 1971) ("[T]he language of a contract must be afforded the meaning derived from the contract by a reasonably intelligent person acquainted with the contemporary circumstances.") (citing Hol-Gar

contains technical terms, those terms are given their meaning within the technical field. Given that this analysis will look to the Terms of Service agreements devoid of specific factual circumstances, a few generalizations must be made about both users and social media websites to help ascertain their respective "principal purpose(s)" for entering into an agreement.

Users utilize social media to stay in touch with friends and family, reconnect with old friends, and connect with others sharing similar hobbies or interests.[86] To engage in such behavior, users will chat directly with one another; post their own pictures, thoughts, and creations; and recommend links to various web pages they personally found interesting. Users agree to Terms of Service agreements in order to gain access to the networks that the websites provide. Social media websites are often operated as corporations and as such, make a profit (usually through advertising or subscriptions) for each new user that the service is able to attract.[87] Social media websites,

Mfg. Corp. v. United States, 169 Ct. Cl. 384, 388 (Ct. Cl. 1965); Deloro Smelting and Refining Co. v. United States, 161 Ct. Cl. 489, 495 (Ct. Cl. 1963)).

[86] Aaron Smith, *Why Americans Use Social Media*, PEW RESEARCH INTERNET PROJECT (Nov. 15, 2011), http://www.pewinternet.org/2011/11/15/why-americans-use-social-media/ (finding that 67% and 64% of polled users responded that staying in touch with current friends and family members, respectively, is a major reason they use social media; 50% also listed reconnecting with old friends a major reason; and 14% listed connecting with others who shared hobbies as a major reason, 35% as a minor reason, for their social media use).

[87] *See* Facebook, Inc., Annual Report (Form 10-K), at 42 (Sept. 30, 2014), *available at* http://investor.fb.com/secfiling.cfm?filingID=1326801-14-7 (explaining that Facebook gained an average revenue per user ("ARPU") of $6.81 in the year 2013); Twitter, Inc., Annual Report (Form 10-K), at 48 (Sept. 30, 2014), *available at* https://investor.twitterinc.com/secfiling.cfm?filingID=950123-14-

then, want to increase the number of users, and likely, the number of ways that active users can ultimately interact; these interactions draw early users to a particular social media site, and the establishment of networks ultimately will bring the hordes.

The principal purpose for users and social media websites to enter into an agreement with one another is inextricably linked: users want to join large networks for the social benefits they provide, and social media sites want to provide large networks for the advertising revenue they generate. Intellectual property is an ancillary bargaining chip of these desires, in that the use of a wide variety of UGC—text posting, chat interaction, videos, pictures, music, et cetera—will draw more users, create larger networks, and allow for more diverse interactions. When interpreting these agreements, then, it is important to keep in mind that users are most likely willing to license their intellectual property in order to gain access to the full benefits that the various social media websites offer.

1. Facebook

The Facebook terms of service regarding posted intellectual property state that the user specifically grants the website a "non-exclusive, transferable, sub-licensable, royalty-free, worldwide license to use any IP content that you post on or in connection with Facebook."[88] The agreement later goes on to state that the user grants Facebook:

3031&CIK=1418091#TWTR-
10K_20131231_HTM_ITEM_7_MANAGEMENT_S_DISCUSSION
(listing various graphs that chart Twitter's advertising income per 1,000 timeline views).
   [88] *Facebook Rights & Responsibilities*, *supra* note 45, § 2.1 It is worth noting that the terms qualify this license as being subject to the user's

> permission to use your name, profile
> picture, content, and information in
> connection with commercial, sponsored,
> or related content (such as a brand you
> like) served or enhanced by us .... you
> permit a business or other entity to pay us
> to display your name and/or profile
> picture with your content or information,
> without any compensation to you.[89]

There are a number of ambiguities contained in the preceding quoted sections that should be discussed and resolved before continuing.

First is the scope of the license that users grant Facebook. The clause "on or in connection with Facebook" could mean two things: either it refers to how Facebook can use posted intellectual property, or it states where UGC must be posted in order for Facebook to receive the license. The definitions listed in the agreement do provide guidance here, as "post" specifically refers to posting on Facebook, thus, this license grants Facebook a right to use UGC "on or in connection with" Facebook. You might find yourself asking, what does it mean for something to be "in

---

privacy settings, which can be changed to restrict access to posts or pictures only to the user's "friends" or even further limited to specific contacts on the website; *see also id.* §§ 18.3, 4, 6, 7 (defining (section 3) "information" as facts and other information about the user, including actions taken by users and non-users who interact with Facebook; (section 4) "content" as anything you or other users post on Facebook that would not be included in the definition of information; (section 6) "post" as post on Facebook or otherwise make available by using Facebook; and (section 7) "use" as use, run, copy, publicly perform or display, distribute, modify, translate, and create derivative works of).

[89] *Id.* §10.1–2. Paragraph 2 of this section states "we do not give your content or information to advertisers without your consent"; a small consolation considering the user's consent is required for them to post content or information. *Id.*

connection with Facebook?" Unfortunately for users, the answer is vague at best.

The phrase "in connection with" is seen with relative frequency in legal writing and seems to be synonymous with "in relation to" or "in association with."[90] Thus, users grant Facebook a broad license to utilize UGC posted on the website for any use in relation to Facebook—including the sale of user information or copyrighted work for profit—with no compensation to the posting user. Any limitations on this IP license are difficult to find. Facebook can simply sublicense UGC to the highest bidder, or it could feature user content in advertising, all without compensation to the user. Users should be wary of the broad license they grant when registering for the website, but unfortunately, such content licenses seem to be the industry standard.

2. Twitter

Much like the Facebook Terms of Service, Twitter's terms first explain that the user retains his or her rights to any content posted on the website.[91] The user goes on to grant Twitter a "worldwide, non-exclusive, royalty-free license (with the right to sublicense) to use, copy,

---

[90] *See* BLACK'S LAW DICTIONARY 165 (9th ed. 2009) (defining "conveyancing" as "the art or science of preparing documents and investigating title in connection with the creation and assurance of interests in land. Despite its connection with the word 'conveyance', the term in practice is not limited to use in connection with old system title but is used without discrimination in the context of all types of title.") (quoting Peter Butt, *Land Law* at 7 (2d ed. 1988)); *id.* at 57 (describing "attribution right" as "[a] person's right to be credited as a work's author, to have one's name appear in connection with a work, or to forbid the use of one's name in connection with a work that the person did not create").

[91] *Twitter Terms of Service, supra* note 45, § 5 ("You retain your rights to any Content you submit, post or display on or through [Twitter's] Services.").

reproduce, process, adapt, modify, publish, transmit, display and distribute [posted] Content in any and all media or distribution methods." [92] This agreement expressly includes:

> [T]he right for Twitter to provide, promote, and improve the Services and to make Content submitted to or through the Services available to other companies, organizations or individuals who partner with Twitter for the syndication, broadcast, distribution or publication of such Content on other media and services, subject to our terms and conditions for such Content use.[93]

The terms and conditions mentioned above do provide some safeguards for users--namely, requiring user permission before: (1) using user content on a commercial durable good or product, (2) creating an advertisement that implies sponsorship or endorsement on the user's behalf, and (3) using content in a manner inconsistent with Twitter's display requirements. [94]

---

[92] *Id.*

[93] *See id.* (defining "Services" as Twitter's various websites, SMS, Application Programming Interfaces (APIs), email notifications, applications, buttons, widgets, ads, and commerce services). The terms further go on to define "Content" as "any information, text, graphics, photos or other materials uploaded, downloaded or appearing on the Services." *Id.*

[94] *Rules of the Road*, TWITTER DEVELOPERS, https://dev.twitter.com/overview/terms/rules-of-the-road (last updated Sept. 16, 2014) ("We encourage you to create advertising opportunities around Twitter content that are compliant with these Rules."); *see also Display Requirements*, TWITTER DEVELOPERS, https://dev.twitter.com/overview/terms/display-requirements (last visited Oct. 16, 2014) (outlining requirements for displaying Tweets— namely, requiring attribution to the author of the tweet, a visible timestamp, the Twitter logo, and that the tweet "must not be altered or modified in any way.").

While the gesture of requiring user permission is admirable, there is no mention of user compensation. There is, however, a clause in the developer terms that states: "In cases where Twitter Content is the primary basis of the advertising sale, we require you to compensate [Twitter]."[95]

The Twitter Terms of Service essentially grant the website a license to exercise every applicable exclusive right granted to a copyright owner.[96] Through this agreement, users allow Twitter to sell or license for profit users' copyrightable material and use any UGC posted material to advertise Twitter's services.[97] While these terms are more defined than those found in the Facebook Terms of Service agreement, the breadth of authorized uses for UGC posted on Twitter is quite astounding. This author, at least, is hard pressed to find uses that could not qualify as the "syndication, broadcast, distribution or publication" of UGC.[98]

3. LinkedIn

Perhaps the most all-encompassing of the discussed Terms of Service agreements was that of LinkedIn, an online professional network with over 300 million users.[99] The social networking site recently modified its

---

[95] *Rules of the Road, supra* note 92.

[96] *Compare* 17 U.S.C. § 106 (2012) (granting copyright owners the right to: (1) reproduce, (2) prepare derivative works, (3) distribute, and (4) display, publicly, the copyrighted work), *with Twitter Terms of Service, supra* note 45, § 5 (the user grants Twitter a license to "use, copy, reproduce, process, adapt, modify, publish, transmit, display and distribute" posted content).

[97] *Twitter Terms of Service, supra* note 45, § 5.

[98] *Id.*

[99] *About Us,* LINKEDIN, https://www.linkedin.com/about-us (last visited Oct. 16, 2014) (boasting users in over 200 countries, LinkedIn's mission is to "connect the world's professionals to make them more productive and successful.").

terms[100] to become much more user-friendly. But until October 23, 2014, users provided LinkedIn the following license for their content:

> [A] nonexclusive, irrevocable, worldwide, perpetual, unlimited, assignable, sublicenseable, fully paid up and royalty-free right to us to copy, prepare derivative works of, improve, distribute, publish, remove, retain, add, process, analyze, use and commercialize, in any way now known or in the future discovered, any information you provide, directly or indirectly to LinkedIn, including, but not limited to, any user generated content, ideas, concepts, techniques, and/or data to the services, you submit to LinkedIn, without any further consent, notice and/or compensation to you or to any third parties.[101]

There are a number of features within this license that make it significantly less desirable for the user than those granted to other users of social media websites.[102]

---

[100] *User Agreement*, LINKEDIN, https://www.linkedin.com/legal/user-agreement (last visited Jan. 31, 2015).

[101] *LinkedIn User Agreement*, *supra* note 43, § 2.2. The agreement does allow users to request the deletion of content/information they post on the website, unless it has been shared with others who have not deleted the content or if it has been copied/stored by other users. *See id.*

[102] It should be noted that LinkedIn is issuing a wide variety of changes to its Terms of Service agreement. Among these changes is a simplification of the contractual language with more limitation on LinkedIn's licensed uses (and the addition of a user ability to revoke the license in any of their content simply by deleting the content from LinkedIn), and additional "layman's" explanations of contractual language. These proposed changes are available at https://www.linkedin.com/legal/preview/user-agreement.

First, the license a user grants to LinkedIn is
irrevocable. Defined as "unalterable," [103] this quality
means that LinkedIn retains a license to UGC even after
users terminate the agreement. Content can only be
deleted upon request and even this is contingent on
whether other users have also deleted the content.[104]
Next, the agreement allows LinkedIn to commercialize
user content "in any way now known or in the future
discovered."[105] In theory, this would seem to allow the
website to publish and sell lists of professionals (users)
in a particular field or location, or compile and sell a
book of business advice written entirely by users,
without compensating the creators of the content.
Lastly, the license allows LinkedIn to use any
information provided "directly or indirectly" by the
user.[106] "Indirectly" is colloquially interchangeable with
"incidentally," meaning that this clause could be
interpreted as granting LinkedIn a license to use
information about a user that was provided by a third
party.[107] The scope of this license greatly exceeds what
would seem to be the norm for Terms of Service
agreements found on social media websites, and
contains what is certainly the broadest content use
license that this author came across in his research.

4. YouTube

Lastly, we look to the Terms of Service agreement
found on YouTube, a widely used social media hub that
"allows billions of people to discover, watch and share

---

[103] BLACK'S LAW DICTIONARY (9th ed. 2009) (defining irrevocable
as "[u]nalterable; committed beyond recall").

[104] *LinkedIn User Agreement, supra* note 43.

[105] *Id.* § 2.2.

[106] *Id.*

[107] This is, admittedly, more of a privacy issue than a copyright
ownership problem.

originally-created videos." [108] The section of the agreement containing the intellectual property license, as would seem to be the industry norm, begins by expressly explaining that "you retain all of your ownership rights in your Content."[109] In what is likely the broadest allowance for commercial use, by signing the agreement, a user grants YouTube:

> [A] worldwide, nonexclusive, royalty-free, sublicenseable and transferable license to use, reproduce, distribute, prepare derivative works of, display, and perform the Content in connection with the Service and YouTube's (and its successors' and affiliates') business, including without limitation for promoting and redistributing part or all of the Service (and derivative works thereof) in any media formats and through any media channels.[110]

What is initially obvious in this license, as compared to those analyzed above, is that YouTube's agreement would have users grant the website the exclusive rights associated with copyright almost verbatim.[111] Moreover,

---

[108] *About YouTube*, YOUTUBE, https://www.youtube.com/yt/about/ (last visited Oct. 16, 2014).

[109] *YouTube Terms of Service, supra* note 45, § 6.C.

[110] *Id.*; *see also id.* § 2.A ("'Content' includes the text, software, scripts, graphics, photos, sounds, music, videos, audiovisual combinations, interactive features and other materials you may view on, access through, or contribute to the Service. The Service includes all aspects of YouTube, including but not limited to all products, software and services offered via the YouTube website such as the YouTube channels, the YouTube 'Embeddable Player,' the YouTube 'Uploader' and other applications.").

[111] *Compare* 17 U.S.C. § 106 (2012) (granting copyright owners the right to: (1) reproduce, (2) prepare derivative works, (3) distribute, (4) perform publicly, (5) and display publicly the copyrighted work), *with*

much like the Facebook Terms of Service, we see that
YouTube is licensed the right to use UGC "in
connection with" its service and business (and the
business of its successors and affiliates).[112] It is consistent
with the canons of statutory interpretation to read this
license as giving YouTube the right to capitalize UGC
for at least "promoting and redistribut[ing]" the
YouTube Service. The breadth with which YouTube can
use UGC would hinge on an interpretation of the
language "including without limitation." There would
seem to be two logical interpretations of that passage as
it appears in the Terms of Service agreement: first, it
could define uses of UGC in connection with the service
as "promoting and redistributing," or second, the phrase
could simply mean that "promoting and redistributing"
are merely types of usages that would fall within the "in
connection with the Service" language—meaning that
the clause is simply illustrative. Case law and Black's
Law Dictionary suggest that the latter interpretation is
correct, and that "promoting and redistributing" the
service are simply examples of how YouTube might
utilize UGC "in connection with the Service."[113] This
license, particularly because it can be used by
YouTube's successors and affiliates business, allows the
website to hugely commercialize, or at least profit from,
UGC. These agreements share many similarities with
one another, and they are all very broad. Especially

YouTube Terms of Service, supra note 45, § 6.C (users license YouTube
the right to "reproduce, distribute, prepare derivative works of,
display, and perform" user uploaded content).

[112] *See supra* Part II.A.1.a.

[113] Optimal Interiors, LLC v. HON Co., 774 F. Supp. 2d 993, 1010
(S.D. Iowa 2011) (quoting BLACK'S LAW DICTIONARY, 831 (9th Ed. 2009)
("[D]efining the word "include" and noting that "some drafters use
phrases such as *including without limitation* and *including but not limited
to*—which mean the same thing". Thus, the phrases 'including,
without limitation,' and 'including, but not limited to' both introduce
items that comprise a *part* of a greater group, class, or aggregate").

given the scale of these IP licenses, a user's ability to terminate the agreements (or licenses) is extremely important to the exercise of their exclusive copyright rights.

B. Termination of the License Granted to Social Media Websites

Most of these agreements do allow the user to terminate them, at any time and for any reason simply by deactivating their account and discontinuing use of the service.[114] However, and again using Twitter's terms as an example, the "Terms will terminate . . . except that the following sections shall continue to apply: 4, 5."[115] Sections 4 and 5 in the Twitter Terms of Service govern the content posted by users and, most notably, includes the license granted to Twitter to use, copy, modify, and distribute the UGC. The application of these terms, then, survives the user's termination of use—meaning that the user effectively has no way to limit how often or with whom Twitter shares the user's content after posting it, so long as any sharing would fall under the Terms of Service. After seeing how broad a license users must give social media websites in order to participate in their online networks, the question of how long such a license lasts begs to be answered.

1. Facebook

Terminating an account on Facebook is relatively straightforward. A user can either disable or completely delete an account at the click (or a few clicks) of a button.[116] However, a user need not even delete his or

---

[114] *See, e.g., Twitter Terms of Service, supra* note 45.

[115] *Id.*

[116] *How Do I Permanently Delete My Account?*, FACEBOOK, https://www.facebook.com/help/224562897555674 (last visited Oct. 2, 2014) (explaining that deactivating your account makes you invisible

her account to remove specific content. As explained by the Terms of Service, "[t]his IP license ends when you delete your IP content or your account unless your content has been shared with others, and they have not deleted it."[117] So while users can delete their content (or entire profile) from Facebook, the ability to actually remove content from Facebook is contingent on whether other users have done so as well.[118] While a user does have the power to severely limit the number of other users who can access their "shared" content, the default settings share a wide variety of content with the user's "friends."[119] Given that the average number of

---

on the website, but your profile information is saved; you can also permanently delete your account, which leaves no option for information recovery).

[117] *Facebook Rights & Responsibilities, supra* note 45, §2.1–2.2 ("When you delete IP content, it is deleted in a manner similar to the recycle bin on a computer. However, you understand that removed content may persist in backup copies for a reasonable period of time (but will not be available to others).").

[118] *How To Post & Share,* FACEBOOK, https://www.facebook.com/help/333140160100643/ (Oct. 2, 2014) ("You can use the audience selector to change who can see stuff you share on your Timeline after you share it. Keep in mind that when you share something on someone else's Timeline, they control the audience for the post.").

[119] Christo Wilson, Bryce Boe, Alessandra Sala, Krishna P.N. Puttaswamy & Ben Y. Zhao, *User Interactions in Social Networks and their Implications,* EUROSYS '09 205–06 (2009), *available at* http://www.cs.ucsb.edu/~ravenben/publications/pdf/interaction-eurosys09.pdf ("By default, a user's profile, including birthday, address, contact information, Mini-Feed, Wall posts, photos, and photo comments are viewable by anyone in a shared network. Users can modify privacy settings to restrict access to only friends, friends-of-friends, lists of friends, no one, or all."); *see also* Larry Magid, *Facebook Changes New User Default Privacy Setting to Friends Only—Adds Privacy Checkup,* FORBES (May 22, 2014, 9:00 AM), http://www.forbes.com/sites/larrymagid/2014/05/22/facebook-changes-default-privacy-setting-for-new-users/ (explaining that Facebook just changed new user default privacy settings last summer from "public" to share content with "friends"; this change "will have no impact on existing users").

friends any given user has on Facebook is 338,[120] the amount of difficulty a single user might face deleting even a single photo from the website seems staggering. To some extent, the ability of a user to remove original UGC from Facebook is out of the user's hands if any other user with whom the content was "shared" has not deleted it as well.

All might not be lost, though, as it would seem that Facebook does limit its ability to utilize UGC after the user's account has been terminated. The provision on account termination states:

> If you violate the letter or spirit of this Statement, or otherwise create risk or possible legal exposure for us, we can stop providing all or part of Facebook to you. We will notify you by email or at the next time you attempt to access your account. You may also delete your account or disable your application at any time. In all such cases, this Statement shall terminate, but the following provisions will still apply: . . . 9.18, 10.3 . . .[121]

Of particular importance is § 10.1, which is noticeably not listed as an active provision following account termination. Provision 10.1 authorizes Facebook to sell user data to businesses or "other entities" without compensation to the user—a very

---

[120] Aaron Smith, *6 New Facts about Facebook*, PEW RESEARCH INTERNET PROJECT (Feb. 3, 2014), http://www.pewresearch.org/fact-tank/2014/02/03/6-new-facts-about-facebook/. Among adults, the average (mean) number of friends is 338, the median is 200; it is also clear that younger generations tend to have larger networks, with 27% of users aged 18-29 having more than 500 friends. *Id.*

[121] *Facebook Rights & Responsibilities, supra* note 45, § 15.

important prospect for users.[122] Most of the provisions
that remain active post-termination concern the use of
Facebook's source code, advertising, and the use of
other users' content and are generally beyond the scope
of this article.[123] The fact that Facebook eliminates its
ability to monetize user content is of the utmost
importance for the user to maintain control over his or
her copyrightable content (and is a little bit surprising).
Lastly, note the unilateral nature with which Facebook
can cease the operations of a particular user's account.
By violating the provisions of the Terms of Service
agreement or otherwise creating "risk or possible legal
exposure," a user's account can be terminated. This
precise provision, and Facebook's action through it, has
been challenged and upheld in court. [124] Given the
unilateral nature that a user can end the agreement with
Facebook, it is not altogether unfair that Facebook can
do the same—it is worth noting that Facebook's
business incentivizes the website to increase the
number of active users on the website and the duration
of their use.

2. Twitter

Twitter's Terms of Service, however, are not so
user-friendly. Users "may end [their] legal agreement
with Twitter at any time and for any reason by

---

[122] *Id.* § 10.1 ("[Y]ou permit a business or other entity to pay us to
display your name and/or profile picture with your content or
information, without any compensation to you.").

[123] *Id.* at § 15. The full list of provisions that continue to apply after
termination are sections: "2.2, 2.4, 3-5, 8.2, 9.1-9.3, 9.9, 9.10, 9.13, 9.15,
9.18, 10.3, 11.2, 11.5, 11.6, 11.9, 11.12, 11.13, and 15–19." *Id.*

[124] *See* Young v. Facebook, Inc., 790 F. Supp. 2d 1110, 1118 (N.D. Cal.
2011) (plaintiff's claim failed because she did not allege that Facebook
terminated her account despite her compliance with the terms; thus
Facebook did not violate the implied covenant of good faith and fair
dealing).

deactivating [their] accounts and discontinuing [their] use of the Services." [125] Following deactivation, about half of the Terms of Service agreement continues to apply, including the section containing the UGC license. [126] This would seem to indicate that, even following account deactivation, Twitter maintains the right to use UGC "with no compensation paid to [the user]." [127] At this point you might ask, can a user do anything to revoke the license granted to Twitter for the use of the content?

When a user deactivates a user account, Twitter only retains the "user data for 30 days from the date of deactivation, after which it is permanently deleted." [128] Having said that, Twitter's Terms of Service do not define what constitutes user data and whether or not user data includes UGC. [129] The agreement defines

---

[125] *Twitter Terms of Service, supra* note 45, § 10 ("You do not need to specifically inform Twitter when you stop using the Services. If you stop using the Services without deactivating your accounts, your accounts may be deactivated due to prolonged inactivity under our Inactive Account Policy."); *see also Inactive Account Policy*, TWITTER, https://support.twitter.com/articles/15362-inactive-account-policy
(last visited Oct. 3, 2014), ("[B]e sure to log in and Tweet (i.e., post an update) within 6 months of your last update. Accounts may be permanently removed due to prolonged inactivity.").

[126] *Twitter Terms of Service, supra* note 45, § 10 ("[Following account deactivation], the Terms shall terminate, including, without limitation, your license to use the Services, except that the following sections shall continue to apply: 4, 5, 7, 8, 10, 11, and 12." The user IP license is contained in section 5.).

[127] *Id.* § 5.

[128] *Deactivating Your Account*, TWITTER, https://support.twitter.com/articles/15358-how-to-deactivate-your-account (last visited Oct. 20, 2014) (containing additionally the simple steps a user must follow to deactivate their Twitter account: (1) sign in, (2) go to account settings and click the "deactivate account" button, (3) read account deactivation information and click "Okay, fine, deactivate account," and (4) enter their password for verification).

[129] Applying canons of statutory interpretation that would require consistency and meaning in each term is inappropriate here, because

content as "any information, text, graphics, photos or other materials uploaded, downloaded or appearing on the services."[130] Data, on the other hand, has a very broad definition.[131] The qualifier "user" seems to indicate that the data can somehow identify a particular user. If this is the case, then "user data" might be synonymous with "personally identifiable information"—which refers to a person's name, address, telephone number, social security number, or credit card information.[132] However, because a user is not required to provide any such information to Twitter when registering an account (indeed, a user can operate an account through a pseudonym), defining "user data" as "personally identifiable information" seems somewhat inapt. But, particularly given that "user data" is referred to when an account is deactivated (as opposed to terminated), the term may be used to refer to account-specific information provided by the user.[133] If this were the case, a more suitable synonym for "user data" might be "user identifiable information" (or "avatar identifiable information"). This class of data would include a user's profile name, profile picture, biographical information, and location as the user chooses to display them on Twitter.[134] If this is the case,

---

the statement regarding the deletion of user data is not contained within the contract.

[130] *Twitter Terms of Service, supra* note 45.

[131] *Data Definition*, MERRIAM-WEBSTER.COM, http://www.merriam-webster.com/dictionary/data (last visited Oct. 20, 2014) (defining data as "information that is produced or stored by a computer").

[132] *E.g.,* 11 U.S.C. § 101(41A) (2012) (providing an equivalent definition for "personally identifiable information" as it applies to the bankruptcy code).

[133] Indeed, termination as contemplated by the agreement most likely takes place at the point that the user data is permanently deleted.

[134] *See generally* Lance Ulanoff, *Twitter's New Profiles: Everything You Need to Know*, MASHABLE (Apr. 8, 2014), http://mashable.com/2014/04/08/twitters-new-profiles-what-you-

then perhaps "user data" refers to some of the user-uploaded content but does not encompass the term.[135]

Assuming that such a conclusion is proper, then Twitter maintains a license to use some user uploaded "Content" even after account termination. The Terms of Service agreement at no point references the ability of a user to remove content from the website, but Twitter does "reserve the right at all times to remove or refuse to distribute any Content on the Services."[136] The stark reality is that users grant Twitter an irrevocable license to use much of the content that they upload on the website, and these same users appear to lack any control over their UGC once it has been posted.

3. LinkedIn

Much of the LinkedIn user agreement also survives account termination. The agreement provides:

> You may terminate this Agreement, for any or no reason, at any time, with notice to LinkedIn pursuant to section 9.3. This notice will be effective upon LinkedIn processing your notice. LinkedIn may terminate this agreement and your

---

need-to-know/ (explaining some changes Twitter made to their profile layouts, as well as how to organize and set up profile information).

[135] *See Twitter Terms of Service, supra* note 45 (defining "Content" to include "any information . . . uploaded, downloaded or appearing on" Twitter; thus, the definition would seem to include a user's profile information).

[136] *Id.* § 8 ("We reserve the right at all times (but will not have an obligation) to remove or refuse to distribute any Content on the Services, to suspend or terminate users, and to reclaim usernames without liability to [the user]."); *see also id.* § 9 ("We reserve the right to remove Content alleged to be infringing without prior notice, at our sole discretion, and without liability to [the user].").

account for any reason or no reason, at
any time, with or without notice . . . .
Upon termination of your LinkedIn
account, you lose access to the Services.
The terms of this Agreement shall survive
any termination, except Section 3 ('Your
Rights') and Sections 4.1., 4.2., and 4.3.
('Our Rights and Obligations'). [137]

The notice requirement as written into the
agreement by LinkedIn is fair, albeit slightly unusual
and seemingly cumbersome for the user. Regardless,
the user content license, as contained in section 2.2 of
the agreement, survives account termination. And
much like the Twitter Terms of Service agreement,
LinkedIn's agreement does not contain any provision
detailing the ability of users to remove their content
from the website. It is worth noting, however, that
LinkedIn is in the process of changing this aspect of its
agreement.[138] Prior to these changes taking effect, the
LinkedIn Terms of Service make no mention of the
ability of the user to remove content from the website.
So, the pending changes to LinkedIn's content
termination policy are extremely user-friendly.

Additionally, the clause granting LinkedIn the
ability to commercialize user content survives account
termination. [139] The maintenance of such a right,

---

[137] *LinkedIn User Agreement, supra* note 43, §§ 7.1, 7.3; *See also id.*
§ 9.3 (providing a link to a question submission form and a mailing
address for providing notice to LinkedIn).

[138] Email from LinkedIn Messages, LinkedIn Customer Service, to
author (Oct. 3, 2014, 9:37 CST) (on file with author) (Effective as of
October 23, 2014, the user will have the ability to remove their
content from the control of LinkedIn. "If you delete something from
our platform, we won't use it anymore.").

[139] *LinkedIn User Agreement, supra* note 43, § 2.2 ("[Y]ou grant
LinkedIn a . . . right to . . . use and commercialize, in any way now
known or in the future discovered, any information you provide,

coupled with the inability of the user to remove posted content from the website, essentially allows LinkedIn to appropriate user content for its own monetary benefit, even long after the user has deleted his or her account from the website. The language granting LinkedIn the right to commercialize user content is completely missing from the pending update to the Terms of Service agreement.[140]

The conclusions to draw here are mixed. On one hand, LinkedIn's Terms of Service agreement as it currently stands exploits user content to a much higher degree than those of similar services; on the other hand, the proposed changes to the agreement are *significantly* more favorable to the user. Here is to hoping that LinkedIn can set the gold standard for years to come, as a harbinger of user-friendly terms of service agreements on social media.

4. YouTube

YouTube's license to user video content posted online, in sharp contrast to the other agreements discussed, is contingent on when the user removes the content from YouTube's website. The Terms of Service agreement provides "licenses granted by [the user] in video Content [submitted] to the Service [to] terminate within a commercially reasonable time after [the user] remove[s] or delete[s] [the] videos from the Service."[141]

---

directly or indirectly to LinkedIn, including, but not limited to, any user generated content, ideas, concepts, techniques and/or data to the services, you submit to LinkedIn, without any further consent, notice and/or compensation to you or to any third parties.").

[140] *See Preview User Agreement*, LinkedIn, https://www.linkedin.com/legal/preview/user-agreement (last visited Oct. 20, 2014) (previewing User Agreement to take effect Oct. 23, 2014).

[141] *YouTube Terms of Service, supra* note 45.

The users "understand and agree, however, that YouTube may retain, but not display, distribute, or perform, server copies of [the] videos that have been removed or deleted."[142] Finally, the licenses" granted by [the user] in user comments [they] submit are perpetual and irrevocable."[143]

More so than the other analyzed agreements, YouTube's Terms of Service allow a user to maintain control over the dissemination of the content they upload to the website. But, what is a "commercially reasonable time?" Both case law and statutory provisions direct that this is to be a highly fact-intensive determination.[144] Certainly, it would be unreasonable for YouTube to continue to distribute a user's video (through the power of the license) six months after the user removed the video from YouTube. How about one month? One week? One day? Given the speed of transactions available via the Internet, a commercially reasonable time likely does not extend beyond one month. Ultimately, however, this determination would only be made if necessitated by litigation—it suffices to say that the language is not facially burdensome for users.

A larger cause for concern arises from the perpetual and irrevocable license in user comments. Certainly, comments are less likely to contain very strong copyright protection interests, but users could claim protection in them, assuming the material is

---

[142] *Id.*

[143] *Id.* § 6(C).

[144] *See* First Nat. Bank of Chicago v. Jefferson Mortg. Co., 576 F.2d 479, 492 (3d Cir. 1978) ("Ordinarily, the circumstances of the particular market involved should determine the duration of a 'commercially reasonable time.'"); U.C.C. §1-205(a) (2013) ("Whether a time for taking an action . . . is reasonable depends on the nature, purpose, and circumstances of the action.").

copyrightable.[145] And quite honestly, YouTube's reason for maintaining a right to the comments is likely more for the purpose of maintaining and facilitating popular discussion topics than monetizing user content. However, the ability to commercialize comments continues to exist, and with it the ability of YouTube to exploit UGC.

IV. THE APPLICATION OF THE UNCONSCIONABILITY DOCTRINE TO SOCIAL MEDIA TERMS OF SERVICE AGREEMENTS

Users, because they have agreed to the terms of service, may look to raise unconscionability as a remedy applicable to contracts generally.[146] Unconscionability requires a showing of two components: (1) procedural––looking for unequal bargaining power and hidden terms; and (2) substantive––"satisfied by overly harsh or one-sided results that 'shock the conscience.'"[147] A determination of unconscionability "cannot be determined merely by examining the face of the contract," but requires inquiry into "the circumstances under which the contract was executed, its purpose, and effect."[148] Given that users certainly do not hold an equal bargaining position as compared to social media websites and the expansive licensing achieved through the Terms of Service agreements could "shock the conscience," users who post UGC on social media sites may have a strong case on their hands.

---

[145] *See supra* Part I.B.1.

[146] *See* Comb v. PayPal, Inc., 218 F. Supp. 2d 1165, 1172 (N.D. Cal. 2002).

[147] *Id.* The two elements interact such that "the more significant one is, the less significant the other need be." *Id.*

[148] *Id.*

A. Procedural Unconscionability

"A contract, or a clause within that contract, is procedurally unconscionable if it is a contract of adhesion."[149] The term *unconscionable* contemplates a contract "imposed and drafted by the party of superior bargaining strength, [which] relegates the subscribing party only the opportunity to adhere to the contract or reject it."[150] Terms of Service agreements are contracts of adhesion––they are presented on a take-it-or-leave-it basis.[151] While there are few market alternatives[152]––as many social media websites have similar terms––the unconscionability inquiry also looks to surprise or the extent to which the "terms of the bargain are hidden."[153] This analysis warrants a case-by-case inquiry, as each websites terms of service are presented differently. However, on the whole, these terms are contracts of adhesion, and some do contain hidden clauses that dictate rights and licenses of user content.

---

[149] Bragg v. Linden Research, Inc., 487 F. Supp. 2d 593, 605 (E.D. Penn. 2007); *see also* Nelson v. McGoldrick, 896 P.2d 1258, 1262 (Wash. 1995) (en banc) ("Procedural unconscionability has been described as the lack of a meaningful choice, considering all the circumstances surrounding the transaction including '[t]he manner in which the contract was entered,' whether each party had 'a reasonable opportunity to understand the terms of the contract,' and whether 'the important terms [were] hidden in a maze of fine print.'" (quoting Schroeder v. Fageol Motors, Inc., 544 P.2d 20, 23 (Wash. 1975) (en banc))).

[150] Armendariz v. Found. Health Psychcare Servs., Inc., 6 P.3d 669, 689 (Cal. 2000) (internal quotation marks omitted).

[151] *See Bragg*, 487 F. Supp. 2d at 606 (explaining that Second Life's terms were a contract of adhesion because a potential participant could either assent to the agreement and enter, or refuse and be denied access).

[152] *See* Ingle v. Circuit City Stores, Inc., 328 F.3d 1165, 1172 (9th Cir. 2003) ("[T]he availability of other options does not bear on whether a contract is procedurally unconscionable.").

[153] *Bragg*, 487 F. Supp. 2d at 606 (internal quotation marks omitted).

1. Oppression

"Oppression arises from an inequality of bargaining power that results in no real negotiation and an absence of meaningful choice."[154] Users, when subscribing to various social media websites, are given no opportunity to negotiate the terms of the contract and are simply required to assent to the terms of the agreement in order to utilize the offered services. Plain and simple, the Terms of Service agreements used by social media websites are "standardized contract[s], imposed upon the subscribing party without an opportunity to negotiate the terms"[155] ––in other words, they are contracts of adhesion. "An adhesion contract fulfills the requirement of procedural unconscionability, although this alone is insufficient to render an arbitration clause unenforceable."[156]

2. Surprise

Surprise looks to whether the particular clause was hidden within the terms of a contract.[157] Considerations affecting this analysis are length of the contract, typeface used, and location of the particular clause

---

[154] Newton v. Am. Debt Servs., Inc., 854 F. Supp. 2d 712, 722–23 (N.D. Cal. 2012) ("While California courts have found that consumer choice can reduce how procedurally unconscionable an arbitration clause is, consumer choice is not determinative of whether there is any procedural unconscionability.").

[155] Shroyer v. New Cingular Wireless Servs., Inc., 498 F.3d 976, 983 (9th Cir. 2007) (quoting Nagrampa v. MailCoups, Inc., 469 F.3d 1257, 1281 (9th Cir. 2006)).

[156] *Newton*, 854 F. Supp. 2d at 723 ("[U]se of a contract of adhesion establishes a minimal degree of procedural unconscionability *notwithstanding the availability of market alternatives*.") (citing Sanchez v. Valencia Holding Co., 135 Cal. Rptr. 3d 19, 31 (Cal. Ct. App. Nov. 23, 2011).

[157] *Id.* at 722–23 ("'Surprise involves the extent to which the supposedly agreed-upon terms are hidden in a prolix printed form drafted by the party seeking to enforce [the disputed terms].'").

within the contract.[158] The intellectual property license found in Terms of Service agreements posted on social media sites could be found to constitute surprise, but the argument is certainly not one-sided. The agreements examined in this paper are well labeled, relatively short, and often include a layman's explanation of contractual language – showing a clear effort to increase access to legally uneducated users.

Facebook's content license is not necessarily a "surprise" clause under legal analysis, but such a finding would not be unreasonable. The clause can be found on page one of a seven page agreement and may be considered "set apart from the rest of the agreement,"[159] in that it is one of five clauses under the specific heading "Sharing Your Content and Information" (which is the second main heading in the agreement).[160] However, the user agrees to the terms by simply clicking a "Sign Up" button when registering his or her account—at no point is a user forced to actually examine the agreement. [161] This specific issue was

---

[158] *See, e.g.,* Estate of Myhra v. Royal Carribean Cruises, 695 F.3d 1233, 1246 (11th Cir. 2012).

[159] *See* Zaborowski v. MHN Gov't Servs., Inc., 936 F. Supp. 2d 1145, 1152 (N.D. Cal. 2013) ("The arbitration clause appears in paragraph twenty of twenty-three paragraphs. It is not set apart from the rest of the agreement in any way, such as highlighting or outlining; the signature line is on the following page, and it does not require a separate signature.").

[160] *Facebook Statement of Rights & Responsibilities, supra* note 45, § 2.

[161] FACEBOOK, https://www.facebook.com/ (last visited Oct. 24, 2014). When a new user visits the website, he or she is prompted to enter a name, email/phone number, password, birthday, and gender. To complete the registration process, a user must click the "Sign Up" button, above which is written: "[b]y clicking Sign Up, you agree to our Terms and that you have read our Data Use Policy, including our Cookie Use." The words "Terms," "Data Use Policy," and "Cookie Use" are all hyperlinked, but, quite literally, are found on different pages. *Id.*

thoroughly discussed in *Fteja v. Facebook, Inc.*[162] In that case, the court explained that Facebook's Terms of Service agreement was not a classic "clickwrap" agreement [163] because it does not "contain any mechanism that that forces the user to actually examine the terms before assenting." [164] The court instead determined that Facebook's Terms of Service agreement was a hybrid clickwrap/"browsewrap" agreement. [165] In reasoning that terms provided via hyperlink were akin to multiple pages of a contract, the court concluded that the user assented to the terms of the agreement in registering a Facebook account— instrumental to this finding was the familiarity the user had with using the Internet.[166] This ruling clearly puts

---

[162] 841 F. Supp. 2d 829, 837–38 (S.D.N.Y. 2012).

[163] *Id.* at 837 ("Yet Facebook's Terms of Use are not a pure-form clickwrap agreement . . . ."). "On the internet, [sic] the primary means of forming a contract are the so-called 'clickwrap' (or 'click-through') agreements, in which website users typically click an 'I agree' box after being presented with a list of terms and conditions of use . . . ." Hines v. Overstock.com, Inc., 668 F. Supp. 2d 362, 366 (E.D.N.Y. 2009).

[164] *Fteja*, 841 F. Supp. 2d at 838; *see also* Register.com, Inc. v. Verio, Inc., 356 F.3d 393, 429 (2d Cir. 2004) ("[U]nder a clickwrap arrangement, potential licensees are presented with the proposed license terms and forced to expressly and unambiguously manifest either assent or rejection prior to being given access to the product.").

[165] *Fteja*, 841 F. Supp. 2d at 838 ("Facebook's Terms of Use are somewhat like a browsewrap agreement in that the terms are only visible via a hyperlink, but also somewhat like a clickwrap agreement in that the user must do something else—click "Sign Up"—to assent to the hyperlinked terms. Yet, unlike some clickwrap agreements, the user can click to assent whether or not the user has been presented with the terms."); *see also Hines*, 668 F. Supp. 2d at 366 (defining a "browsewrap" agreement as one "where website terms and conditions of use are posted on the website typically as a hyperlink at the bottom of the screen").

[166] *Fteja*, 841 F. Supp. 2d at 839–41 ("[A]t least for those to whom the internet is in [sic] an indispensable part of daily life, clicking the hyperlinked phrase is the twenty-first century equivalent of turning over the cruise ticket. In both cases, the consumer is prompted to

the burden on the user to show that the IP license was a surprise, but much like Atlas, the weight of the world often rests on the shoulders of a single, average Internet user.

The crux of this argument would lie in differentiating a forum selection clause from an intellectual property license. As a preliminary matter, "[t]he general rule is that forum selection clauses are regularly enforced."[167] While such has never been said in regards to copyright licenses, grants of nonexclusive licenses do not require a writing (the exclusive transfer of copyrights do). [168] Given that a "nonexclusive copyright license may be granted orally or by implication," [169] it would seem difficult to require separate assent for the license when a user agrees to the Terms of Service agreement. However, implied copyright licenses "simply permit the use of a copyrighted work in a particular manner"[170] and are extremely uncommon.[171] Obviously the license at issue is a written one, but trouble may arise because users are

---

examine terms of sale that are located somewhere else. Whether or not the consumer bothers to look is irrelevant.").

[167] Elite Parfums, Ltd. v. Rivera, 872 F. Supp. 1269, 1271 (S.D.N.Y. 1995) (citing Carnival Cruise Lines, 1 S.Ct. 1522 (1991); *see, e.g.,* Stewart Org., Inc. v. Ricoh Corp., 487 U.S. 22, 29 (1988); The Bremen v. Zapata Off-Shore Co., 407 U.S. 1, 92 (1972); Weiss v. Columbia Pictures Television, Inc., 801 F. Supp. 2d 1276, 1282 (S.D.N.Y.1992)).

[168] Foad Consulting Group, Inc. v. Azzalino, 270 F.3d 821, 825 (9th Cir. 2001) ("[G]rants of nonexclusive copyright licenses need not be in writing."); *see* 17 U.S.C. § 204(a) (2012) ("A transfer of copyright ownership, other than by operation of law, is not valid unless an instrument of conveyance, or a note or memorandum of the transfer, is in writing and signed by the owner of the rights conveyed . . . .").

[169] *Foad,* 270 F.3d at 826.

[170] I.A.E., Inc. v. Shaver, 74 F.3d 768, 775 (7th Cir. 1996).

[171] Estate of Hevia v. Portrio Corp., 602 F.3d 34, 41 (1st Cir. 2010) ("We do not mean to suggest that implied licenses are an everyday occurrence in copyright matters. The opposite is true: implied licenses are found only in narrow circumstances.").

not forced to read—or even look at—the agreement before assenting to a license (an entire agreement, really) that is found on a separate page.[172] This factor was important when analyzing the surprise of an arbitration clause.[173] A copyright license, particularly one as broad as the implied one, should be given due consideration—I do not see why social media websites should be spared for making clear what its users are agreeing to.

The IP license in Twitter's Terms of Service is contained in section 5 of the contract, which is titled "Your Rights" and found on page two of a seven-page agreement.[174] Immediately below the license, Twitter writes a "tip" that states: "This license is you authorizing us to make your Tweets available to the rest of the world and to let others do the same."[175] The desire to inform users as to what the agreement states is admirable, and a showing that a user understood the contract can weigh against a finding of procedural

---

[172] *See* Fteja, 841 F. Supp. 2d at 837–38 ("While the Terms of Use require the user to click on 'Sign Up' to assent, they do not contain any mechanism that forces the user to actually examine the terms before assenting.").

[173] *See* Bragg v. Linden Research, Inc., 487 F. Supp. 2d 593, 605 (E.D. Penn. 2007); *see also* Lau v. Mercedes-Benz, No. CV 11-1940, 2012 WL 370557, at *8 (N.D. Cal. 2012) ("Although the paragraph on the front mentions the arbitration clause on the back, the language lies imbedded inconspicuously within a paragraph of the same font size, and on the opposite side of the page where the Mr. Lau's signature was required.").

[174] *Twitter Terms of Service, supra* note 45, § 5.

[175] *Id.* (The tip is referring to the IP license: "By submitting, posting or displaying Content on or through the Services, you grant us a worldwide, non-exclusive, royalty-free license (with the right to sublicense) to use, copy, reproduce, process, adapt, modify, publish, transmit, display and distribute such Content in any and all media or distribution methods (now known or later developed).").

unconscionability. [176] However, Twitter's "tip" doesn't adequately describe the license. While Twitter is likely explaining a majority of its uses under the license, the actual conveyance of rights is far greater than what a reader might assume. Further, there is no explanation of the terms explaining that users will receive no compensation for the use of their work. While the comparison might leave something to be wanting, I would argue that an IP clause should require the same kind of treatment within a contract as a class-action waiver. In such scenarios, courts have required that the particular clause be in all-caps font and presented in a "conspicuous manner." [177] The IP license could be labeled with more clarity, explained more honestly, and all-caps font could be used to focus readers in on more important parts of the license. While none of this is done, as explained above, it is quite clear that a nonexclusive copyright grant is not as central of a right to a user as the ability to participate in a class-action lawsuit. Ultimately, the element of surprise is most likely not fulfilled, as the IP license is easy to find and easy to read (the same can be said of the other analyzed Terms of Service agreements).

---

[176] Nelson v. McGoldrick, 896 P.2d 1258, 1262 (Wash. 1995) (en banc) (weighing against a finding of procedural unconscionability because there was no indication that McGoldrick lacked adequate time to study the contract, and there was no indication that she did not understand the contract language).

[177] Pleasants v. Am. Express Co., 541 F.3d 853, 857 (8th Cir. 2008) (citing Pleasants v. Am. Express Co., No. 4:06–CV–1516, 2007 WL 2407010, at *5 (E.D. Mo. Aug.17, 2007) ("[T]he class-action waiver was in all-caps font and found that the 'conspicuous manner in which the arbitration clause was presented distinguishes this case from those which found the clauses invalid.'").

B. Substantive Unconscionability

Substantive unconscionability focuses on the one-sidedness of the contract terms considering a number of different factors, but the most fundamental requirement is that it "shock the conscience."[178] Many cases on substantive unconscionability dealt with arbitration clauses instead of copyright license agreements, making their analyses somewhat inapplicable to these circumstances. Yet, an important factor that has previously been considered is that of mutuality, or whether the contractual terms contain a "modicum of bilaterality."[179] This analysis considers the facial neutrality of the contract as well as "the actual effects of the challenged provision."[180] In this particular field, other elements are certainly of importance: the user's right to regulate the dissemination of his or her content beyond the authorized company and profits made using UGC. An application of these standards and a discussion of other relevant considerations will result in a finding that the terms of usage are substantively unconscionable.

---

[178] Newton v. Am. Debt Servs., 854 F. Supp. 2d 712, 724 (N.D.Cal. 2012); *see also* Nagrampa v. MailCoups, Inc., 469 F.3d 1257, 1280 (9th Cir. 2006) (quoting Armendariz v. Found. Health Psychcare Servs., Inc., 24 Cal.4th 83, 114, 99 Cal.Rptr.2d 745, 6 P.3d 669 (2000) ("An arbitration provision is substantively unconscionable if it is 'overly harsh' or generates 'one-sided results.'").

[179] *Id.*; *see also* Abramson v. Juniper Networks, Inc., 115 Cal. App. 4th 638, 657 (Cal. 6th Dist. Ct. App. 2004) ("[T]he paramount consideration in assessing conscionability is mutuality.").

[180] Ting v. AT&T, 319 F.3d 1126, 1149 (9th Cir. 2003) (finding an arbitration provision in a contract unconscionable because the terms allowed the defendant to "impose the arbitration forum on the weaker party without accepting that forum for itself").

Class action waivers found in consumer contracts have been found to be substantively unconscionable.[181] A primary distinction between a class action waiver and the intellectual property license at bar is, of course, that a waiver denies a right, while a license assigns rights to another. Regardless, the one-sided terms contained within the Terms of Service agreements concern termination of the IP license. Of particular issue are Facebook's content deletion barrier and the lack of license revocation in Twitter's and LinkedIn's terms of service. [182] But for this particular analysis, Twitter's termination clause presents the best case for substantive unconscionability.[183]

A lack of mutuality is important when considering substantive unconscionability.[184] The Terms of Service agreement here, particularly with respect to the IP license, is absolutely one-sided.[185] But most important is

---

[181] *See* Chalk v. T-Mobile USA, Inc., 560 F.3d 1087, 1096 (9th Cir. 2009) (explaining that the class action waiver in T-Mobile's service agreement was substantively unconscionable because it is unilateral in effect, and it discourages consumers from litigation, effectively robbing them of their right to be compensated for a claim); *see also* Vasquez-Lopez v. Beneficial Oregon, Inc., 152 P.3d 940, 950 (Or. Ct. App. 2007) ("[T]he opportunity that the class action ban denies to borrowers is, in many instances, a crucial one, without which many meritorious claims would simply not be filed.").

[182] *See supra* Part III.B.1–3.

[183] When a user terminates his or her Facebook profile, Facebook loses its ability to monetize user content. Twitter does no such thing. Additionally, because LinkedIn's Terms of Service will soon be undergoing a radical change, it makes little sense to analyze the current agreement for unconscionability. Email from LinkedIn Messages, LinkedIn Customer Service, to author (Oct. 3, 2014, 9:37 CST) (on file with author).

[184] Grabowski v. Robinson, 817 F. Supp. 2d 1159, 1173 (S.D. Cal. 2011) (a "lack of mutuality is relevant in analyzing" substantive unconscionability).

[185] But perhaps it is necessary. Twitter could not hand away its IP content and stay in business for very long.

whether the agreement is "so one-sided as to *shock the conscience*."[186] A user, when agreeing to the Terms of Service, licenses Twitter a "worldwide, non-exclusive, royalty-free license (with the right to sublicense) to use, copy, reproduce, process, adapt, modify, publish, transmit, display and distribute [posted content] in any and all media or distribution methods."[187] For this license, the user gains access to the Twitter network and any specific activities associated with such access—the agreement expressly states that Twitter will not compensate the user for the use of his or her content.[188] And, when a user decides to remove content from Twitter, the termination provision makes no guarantee that Twitter will end its use of UGC.[189] In this situation, the party with more bargaining power and sophistication has acquired a large bundle of rights through the veil of a nonexclusive license. This result certainly shocks the conscience because a user to the website has traded the ability to monetize an indefinite amount of uploaded material in exchange for access to a service (that will commercialize the user's content in his stead). Given the right facts, where Twitter has substantially profited from the unsolicited use (outside the Terms of Service agreement) of a user's content, the website's agreement could be found both procedurally and substantively unconscionable, rendering it legally unenforceable. However, because Twitter's terms are significantly more one-sided, and the facts necessary are quite specific, this result would likely not apply to the agreements employed by Facebook or YouTube or LinkedIn.

---

[186] *Grabowski*, 817 F. Supp. 2d at 1173 (quoting Davis v. O'Melveny & Myers, 485 F.3d 1066, 1075 (9th Cir. 2007)).

[187] Agence Fr. Presse v. Morel, 934 F. Supp. 2d 547, 560 (S.D.N.Y. 2013).

[188] *Id.*

[189] *See supra* Part III.B.2.

V. SOCIAL MEDIA TERMS OF SERVICE
AGREEMENTS AS AGAINST COPYRIGHT
POLICY

In the case that a court would find the social media Terms of Service agreements conscionable, and thus valid under contract law, this author would like to argue in the alternative that enforcing these Terms of Service agreements ultimately undermines the purpose of copyrights.[190] By disseminating the content of users beyond any expectation they might have when originally registering to use the service, these social media websites are lowering the incentive of users to create original work and post it to these online communities. The primary objective of copyright law is to secure to the public "the benefits derived from authors' labors"—it is well accepted that part of this benefit is gained when original works are created.[191] Additionally, copyright laws exist to "facilitate the flow of ideas in the interest of learning."[192] Protection for works, then, is granted in order to incentivize artistic creativity through the grant of a temporary monopoly over the work.[193] It has been said by the Supreme Court

---

[190] Eldred v. Ashcroft, 537 U.S. 186, 247 (2003) ("copyright statutes must serve public, not private, ends; that they must seek 'to promote the Progress' of knowledge and learning; and that they must do so both by creating incentives for authors to produce . . . .") (quoting 2 S. JOHNSON, A DICTIONARY OF THE ENGLISH LANGUAGE 1151 (4th rev. ed. 1773)).

[191] H.R. REP. NO. 100-609, at 17 (1988) ("Under the U.S. Constitution, the primary objective of copyright law is not to reward the author, but rather to secure for the public the benefits derived from the authors' labors. By giving authors an incentive to create, the public benefits in two ways: when the original expression is created and . . . when the limited term . . . expires and the creation is added to the public domain.").

[192] *Id.* at 22.

[193] Cnty. of Suffolk v. First Am. Real Estate Solutions, 261 F.3d 179, 194 (2d Cir. 2001) ("Copyright benefits the public by providing an

that "[t]he sole interest of the United States and the primary object in conferring the monopoly lie in the general benefits derived by the public from the labors of authors."[194]

Are the terms of these agreements not effectively robbing lay users of the exclusive rights associated with their copyrights? Given that the Terms of Service agreements analyzed here confer a license that includes every single exclusive right granted to copyright owners, the user has lost control over the monopoly granted to them by the Constitution.[195] This economic incentive, the "sole interest" in providing copyright protection at all, rests in the ability of the owner to control the reproduction and dissemination of his or her work. The simple fact is that lay Internet users do not fully understand the copyrights they hold, particularly because life in a digital world demolishes the fixation barrier precluding copyright protection to mere conversations. The invention of the computer coupled with widespread internet usage means that copyrightable material is easier than ever to create, and harder than ever to control. [196] And, while it may certainly be argued with some legitimacy that Internet users should understand the risks of posting any

---

incentive to stimulate artistic creativity through the grant of a temporary monopoly to a copyright owner.").

[194] Fox Film Corp. v. Doyal, 286 U.S. 123, 127 (1932).

[195] U.S. CONST. art. I, § 8, cl. 8; 17 U.S.C. § 106 (2012); *see supra* Part II.A.1.a–d.

[196] Internet Watch Foundation, *Study of Self-Generated Sexually Explicit Images & Videos Featuring Young People Online*, p. 6, *available at* https://www.iwf.org.uk/assets/media/resources/IWF%20study%20-%20self%20generated%20content%20online_Sept%202012.pdf (finding that 88% of content assessed appeared on "parasite" websites, demonstrating the startling lack of control capable of being exercised once content has been circulated online).

content online (regardless of location), the crux of the issue lies with commercialization of UGC.

By establishing a marketable right to monetize an author's creative expression, "copyright supplies the economic incentive to create *and* disseminate ideas."[197] While a large majority of UGC posted on social media websites is uploaded and forgotten with little financial impact, social media websites clearly profit from the trafficking and distribution of the content—if they did not, why would their Terms of Service agreements include express provisions allowing the websites to sell user information and content? [198] Under these circumstances, the incentive to disseminate still exists, but it has changed hands through the granting of a license. It is true that social media websites are better situated to profit off UGC, but is it fair to strip the providers of this content of any compensation for their original works? Ultimately, the IP license found in social media Terms of Service agreements eliminate the individualized incentive to create new works, swindle users out of any due compensation, **and should be found to violate the copyright clause of the Constitution.**

It might be said that many users would be willing to surrender their control over UGC that they submit; that it is understood as a price to be paid in order to participate in social media and social networking generally. And while this may be true—forums and

---

[197] Harper & Row Publishers, Inc. v. Nation Enters., 471 U.S. 539, 558 (1985); *see also* Mazer v. Stein, 347 U.S. 201, 219 (1954) ("The economic philosophy behind the clause empowering Congress to grant patents and copyrights is the conviction that encouragement of individual effort by personal gain is the best way to advance public welfare through the talents of authors and inventors in 'Science and useful Arts.'").

[198] *See supra* Part III.A.

message boards are certainly social media hubs for beginning and participating in discussions—users at the very least should be informed of the property rights they ultimately relinquish. If nothing else, users should be aware of the copyrights they own and should be required to explicitly agree to each commercial use of their UGC—ideally with the ability to negotiate for fair compensation. This would seem to strike a balance between creation incentives and corporate monetization interests. By allowing users to refuse to commercialize their content, they would retain control over the dissemination of their work beyond the specific social media website on which it was posted.

Control. In a digital age, the ability to control your content is paramount, and allowing users retain this right is the best way to serve copyright interests.

VI. CONCLUSION

Right now, as humanity experiences an Internet revolution, or better yet, a digital renaissance, it is more important than ever to adapt our intangible property laws with the times. Widespread Internet usage presents a vast array of unique and troubling copyright problems, many of which have yet to be solved or struggle to function under antiquated laws. Users across the world participate in social media and submit content, which is subject to copyright protection, online for free and without the expectation of compensation. Social media sites hosting the material manage to commercialize user content and reap substantial benefits from its utilization. Contract law is unable to solve the problem created under these circumstances, but a fix should be rooted in the underlying policy of copyright law. A compromise will best temper the competing interests of user rights and social media (corporate) interests. By granting users the right of first refusal in regard to monetizing their content, we can keep the control of copyrightable works where it belongs, in the hands of the creator. Social media offers a beautiful beacon of human creation—of pure, raw expression—we need only protect its potential, and the rest, as they say, is #history.

HOW SPOTIFY KILLED THE RADIO STAR: AN ANALYSIS ON HOW THE SONGWRITER EQUITY ACT COULD AID THE CURRENT ONLINE MUSIC DISTRIBUTION MARKET IN FAILING ARTISTS

CAITLIN KOWALKE†

† J.D. Candidate 2016, William Mitchell College of Law. The author would like to thank Professor Kenneth Port for his advice and feedback on this article's formative drafts; the entire Staff and Board of *Cybaris®* for their comprehensive editing efforts; and in particular Sarah Howes and Nadja Baer for serving not only as editors but also mentors throughout the writing process. Many thanks also to the many family members and friends who have supported me throughout the creation of this piece.

I. Introduction

As technology continually evolves, unique challenges and opportunities are constantly presented to the music industry.* In today's music market, the Internet is creating a new crossroad for music distributors as well as consumers. The more readily available music becomes, the more rapidly consumers will expect it; and as is often the case with emerging technologies, copyright law has not been able to keep pace with such drastic changes.[1]

Additionally, it appears that the economic value placed on music has decreased in our society. While legitimate music markets still exist, it is clear that consumers are just not willing to pay what they used to for physical albums.[2] Today's music industry is so centered on earning profits through album sales that it is missing out on the steadily growing number of people whose valuations for music have fundamentally shifted. While sharing music has always been a significant social practice[3]—with the increase of illegal

---

* For a shockingly accurate overview of the prominent issues in today's music market and how they should be confronted, see *The State of the Music Industry*, Oatmeal, http://theoatmeal.com/comics/music_industry (last visited Jan. 24, 2015).

[1] *See infra* Part III.A.

[2] According to a study by *Billboard Magazine*, overall album sales dropped 8.4% in 2013, decreasing by 26.6 million units over the course of the year. The report also indicates that physical CD sales "declined 14.5% to 165.4 million units, down from 193.4 million in the prior year." Physical album sales still comprise 57.2% of music sales in the U.S.; however, digital sales account for 40.6% of album revenue. Ed Christman, *Digital Music Sales Decrease for First Time in 2013*, BILLBOARDBIZ (Jan. 3, 2014), http://www.billboard.com/biz/articles/news/digital-and-mobile/5855162/digital-music-sales-decrease-for-first-time-in-2013.

[3] When discussing music piracy, many consumers automatically jump to consideration of online file sharing and downloading. However, according to the Recording Industry Association of America, "[r]egardless of the format at issue, the same basic principle

downloading sites, and the growing ease of sharing
music with friends[4] through digital media
connections—the importance of creating a marketplace
that is mutually beneficial to publishers and consumers
is increasingly important.[5] In short, the current music
market is in dire need of an *effective* response to online
music piracy.

While the negative effect of online music piracy
cannot be overstated, fair compensation issues do not
cease with societal habits of illegal downloading. When
evaluating today's online music market, it is clear that

---

applies: music sound recordings may not be copied or distributed
without the permission of the owner." This includes not only Internet
copying, but also burning and distributing physical CDs. *The Law*,
RIAA,
http://www.riaa.com/physicalpiracy.php?content_selector=piracy_on
line_the_law (last visited Nov. 11, 2014). For a more comprehensive
discussion of how CD burning contributed to loss in revenue in the
music industry before widespread online file-sharing, see Gwendolyn
Mariano, *Music Industry Sounds Off on CD Burning*, CNET NEWS (June
11, 2002), http://news.cnet.com/Music-industry-sounds-off-on-CD-
burning/2100-1023_3-935120.html. Additionally, for a brief overview
of unauthorized copying of music pre-Internet piracy, see Danwill
David Schwender, *Reducing Unauthorized Digital Downloading of Music
by Obtaining Voluntary Compliance with Copyright Law Through the
Removal of Corporate Power in the Recording Industry*, 34 T. JEFFERSON L.
REV. 225, 235-38 (2012).
    [4] Not only has online music piracy become a more accessible
option for consumers, industry experts also suggest that today's
society is failing to recognize music as intellectual property. Danwill
David Schwender provides a helpful example in stating, "a person
who purchases music on a compact disc, listens to it, and then gives
the album to a friend can no longer listen to that compact disc until it
is returned or repurchased. But a person sharing a digital music file
over a peer-to-peer network does not sacrifice the original digital
music file." Schwender, *supra* note 3, at 244.
    [5] Successful songwriter Rivers Rutherford stated that "[t]he irony
of the digital age is it's getting harder and harder to make a living as a
songwriter, even though our music is being heard by more people in
more places than ever before." Andrew Watt, *Songwriter Equity Act*,
GIBSONS   NEWS   (May   30,   2014),
http://www.gibsonssolicitors.com.au/news/songwriter-equity-act/.

the business model that top-distribution services are utilizing is also failing artists.[6] In February 2014, members of Congress and advocates of increasing artist compensation joined forces to create the Songwriter Equity Act of 2014 (SEA). Proposed changes would alter both sections 114(i) and 115 of the Copyright Act, which proponents of the bill believe prevent songwriters from receiving royalty rates that reflect a fair market value for the use of their intellectual property.[7] There is very little industry debate over the necessity of section 114(i) reform, which currently limits federal rate courts from considering royalty rates as a relevant standard for regulating performance royalty rates for songwriters and composers.[8] However, the proposed increase to the mechanical royalty rate under section 115 is significantly more problematic and would likely cause a detrimental spike in costs across the music industry.[9] While SEA is admirable in its mission to grant artists more financial return for their work, it would add considerably to music production costs—including transaction costs, which music pirates are already avoiding.

A more efficient approach to battle artist compensation issues in the music industry would be to convert to a model emulating television's recent switch to online streaming distribution.[10] At a nominal fee, consumers may be more willing to compromise between paying for full, physical albums and illegally obtaining music.[11] While the current online music

---

[6] *See infra* Part VI.C.i.a.

[7] *See infra* Part IV.A.

[8] *See infra* Part II.C.

[9] *See infra* Part V.A.

[10] *See generally,* Scott Hervey, *The Future of Online Music: Labels and Artists,* 15 Transnat'l Law. 279, 284 (2002).

[11] A report by CNN suggests that younger generations are more apt to stream music rather than own it outright. According to Paul Resnikoff, publisher and editor-in-chief of Digital Music News, "[w]e are already seeing a trend on the aggregate with the lack of music

distribution market is on the right track, there is still significant work to be done in advancing the industry's business practices to provide adequate payment for the artist whose work is currently being accessed by millions of consumers at little or no cost.[12]

II. WHAT OWNERSHIP RIGHTS ARE SONGWRITERS GUARANTEED UNDER CURRENT COPYRIGHT LAW?

A. Mechanical Licenses

Copyright protection has been a matter of relentless controversy throughout modern history. Technological advancements have also greatly affected copyright protection and fair compensation for artists. Debates concerning copyright protection in an evolving musical industry first arose in 1908, when composers began to lobby Congress for a legislative change granting them exclusive rights to authorize the mechanical reproductions of their works in response to *White-Smith Music Publishing Co. v. Apollo Co.*[13] At this time, the player piano was popular in the United States, and copyright owners had concerns about their right to control the reproduction of their works on piano rolls. The

---

ownership." Jareen Imam, *Young Listeners Opting to Stream, Not Own Music,* CNN TECH (June 16, 2012), http://www.cnn.com/2012/06/15/tech/web/music-streaming/.

[12] *See infra* Part VI.C.i.b.

[13] 209 U.S. 1, 18 (1908). In *White v. Apollo*, the Supreme Court ruled that manufacturers of music rolls for player pianos did not have to pay royalties to the composers. The Court stated that piano rolls were parts of the machine that reproduced the music, rather than copies of the plaintiffs' copyrighted sheet music. *Id.* The case likely caused Congress's intervention to create a compulsory license for the manufacture and distribution of such "mechanical" embodiments of musical works through an amendment to the Copyright Act of 1909. *See* EDWARD SAMUELS, THE ILLUSTRATED STORY OF COPYRIGHT, 33–38 (2000), *available at* http://www.edwardsamuels.com/illustratedstory/isc2.htm.

technology used to broadcast audio transmissions was also not widely available at the time the 1909 Copyright Act was debated. Congress did not extend copyright protection to sound recordings on records even though this medium was becoming more widespread because the average consumer did not have the ability to copy records.[14]

In addition to technological limitations to potential infringement, it is also possible that Congress did not consider sound recordings to be "writings" as provided for in the Constitution at the time of drafting. Congress was mainly concerned with providing protection for musical compositions on a written page, "securing to the composer an adequate return for all use made of his composition and at the same time prevent[ing] the formation of oppressive monopolies."[15] Accordingly, copyright protection did not extend to recordings of a composition onto a physical medium but only the written composition itself. Therefore, when the United States Supreme Court held that piano rolls were not "copies" of the composers' works, but physical parts of the piano itself, Congress was forced to tailor the Copyright Act of 1909 to include a compulsory license for the manufacture and distribution of such "mechanical" embodiments of musical works. Under modern copyright law, section 115 of the 1976 Copyright Act[16] grants songwriters the right, with certain

---

[14] Even forty years later, it was more efficient to record a live performance onto vinyl than to copy a record. *See* Robert P. Merges, *One Hundred Years of Solicitude: Intellectual Property Law, 1900–2000*, 88 CALIF. L. REV. 2187, 2195 (2000).

[15] *See, e.g.*, Proposed Conclusions of Law, Jointly Submitted by Sirius Satellite Radio, Inc. and XM Satellite Radio Inc. at 10, n.2, Adjustment of Rates & Terms For Preexisting Subscription Servs & Satellite Digital Audio Radio Servs, No. 2006-1 CRB DSTRA (October 1, 2007), *available at* http://www.loc.gov/crb/proceedings/2006-1/pff-cl/10-1-07-sdars-joint-proposed-conclusions-of-law.pdf.

[16] Copyright Act of 1976, Pub. L. No. 94–553, 90 Stat. 2556 (1976).

restrictions,[17] to make and distribute "mechanical reproductions"[18] of their compositions.[19]

B. Compulsory Licenses

In addition to the creation of mechanical licenses, Section 115 of the Copyright Act established a compulsory license for the reproduction and distribution of nondramatic musical works.[20] Under the compulsory licensing system, a songwriter has the exclusive right to make the first mechanical

---

[17] 17 U.S.C. § 115(a)(1) (2012) ("A person may obtain a compulsory license only if his or her primary purpose in making phonorecords is to distribute them to the public for private use, including by means of a digital phonorecord delivery. A person may not obtain a compulsory license for use of the work in the making of phonorecords duplicating a sound recording fixed by another, unless: (i) such sound recording was fixed lawfully; and (ii) the making of the phonorecords was authorized by the owner of copyright in the sound recording or, if the sound recording was fixed before February 15, 1972, by any person who fixed the sound recording pursuant to an express license from the owner of the copyright in the musical work or pursuant to a valid compulsory license for use of such work in a sound recording.").

[18] Originally, reproductions were referred to as "mechanical" because the composition was being "mechanically" recorded on media such as a phonography record or piano roll. Today, "mechanical reproductions" are referred to as "phonorecords" and come in formats such as compact discs, cassette tapes, records, and even digital phonorecords such as MP3s. *See Section 115 Compulsory License: The Register of Copyrights Before the Subcommittee on Courts, the Internet and Intellectual Property of the House Committee on the Judiciary,* 108th Cong. (2004) (statement of Marybeth Peters, Register of Copyrights, Copyright Office), *available at* http://www.copyright.gov/docs/regstat031104.html.

[19] 17 U.S.C. § 115 (2012).

[20] 17 U.S.C. § 115(a)(1) (2012) ("When phonorecords of a nondramatic musical work have been distributed to the public in the United States under the authority of the copyright owner, any other person, including those who make phonorecords or digital phonorecord deliveries, may, by complying with the provisions of this section, obtain a compulsory license to make and distribute phonorecords of the work.").

reproduction of his or her work.[21] Once the original copy of the composition has been published, however, the copyright owner is compelled to license his or her work to any party who meets the requirements of the license.[22] This right is primarily associated with performers recording "covers" of songs composed and originally performed by another artist.[23]

Songwriters have the exclusive right to publicly perform their own compositions.[24] "Traditionally, this right was primarily implicated by broadcast analog radio and television . . . ."[25] However, in today's ever-evolving tech-savvy society, digital broadcasters, webcasting, satellite radio, and some online music services frequently implicate this right.[26] In order to better "administer these rights on behalf of songwriters," entities known as Performance Rights

---

[21] *Id.*; *see* Mary Jane Frisby, *Rockin' Down the Highway: Forging a Path for the Lawful Use of MP3 Digital Music Files*, 33 IND. L. REV. 317, 325 (1999).

[22] Generally, these requirements include royalty payment to the copyright owner at a set statutory rate, adequate notice of a request to use the compulsory license, and adequate reporting of the provisions from the license. *See* 17 U.S.C. § 115(b)(1)—(c) (2012).

[23] This right does not extend to artists who merely publish works similar in nature or content to the original copyrighted work. *See, e.g.*, Peters v. West, 692 F.3d 629, 633 (7th Cir. 2012).

[24] As held in *Hulex Music v. Santy*, "[i]n order to show copyright infringement, a plaintiff must establish five elements: (1) the originality and authorship of the works involved, (2) compliance with the formalities of federal copyright law, (3) rightful proprietorship of the copyrights as issue, (4) that the copyrighted works were performed publicly for profit, and (5) a lack of authorization by the owner of the owner's representative for the alleged infringer to publicly perform the works." 698 F. Supp. 1024, 1030 (D.N.H. 1988).
For a more current example illustrating songwriters' exclusive right to publicly perform their own compositions, see Severe Records, LLC. v. Rich, 658 F.3d 571 (6th Cir. 2011).

[25] Skyla Mitchell, *Reforming Section 115: Escape from the Byzantine World of Mechanical Licensing*, 24 CARDOZO ARTS & ENT. L.J. 1239, 1252 (2007).

[26] *Id.*

Organizations (PROs) were established.[27] Currently
there are three operating PROs: the American Society
of Composers, Authors, and Publishers (ASCAP),[28]
Broadcast Music, Inc. (BMI),[29] and the Society of
European Stage Authors and Composers (SESAC).[30]
Combined, ASCAP and BMI represent roughly 97% of
all American compositions.[31] All three PROs offer radio
stations the use of a blanket license, which is a set fee
that allows each station the use of any composition
represented by the PRO.[32] After deducting overhead

---

[27] *Id.*

[28] *Id.* In 2013, ASCAP collected over $945 million in licensing fees
and distributed $851 million in royalties to its members. While ASCAP
is a not-for-profit organization, it ran with a 12.1% operating expense
ratio in 2013. The American Society of Composers, Authors and
Publishers, 2013 Annual Report 17 (2013). As of July 2013, ASCAP
membership included over 500,000 songwriters, composers, and
music publishers. The American Society of Composers, Authors
and Publishers, http://www.ascap.com/about (last visited Nov. 14,
2014).

[29] In fiscal year 2013, BMI collected over $944 million in licensing
fees and distributed $814 million in royalties. Broadcast Music Inc.,
http://www.bmi.com/press/entry/563077 (last visited Nov. 14, 2014).
BMI tracks public performances for 8.5 million works, and collects
and distributes licensing revenues for those performances as royalties
to the over 650,000 composers, songwriters, and music publishers it
represents. Broadcast Music Inc., www.bmi.com/about (last visited
Nov. 14, 2014).

[30] SESAC is the smallest of the three PROs in the United States,
representing just over 9,000 authors and composers. However,
SESAC is also the fastest-growing PRO in the United States. Unlike
ASCAP and BMI (both not-for-profit organizations), SESAC retains
some income as profit. Additionally, unlike the other prominent
PROs, SESAC does not offer open membership. In order to benefit
from the organization, members must be approved to join. SESAC,
www.sesac.com/About (last visited Nov. 14, 2014).

[31] Mitchell, *supra* note 25, at 1252 (citing Michael A. Einhorn,
Intellectual Property and Antitrust: Music Performing Rights in
Broadcasting, 24 Colum. J.L. & Arts, 349, 349 (2001), *available at* http://
www.musicdish.com/mag/index.php3?id=3823).

[32] *Id.* For a more detailed explanation of how blanket license
agreements are executed, see Neil Conley, *The Future of Licensing Music
Online: The Role of Collective Rights Organization and the Effect of*

costs, the profits made from each blanket license agreement are then distributed as royalty payments to all represented songwriters.[33]

In 2004, The Copyright Royalty and Distribution Reform Act[34] created a board of Copyright Royalty Judges (CRJs, or sometimes referred to simply as the Copyright Royalty Board (CRB)) responsible for determining the rates and terms for statutory licenses.[35] Under the Copyright Royalty and Distribution Reform Act, "statutory rates" are set through either voluntary negotiations or trial-type hearings before the panel of three CRJs.[36] When calculating royalty rates, CRJs are expected to focus on four main objectives.[37] In order to maintain an equal balance between artists and distribution companies, royalty rates must be set to maximize availability of song uses; afford a fair return to the copyright owner and a fair income to the song user that reflects the roles of each; and minimize the disruptive impact on the structure of the industries involved.[38]

Territoriality, 25 J. MARSHALL J. COMPUTER & INFO L. 409, 422–23 (2008).

[33] Mitchell, *supra* note 25, at 1253. Generally, there is a 50/50 distribution of royalty payments between writers and publishers. Conley, *supra* note 32, at 423.

[34] Copyright Royalty and Distribution Reform Act of 2004, Pub. L. No. 108-419, 118 Stat. 2341 (enacted through 17 U.S.C. §114(f) (2006)), *available at* http://copyright.gov/title17/92appc.pdf. *See also,* Peter Dicola & Matthew Sag, *An Information- Gathering Approach to Copyright Policy*, 34 CARDOZO L. REV. 173, 231–33 (2012) (discussing the Copyright Royalty and Distribution Reform Act of 2004 and its impact on the current music industry).

[35] Mitchell, *supra* note 25, at 1250.

[36] 17 U.S.C. § 115(c)(3)(C) (2010); 17 U.S.C. § 803 (2010).

[37] Mitchell, *supra* note 25, at 1250 n.69 (quoting 17 U.S.C. § 801(b)(1)); Recording Indus. Ass'n of Am. v. Copyright Royalty Tribunal, 662 F.2d 1, 13 (1981).

[38] Recording Indus. Ass'n of Am. v. Copyright Royalty Tribunal, 662 F.2d 1, 13 (1981).

While the CRB is aware of copyright holder and
user needs when setting the statutory royalty rate, due
to burdensome monthly payment provisions of Section
115 and competition among composers, the statutory
terms are rarely followed.[39] The statutory mechanical
rate merely represents a ceiling[40] for voluntary
negotiations between a music publisher, the
composition's copyright holder, and the licensee.[41]

C. Section 114 Limitations

Not only are composers burdened by the potential
for less-than-desirable royalty payments under Section
115, they are also subject to further rate limitations
under section 114 of the Copyright Act. In cases where
the royalty rate is reached through negotiation,
interested parties discuss rates and terms with

---

[39] *See* Howard B. Abrams, *Copyright's First Compulsory License*, 26
SANTA CLARA COMPUTER & HIGH TECH. L.J. 215, 234–39 (2010).

[40] There are many advocates pushing for an alteration of the
mechanical royalty rate system, in that a minimum rate would be
established, replacing the current maximum rate (i.e., a floor rather
than a ceiling). Mitchell, *supra* note 25, at 1243.While this is not an
entirely deficient idea, it does have some flaws. Due to unevenness in
bargaining power, artists do frequently agree upon a mechanical rate
significantly lower than the statutory rate. Mitchell, *supra* note 25, at
1249; Abrams, *supra* note 39, at 235. Record companies have the power
to force artists to settle at a low rate, and should a minimum royalty
rate be the new industry standard, it is likely that most record
companies would still be able to negotiate agreements at the lowest
legal limit. *Id.* at 235.

[41] Most record contracts pay mechanical royalties at
approximately three-fourths of the statutory rate. Hervey, *supra* note
10, at 289. Additionally, through controlled compositions clauses,
artists are frequently limited in the number of tracks on which
mechanical royalties will be paid (typically ten out of the average
twelve songs on an album). *Id.* This will result in an additional loss in
profits to the artist. For more information on controlled composition
clauses in contractual agreements in the music industry, see Hervey,
supra note 10, at 289.

SoundExchange,[42] and present those to the CRJs for adoption. If the judges adopt the agreement, it will be available for opt-in by any similarly situated parties. Any parties who have not negotiated agreements through SoundExchange may present their agreement to the CRJs, who will conduct a rate setting arbitration to establish royalty rates. However, under Section 114(i) of the Copyright Act,[43] federal rate courts are forbidden from considering sound recording royalty rates when determining what performance royalty rates should be for songwriters and composers. Not only does Section 114(i) prevent the rate courts from using mechanical royalties as a standard for performance royalties, this section also precludes PROs from presenting this as an

---

[42] Prior to 1995, (under 17 U.S.C. 114(g)(2)(A)), recording companies and their artists were not entitled to receive payment for the public performance of their sound recordings. However, as a result of The Digital Performance Right in Sound Recordings Act of 1995 and The Digital Millennium Copyright Act of 1998, a performance right for sound recordings was granted. Digital Performance Right in Sound Recordings Act of 1995, Pub. L. No. 104-39, 109 Stat. 336 (1995); The Digital Millennium Copyright Act of 1998, Pub. L. No. 105-304, 112 Stat. 2860 (1998). Accordingly, under current copyright law it is now required that users of music pay the copyright owner of the sound recording for the public performance of that music. 17 U.S.C. § 114 (2012). This notably includes any online music transmissions of the recording. SoundExchange is a not-for-profit organization that collects royalties on behalf of sound recording copyright owners and features artists for non-interactive digital transmissions, including satellite and Internet radio. For more information about the licenses granted by SoundExchange and its royalty distribution process, see SoundExchange General FAQ, www.soundexchange.com/generalfaq (last visited Sep. 6, 2014).

[43] 17 U.S.C. § 114(i) (2012). ("License fees payable for the public performance of sound recordings under section 106(6) shall not be taken into account in any administrative, judicial, or other governmental proceeding to set or adjust the royalties payable to copyright owners of musical works for the public performance of their works. It is the intent of Congress that royalties payable to copyright owners of musical works for the public performance of their works shall not be diminished in any respect as a result of the rights granted by section 106(6).").

argument in a court of law.[44] As a result, "digital streaming services often pay an unfair royalty rate to the artists that they feature."[45]

III. INDUSTRY LIMITATIONS ON MUSICAL COPYRIGHT TODAY

A. Emerging Technology as a Constant Threat to Copyright Protections

Rapidly emerging avenues of technology are readily rendering Section 115 more ineffective against copyright challenges. The decentralized nature of the Internet poses a significant difficulty in tracking and policing online copyright infringement, especially since most illegal music distribution takes place through peer-to-peer file sharing.[46] No central authority exists to help control the relentlessly expanding scope of online behavior.[47] This, coupled with the seemingly virtual anonymity of the Internet, contributes to the constant

---

[44] Kyle Duncan, *The Songwriter Equity Act*, AMPED BLOG (June 24, 2014), http://theampedblog.com/2014/06/songwriter-equity-act/.

[45] *Id.*

[46] Most piracy activity occurs through peer-to-peer (P2P) file sharing. P2P file sharing occurs when digital media is distributed using a software program that searches for other connected users wishing to trade electronic books, music, movies, or games. Since P2P file sharing transactions occur between individual users, it is difficult to track every illegal interaction, especially considering the widespread nature of the practice. John C. Boehm, *Copyright Reform for the Digital Era: Protecting the Future of Recorded Music Through Compulsory Licensing and Proper Judicial Analysis*, 10 TEX. REV. ENT. & SPORTS L. 169 at 179 (2009); *see also* Hisanari Harry Tanaka, *Post-Napster: Peer-to-Peer File Sharing Systems Current and Future Issues on Secondary Liability Under Copyright Laws in the United States and Japan*, 22 LOY. L.A. ENT. L. REV. 37 at 40–42 (2001).

[47] While deterrence against pirating music online through increased penalties to individuals has been visited, such drastic measures are unlikely to be adopted. Boehm, *supra* note 46, at 207–08.

infringement of copyrights, in particular music sharing.[48]

Napster was the predominant pioneer among peer-to-peer file-sharing software.[49] However, on December 6, 1999, several record companies filed an action against Napster for vicarious and contributory copyright infringement.[50] After proving that individual users of Napster were the primary infringers of copyright law, the Ninth Circuit held that Napster users, by illegally uploading and downloading music files, were in violation of copyright holders' exclusive rights of reproduction and distribution.[51] While the court did not entirely shut down Napster, the court did place several heavy constraints on the system.[52] After three months of monitoring by the district court, it determined that Napster was not in satisfactory compliance with the requirements of the enforced injunction. After the

---

[48] *Id.* at 198.

[49] Napster's MusicShare software, which was available as a free download from Napster's website, allowed users to search for and trade MP3 music files among anyone else using the software. *See* A&M Records, Inc. v. Napster, Inc., 239 F.3d 1004, 1011 (9th Cir. 2001), aff'd, 284 F.3d 1091 (9th Cir. 2002).

[50] A&M Records, Inc. v. Napster, Inc., 114 F. Supp. 2d 898, 900 (N.D. Cal. 2000) ,aff'd in part, rev'd in part sub, 239 F.3d 1004 (9th Cir. 2001), aff'd, 284 F.3d 1091 (9th Cir. 2002).

[51] *Napster*, 239 F.3d at 1014. The court found that Napster had contributory liability, because it knew, or had reason to know, of direct copyright infringement by its users. *Id.* at 1020–24. Additionally, the court held that the site had a right to supervise and direct financial interest in the activities of its users. *Id.*

[52] *Id.* at 1028. Napster was required to remove any user file from the system's music index if Napster had reasonable knowledge the file contained a plaintiffs' copyrighted works. A&M Records, Inc. v. Napster, Inc., No., 2001 WL 227083, at 1 (N.D. Cal. 2001) aff'd, 284 F.3d 1091 (9th Cir. 2002). In turn, the plaintiffs were ordered to give Napster notice of specific files they knew to be infringed upon. *Id.*

unsuccessful trial period, the court ordered Napster to close.[53]

While Napster is no longer in existence, there is a continued abundance of illegal online peer-to-peer file-sharing hosts. Lawsuits similar to the one brought against Napster are fairly common; however, with the ever-evolving nature of technology, it is difficult to keep up with every new avenue of illegal online distribution.[54] Due to the vast availability of unauthorized copies of digital phonorecords, consumers are now able to download nearly any sound recording they wish, usually free of charge. While there is a successful legitimate online market[55] for downloaded music, it fails to keep up with the never-ending number of sites providing free downloads.[56]

---

[53] A&M Records, Inc. v. Napster, Inc., 239 F.3d 1004, 1014 (9th Cir. 2001).

[54] For further examples of post-Napster litigation surrounding illegal online music distribution, see *MGM Studios, Incorporated v. Grokster, Limited*, 259 F. Supp. 2d 1029, 1031-33 (C.D. Cal. 2003) (holding that when a party distributes a device that can be used to infringe copyright, it is liable for the resulting acts of infringement by third parties) and *In re Aimster Copyright Litigation*, 334 F.3d 643 (7th Cir. 2003).

[55] iTunes, a media player, library, and mobile device application developed by Apple Inc., legally generated over $12 billion in downloaded music profits in 2013 alone. Owen Thomas, *iTunes is a Bigger Business Now than Apple was in 2004*, BUS.. INSIDER (JAN. 9, 2013, 10:33 PM), http://www.businessinsider.com/itunes-sales-2013-1; *see also* APPLE INFO, www.apple.com/about (last visited Nov. 11, 2014) (describing current company news and profit information).

[56] According to Billboard Biz (the online music business extension of Billboard Magazine), in 2013, digital track sales fell 5.7% from 1.34 billion units to 1.26 billion units. This was the first time in iTunes' thirteen-year history that the store finished the year with a decrease in digital music sales. Ed Christman, *Digital Music Sales Decrease for First Time in 2013*, BILLBOARD MAG. (Jan. 3, 2014, 9:21 AM EST), http://www.billboard.com/biz/articles/news/digital-and-mobile/5855162/digital-music-sales-decrease-for-first-time-in-2013.

For those seeking legitimate copyright usage of a particular work, frustration and uncertainty are often experienced due to complicated notice and reporting procedures, which frequently lead to prohibitive transactional costs and delays. In addition to a general lack of clarity regarding which activities require which licenses, Section 115 has hindered online music providers in their attempts to effectively combat piracy.[57] Since businesses that wish to take advantage of a compulsory license must engage in a costly search[58] for the song's copyright owner, Section 115 notice provisions are burdensome on potential licensees. Should a business fail to locate the correct copyright holder, it must file an intent-to-use claim with the Copyright Office for a twelve-dollar fee.[59] In

---

[57] *See* Mitchell, *supra* note 25, at 1257.

[58] 17 U.S.C. § 115(b)(1) (2006). In order to independently search for a copyright owner, a party must manually check the Copyright Office's records, a task that can only be performed by traveling to the Copyright Office in Washington D.C. Should the party wish to avoid the necessary trip to Washington, the Copyright Office will undertake the burden of the record search. However, while estimates vary, the expense of a search is typically $200 per hour, with a two-hour minimum. While some parties, particularly large distribution corporations, are financially able to pay these exorbitant fees, not all copyright owners file ownership rights with the Copyright Office. Therefore, after the time and expense allotted for the search, the party may still be unclear as to whom royalty payments are owed. In considering these substantial costs, which are all incurred in pursuit of a nine-cent license, it is obvious why potential licensees would be deterred from seeking a license under section 115, let alone a massive collection of them needed to create appealing options for consumers. U.S. COPYRIGHT OFFICE, CIRCULAR 4: COPYRIGHT OFFICE FEES (2014) (discussing fees associated with Copyright Office), *available at* http://copyright.gov/circs/circ04.pdf.

[59] Compulsory License for Making and Distributing Phonorecords, Including Digital Phonorecord Deliveries, 69 Fed. Reg. 11,566 (March 11, 2004). A party may not take advantage of this option if she has not already executed the manual copyright search. While it may seem a twelve-dollar fee alone is not particularly significant, when multiplied by the thousands of songs that an online provider

accumulating initial search and Copyright Office administrative fees, use of a compulsory license can be exorbitantly expensive and time consuming. Additionally, Section 115's reporting requirements that require a licensee to submit monthly and audited annual statements of accounts to the copyright owner are extensive and complex.[60]

B. Unequal Bargaining Positions Between Songwriters and Music Publishers

Not only are composers faced with the harsh reality of expanding online music piracy, they are also continually forced to confront severe disparity in publishing negotiations. While changes in technology have caused major changes in music distribution, many artists still seek a traditional relationship with a publishing company.[61] In all relationships formed between a songwriter and music publisher, the songwriter provides the creative product and the music publisher holds the capital and managerial ability.[62]

---

may wish to make available, it is clear how quickly the cost could become prohibitive.

[60] 37 C.F.R. § 201.19 (2006).

[61] In today's online society, where it can feel as if fame is one MySpace posting away, it may seem that a music publisher's role has diminished. However, Budi Voogt, author of *The Soundcloud Bible* and founder and president of Heroic Recordings, comments on the continued importance of this role in the digital age, "They [the publishers] will register your works with the right associations, administer your royalty income and most importantly, create commercial opportunities. . . . Of course, you can decide not to do this and manage your repertoire independently. Beware that this is a very time consuming and diligent task, as the publishing landscape is intricate and highly technical." Paul Resnikoff, *Now You Know Everything About Music Publishing...*, DIGITAL MUSIC NEWS (Feb. 28, 2014) http://www.digitalmusicnews.com/permalink/2014/02/28/understandpublishing.

[62] *See* Don E. Tomlinson, *Everything that Glitters is Not Gold: Songwriter-Music Publisher Agreements and Disagreements*, 18 HASTINGS COMM. & ENT. L.J. 85, 93–101 (1995).

Since most songwriters (essentially all songwriters at the beginning of their careers) do not have the financial resources to self-publish their compositions,[63] it is practically required that the songwriters seek the assistance of a music publisher. This somewhat forced relationship automatically places professional songwriters at an extreme bargaining disadvantage.[64]

---

[63] Many modern music fans are beginning to believe successfully creating and marketing an album is as easy as setting up a webcast or starting an online fan page to sell albums. However, even the most simplistic of albums require a great deal of financial support to stand a chance at profitable success. Recording spaces and quality equipment are essential to an album's success, and it is not uncommon for different parts of each record to require separate recordings of each element laid into each musical track. Once all the elements for each track are recorded, a sound mixing process must occur. Professional mixers estimate this process can take roughly six to eight hours per song, which, should an artist choose to splurge on this process, would add significant time and cost.

So realistically, what could be the cost of producing an album? According to John Feldmann, who has served as executive producer for bands such as Panic! At the Disco, The Used, and Good Charlotte, "I think to record a full-length album, [the budget is] anywhere between $40,000 and $150,000. But for me to do a record for $50,000, I've got to be pretty passionate about the music." While being less sure of an album's going rate, Producer Mark Trombino, who has worked with bands such as Blink-182 and Jimmy Eat World, agrees album production is no small undertaking. "The cost of recording these days can vary so wildly that I have no idea what the average is," he says. "I know some major labels are still spending a couple hundred thousand dollars on albums, while most indies are spending $30,000. My budgets are typically somewhere in between." While there will always be individuals creating albums in their basements, it's doubtful the quality will ever reach a professional level. In an already competitive market, a sub-par product is unlikely to yield great profits. Emily Zemler, *On the Record: The True Cost of Recording*, The   Alternative   Press   (Feb.   28,   2011) http://www.altpress.com/features/entry/on_the_record_the_true_cost_of_record ing.

[64] Schwender, *supra* note 3, at 232. ("Theoretically, copyright law in the United States strikes a balance between artists and consumers—granting limited, exclusive, private rights to induce creators to produce original works in return for a vast public domain of works.

Historically, in contracts between songwriters and music publishers, very few terms are negotiable.[65] Courts have little issue identifying the problems associated with unequal bargaining positions in the formation of a contract between songwriters and music publishers;[66] however, before showing a party in the weaker position any contractual leniency, courts insist that the party prove substantive unconscionability or unfairness in the terms of the contract itself.[67] While

---

The balance, however, actually weights heavily in favor of publishers, especially in the music recording industry.").

[65] Hal I. Gilenson, *Badlands: Artist-Personal Manager Conflicts of Interest in the Music Industry*, 9 CARDOZO ARTS & ENT. L.J. 501, 535 (1991).

[66] *See* Harry Fox Agency, Inc. v. Mill Music, Inc., 543 F. Supp. 844, 859 (S.D.N.Y. 1982), ("Because of the impossibility of predicting the commercial value of a work upon its creation and because of the weak bargaining position of [songwriters], they are sometimes assigned their copyrights in return for very little remuneration, such as small lump-sum payments or inadequate royalty rates, and were thus prevented from sharing fairly, if at all, in the rewards from works that later became commercial successes.").

[67] Unlike procedural unconscionability, which relates to unfair business procedure in relation to the transaction, substantive unconscionability requires unfairness of the contract itself. In *Croce v. Kurnit*, 565 F. Supp. 884, 893 (S.D.N.Y. 1982), *aff'd*, 737 F.2d 229 (2d Cir. 1984), Ingrid Croce, widow of a singer-songwriter Jim Croce, argued that the relationship between her husband and his music publisher at the beginning of his career was unconscionable. The court concluded that the contracts formed between the two parties could not be rescinded on the basis of unconscionability: "[T]he contracts were hard bargains, signed by an artist without bargaining power, and favored the publishers, but as a matter of fact did not contain terms which shock the conscious or differed so grossly from industry norms as to be unconscionable by their terms. . . . Because of the uncertainty involved in the music business and the high risk of failure of new performers, the contracts, though favoring the defendants, were not unfair." *Id.* at 893.

While the holding of this case is clear, should we really conform songwriter-music publisher contracts to an industry standard that may be unfair to creative professionals? In creating a system where one "side" of the industry has an extreme bargaining advantage over the other, it appears courts determining the validity of these contracts

some artists seek the assistance of a publisher mainly for promotional purposes,[68] when it comes to collecting royalty profits, composers are getting a raw deal.[69] This is especially relevant when considering the exceptionally low royalty payments provided for artists through up-and-coming online streaming sites.[70]

IV. Proposed Reformation Efforts of the Songwriter Equity Act

A. Changes Proposed by the Songwriter Equity Act

The Songwriter Equity Act (SEA) intends to revise both Section 115 and Section 114 of the Copyright Act. Advocates of SEA suggest that alterations would allow songwriters to receive better performance and mechanical royalty rates.[71] Since Representative Doug

---

are entirely ignoring the issue of unconscionability. For further information concerning contracting unfairness in the music industry, see Gilenson, *supra* note 65, at 515–19.

[68] Douglas Wolk, music industry author and critic, states that only 6% of performers actually make money from recording revenues. "Recordings are how listeners generally spend the most *time* experiencing music, but not how we spend the most *money* experiencing music. In practice, recordings mostly serve as promotion for the other ways musicians make money: performing, most of all, but also salaries for playing in orchestras and other groups, session work, and so on." Douglas Wolk, *How Ashamed Should You Feel About Using Spotify?*, Slate Group (Aug. 21, 2013, 6:30 AM) http://www.slate.com/articles/business/moneybox/2013/08/spotify_and_pandora _artist_payments_not_as_exploitative_as_they_re_made.html.

[69] Many artists are now turning to social media to speak out against the despairingly low royalty payments they are afforded, particularly by newer online streaming sites. *See infra* Part VI.C.i.a. *See also* Paul Resnikoff, *16 Artists That Are Now Speaking Out Against Streaming...*, Digital Music News (Dec. 2, 2013) http://www.digitalmusicnews.com/permalink/2013/12/02/artistspirac y.

[70] *See infra* Part VI.C.i.a.

[71] *See* Press Kit, Rep. Doug Collins, Paul Williams, David Israelite, Michael O'Neill & Daryl Friedman, Songwriter Equity Act Press Kit (Feb. 25, 2014), http://www.bmi.com/images/news/2014/SEA_press_kit.pdf

Collins[72] introduced SEA on February 25, 2014, it has
gained "sixteen co-sponsors in the House and has been
referred to the subcommittee on courts, intellectual
property, and the Internet."[73] Following SEA's first
introduction in the U.S. House of Representatives, the
bill also gained momentum with three Senators
introducing their version for the Senate.[74] While
Senators Lamar Alexander,[75] Bob Corker,[76] and Orrin
Hatch[77] still acknowledge the importance of the existing

[hereinafter Songwriter Equity Act Press Kit]; *see also* Duncan, *supra* note
44.

[72] Doug Collins serves as a Republican Congressman for the 9th District
of Georgia. *Biography*, CONGRESSMAN DOUG COLLINS,
http://dougcollins.house.gov/biography (last visited Nov. 15, 2014).

[73] Ed Christman, *Songwriter Equity Act Picks Up Momentum in Senate,
Aims to Modernize Copyright Law*, BILLBOARD (May 12, 2014, 8:39 PM),
http://www.billboard.com/biz/articles/news/publishing/6084822/songwrit
er-equity-act-senate-copyright-law; *see Collins Introduces Songwriter Equity
Act*, CONGRESSMAN DOUG COLLINS (Feb. 25, 2014),
http://dougcollins.house.gov/press-releases/collins-introduces-songwriter-
equity-act/; *see also* Nate Rau, *Ga. Congressman Doug Collins Vows to Fight for
Songwriters*, TENNESSEAN (Mar. 19, 2014, 6:14 PM),
http://www.tennessean.com/story/news/politics/2014/03/19/ga-
congressman-doug-collins-vows-to-fight-for-songwriters/6630207/.

[74] *See* Songwriter Equity Act of 2014, S. 2321, 113th Cong. § 2
(2014); 160 Cong. Rec. S 2910 (daily ed. May 12, 2014) (introduction of
senate bill 2321, Songwriter Equity Act of 2014); Christman, *supra* note
73.

[75] Andrew Lamar Alexander is a Republican United States Senator
from Tennessee, having served since 2003. *See About/Lamar Alexander*, U.S.
SENATOR LAMAR ALEXANDER,
http://www.alexander.senate.gov/public/index.cfm/lamaralexander (last
visited Nov. 15, 2014).

[76] Bob Corker is a Republican United States Senator from
Tennessee, having served since 2007. *See Biography*, U.S. SENATOR BOB
CORKER, www.corker.senate.gov/public/index.cfm/biography (last
visited Nov. 15, 2014).

[77] Having served seven terms as a member of the Republican
Party, Orrin Grant Hatch is a United State Senator from Utah and the
most senior Republican Party member in the United States Senate. *See
Biography*, U.S. SENATOR ORRIN HATCH,
http://www.hatch.senate.gov/public/index.cfm/biography (last visited
Nov. 15, 2014). Hatch has also worked as a professional songwriter,

four considerations used by the CRB when determining royalty rates, their proposed legislation also stresses the need to "achieve fair market value when setting songwriter publishing rates on digital music services."[78]

SEA proposes an amendment to federal copyright law regarding the exclusive rights of sound recording copyright owners to remove a provision under Section 114 of the Copyright Act that prohibits license fees payable for the public performance of sound recordings from being taken into account in any administrative, judicial, or other governmental proceeding to set or adjust the royalties payable to copyright owners of musical works for the public performance of their works.[79] In amending Section 114(i) of the Copyright Act, a rate court would be allowed to consider all relevant evidence presented by the parties when determining songwriter compensation.[80] This amendment would grant each individual rate court discretion in how evidence provided in each case

---

writing mostly worship songs, but also achieving mainstream success. *See* Jesse Fox Mayshark, *Orrin Hatch, Lyricist*, N.Y. TIMES (July 16, 2006), www.nytimes.com/2006/07/16/weekinreview/16word.html. For information on Senator Hatch's political career, see U.S. SENATOR ORRIN HATCH, www.hatch.senate.gov/public (last visited Nov. 9, 2014). To read more about Hatch's career in songwriting and music management, see Jesse Fox Mayshark, *Orrin Hatch, Lyricist*, N.Y. TIMES (July   16,   2006), http://www.nytimes.com/2006/07/16/weekinreview/16word.html.

[78] Christman, *supra* note 73 ("The new legislation aims to charge the CRB with replicating the rate levels that would be achieved in a market with a willing seller and a willing buyer."); *see also* Songwriter Equity Act Press Kit, *supra* note 71.

[79] *See* Songwriter Equity Act Press Kit, *supra* note 71.

[80] "Section 114(i) of title 17, United States Code, is amended to read as follows:(i) Effect on Royalties for Underlying Works. It is the intent of Congress that royalties payable to copyright owners of musical works for the public performance of their works shall not be diminished in any respect as a result of the rights granted in section 106(6)." H.R. 4079, 113th Cong. § 2 (2014), *avalible at* https://www.congress.gov/bill/113th-congress/house-bill/4079/text.

should be considered in the decision-making process.[81]
Advocates of the SEA proposal have high hopes that
when establishing rates and terms for each agreement,
CRJs will base their decisions on economically fair
marketplace quotas as well as information presented by
the participating parties.[82] In theory, mechanical rates
would be based on what a willing consumer would pay
the artist for their work, and in turn, a more objective
mechanical rate would be used to establish performance
rates paid by digital streaming services.[83]

SEA also suggests replacement of the insufficient
royalty rate currently used by the CRB; the new rate to
determine mechanical royalties would more accurately
reflect free-market conditions.[84] However admirable
this goal may be, SEA omits any suggestions on how the
government should establish a fair market value for
royalty payments of each song.

---

[81] *See* Songwriter Equity Act Press Kit, *supra* note 71.

[82] *See* Songwriter Equity Act Press Kit, *supra* note 71. "We are
simply asking Congress to take the evidentiary blinders off of the
judges who control a significant portion of our writers' income. We
believe that an open and full picture of the market will permit our
rate court to recognize the value of musical works." *Id.* (quoting BMI
CEO Michael O'Neill).

[83] *See id.*

[84] *See id.* The standard royalty rate per song made and distributed
on or after January 1, 2006, is 9.1¢ per song or 1.75¢ per minute of
playing, whichever amount is greater. 37 C.F.R. § 255.3(m) (2014). For
more information about how compulsory license rates for sound
recordings of nondramatic musical works have been altered over
time, see 1 HOWARD B. ABRAMS, THE LAW OF COPYRIGHT § 5.28 (2d ed.
2013).

According of advocates of the bill, "[t]his minimal increase is due
to current law, which directs the Copyright Royalty Board (CRB)—the
government body responsible for setting the rate—to apply a standard
that does not reflect market value." Songwriter Equity Act Press Kit,
supra note 71.

B. Reactions to the Songwriter Equity Act

For songwriters, this pending legislation appears to be nothing but good news.[85] Even with potentially higher streaming prices for consumers, changes would reflect a marketplace in which those responsible for music composition would be more reasonably compensated for their work.[86] In a press kit presented by the House,[87] David Israelite, President and CEO of the National Music Publishers Association,[88] illustrated the importance of improvement concerning the manner in which the CRB evaluates songwriter royalties. Israelite noted that while a mechanical royalty rate of two cents per song was set in 1909,[89] the same rate has only increased to 9.1 cents in today's market.[90] While a seven-cent difference may not seem staggering, he continues to illustrate a shocking parallel in that

---

[85] Songwriter Equity Act Press Kit, *supra* note 71. As Paul Williams, President and Chairman of the Board for ASCAP, has stated, "'[b]y updating the outdated provisions of the Copyright Act in Sections 114(i) and 115, Congress has an opportunity to modernize the music licensing system so that songwriters and composers can thrive alongside the businesses that use our music.'" *Id.*

[86] While many sources are quick to jump to the conclusion that an increased mechanical royalty rate will benefit composers, there is currently no authority on how great an impact there could be.

[87] Songwriter Equity Act Press Kit, *supra* note 71.

[88] The National Music Publishers Association (NMPA) is a trade association for the American music publishing industry. With over 3,000 members, the organization aims to "protect its members' property right on the legislative, litigation, and regulatory fronts". The NMPA has pursed litigation against numerous organizations participating in illegal music distribution, including YouTube, LimeWire, Kazaa, and Napster. *NMPA Mission Statement*, NAT'L MUSIC PUBLISHERS ASS'N, http://www.nmpa.org/aboutnmpa/mission.asp (last visited Nov. 15, 2014).

[89] Copyright Act of 1909, Pub. L. No. 60-349, § 1(e), 35 Stat. 1075 (1909).

[90] Mechanical and Digital Phonorecord Delivery Rate, No. 2006-3 CRB   DPRA,   (2006)   *available   at* http://www.loc.gov/crb/proceedings/2006-3/dpra-public-final-rates-terms.pdf

while a dozen eggs would have cost fourteen cents in 1909, the same amount of product would cost roughly three dollars in today's grocery stores.[91] "[T]he standard rates of inflation seem to somehow not apply to songwriter," Israelite stated. "We must inject fairness into an outdated process that is undeniably stacked against songwriters and publishers, ensuring they are rightly compensated for their work."[92]

In addition to the National Music Publishers Association, all three PROs have stated public support for SEA. Pat Collins, President and CEO of SESAC, gave overwhelming support for the bill, saying: "[o]ur goal is to maximize the value of the copyrights we represent on behalf of our songwriters and publishers. Passing this important legislation will help sustain that value and safeguard the intellectual property of our creators and copyright proprietors."[93] BMI CEO Michael O'Neill has also publicly praised the need for legislative change to copyright law, stating, "[t]his bill is an important step on the road to fairness for songwriters and music publishers. The current environment, where performance of sound recordings are valued at twelve times those of the musical compositions that underlie them, is untenable."[94] Paul Williams, President and Chairman of the ASCAP Board, concurs with fellow PRO executives: "The Songwriter Equity Act is an important first step toward a more effective and efficient licensing system that will benefit everyone— consumers, music licensees and the songwriters and

---

[91] Christman, *supra* note 73.

[92] Neil Portnow, President and CEO of The Recording Academy, supports Israelite's stance in saying, "The Songwriter Equity Act will bring more fairness to those who write and compose the music loved worldwide . . . . All music creators deserve to be paid fair market value for their talents . . . ." Songwriter Equity Act Press Kit, *supra* note 71.

[93] *Id.*

[94] *Id.*

composers who are the foundation of the rapidly changing music environment."[95]

While there is adamant support of the proposed legislation, not everyone in the industry is so hastily welcoming the legislation's proposals. The National Association of Broadcasters[96] (NAB) is in public opposition of the pending legislation.[97] According to NAB Executive Vice President of Communications Dennis Wharton, the proposed legislation has the potential to impose "new costs on broadcasters that jeopardize the future of our free locally-focused service."[98] Additionally, Wharton stated, "[w]hile this legislation raises important issues about the changes confronting the songwriter community, NAB objects to changes in law that would deal with the financial imbalance between songwriters and artists by subjecting free broadcast radio stations to new fees."[99]

---

[95] *Id.*; *see also*, *ASCAP Applauds the Introduction of the Songwriter Equity Act*, AM. SOC'Y COMPOSERS, AUTHORS & PUBLISHERS (Feb. 25, 2014), http://www.ascap.com/press/2014/0225-ascap-statement-on-sea.aspx.

It is important to recognize ASCAP's support of the bill is purely based on its belief that legislative changes will benefit the artists they support. Since ASCAP does not collect mechanical royalties, it is the one PRO that would see no financial gain in the bill's possible passing. Ari Herstand, *Congress Wants to Hear Your Songs and Stories to Help Fix the Copyright Law*, DIGITAL MUSIC NEWS (Apr. 28, 2014), http://www.digitalmusicnews.com/permalink/2014/04/28/songwriter-equity-act.

[96] The National Association of Broadcasters (NAB) is a trade association, workers union, and lobby group that represents the interests of for-profit, over-the-air radio and television broadcasters in the United States. The NAB represents more than 8,300 radio and television stations and broadcast networks. NAT'L ASS'N OF BROADCASTERS, http://www.nab.org (last visited Nov. 15, 2014).

[97] *See*, Christman, *supra* note 73.

[98] *Id.*

[99] *Id.*

Despite relatively minor concerns raised by organizations within the music industry, it is somewhat hard to detect a downside to the SEA proposal. However, while many regular citizens would likely be in support of fair compensation for composers, there is a substantial likelihood that prices for music streaming services would significantly increase with legislative changes. "Raising the price of digital streaming would be the wrong technology call," stated a recent editorial in *The Washington Times*, "the higher rates would be passed on to consumers."[100] But why does it matter that streaming service costs could increase? Many consumers, while not completely enthused about raised prices, would still support fair compensation for the artists whose works they enjoy. However, should SEA proposals succeed, there is great potential for an abundance of artist compensation issues to accompany the legislative changes.

V. MUSIC INDUSTRY RECTIFICATION THROUGH THE SONGWRITER EQUITY ACT

Historically, changes in the music industry have been incremental; however, with the evolution of digital music, a more transformative change is necessary. Until recently, record companies had four major costs: recording, manufacturing, distribution, and promotion.[101] While all four functions are necessary to

---

[100] Daniel Horowitz, *Editorial: Songwriter Equity Act Inequity*, WASH. TIMES (June 6, 2014), http://www.washingtontimes.com/news/2014/jun/6/editorial-songwriter-inequity/.

[101] Steve Lawson, *Transformative Vs. Incremental Change*, MUSIC THINK TANK (Nov. 14, 2009), http://www.musicthinktank.com/blog/transformative-vs-incremental-change.html (explaining why changes in the music industry must occur at a quicker pace to keep up with current changes to online distribution services).

the industry, all but recording have been removed or modified due to recent technological advancements in the Internet age.[102] Solutions to correct issues within the music industry generally fall into three categories: statutory, administrative, and free-market approaches.[103] While there are strong advocates for each type of reformation within the music industry, administrative and free-market solutions are likely to be highly time intensive without producing many benefits for the affected parties. Statutory changes, such as SEA, are increasing in popularity. However, these solutions would likely also be ineffective due to increased costs to consumers, which would only further society's tendency to resort to piracy.[104] A more realistic approach to combat the compensation issues present in the industry would be to switch over to a model mirroring television's recent switch to online streaming. For a nominal fee, consumers might be more willing to compromise between paying for full, physical albums

---

[102] *Id.*

[103] Jared S. Welsh, *Pay What You Like—No, Really: Why Copyright Law Should Make Digital Music Free for Noncommercial Uses*, 58 EMORY L.J. 1495, 1528–30 (2009).

[104] *See Ram* D. Gopel, G. Lawrence Sanders, Sudip Bhattacharjee, Manish Agrawal & Suzanne C. Wagner, *A Behavioral Model of Digital Music Piracy*, 14 J. ORGANIZATIONAL COMPUTING & ELECTRONIC COMMERCE 89 (2004) ("Economic incentives to pirate digital audio include the high costs of purchasing legitimate copies of audio CDs . . . higher music purchasing cost would increase the payoff from piracy, *ceteris paribus*. Such an increase in the payoff would naturally increase the likelihood for piracy.").

Additionally, as a general note, statutory amendments do not historically always lead to changes in social practice. For example, the Civil Rights Act of 1968 outlawed discrimination based on race. While much of today's society would agree racial discrimination is an issue of the past, it still runs rampant in today's culture. *See, e.g.*, Deuel Ross, *Pouring Old Poison Into New Bottles: How Discretion and the Discriminatory Administration of Voter ID Laws Recreate Literacy Tests*, 45 COLUM. HUM. RTS. L. REV. 362, 364 (2014).

outright and illegally obtaining music. While there currently are popular online distribution services available to consumers, these services are inadequate due to their inability to reasonably compensate artists.

A. Statutory Reformation: The Songwriter Equity Act is Not the Answer

While restructuring the Copyright Act is generally debated, there is little argument to proposed section 114(i) alterations. Section 114(i) prevents the establishment of a fair and efficient rate-setting procedure, but "there is no policy justification for retaining this provision, which favors one group of rights holders over another based solely on being the first to achieve their 'place at the table.'"[105] By allowing artists and PROs to present mechanical royalties as a standard for performance royalties, there is a greater likelihood that the music market will more fairly compensate artists.

Unlike the section 114(i) reformation, which has been fairly well received, the statutory change in section 115 of the Copyright Act is a hot-button topic in Congress and among today's music industry professionals. In a statement for the July 2005 Senate hearing, the Register of Copyrights, Marybeth Peters, argued that the bulk of consumers would choose to use a legal downloading service over illegal file sharing options if the service could offer an equivalent product:

> Right now, illegitimate services clearly offer something that consumers want: lots of music at little or no cost. They can do this because they offer people a means to

---

[105] Mary LaFrance, *From Whether to How: The Challenge of Implementing a Full Public Performance Right in Sound Recordings*, 2 HARV. J. SPORTS & ENT. L. 221, 261 (2011).

obtain any music they please without obtaining the appropriate licenses. However, under the complex licensing scheme engendered by the present section 115, legal music services must engage in numerous negotiations with publishers and record companies, which result in time delays and increased transaction costs. In cases where they cannot succeed in obtaining all of the rights they need in order to make a musical composition available, the legal music services simply do not offer that selection, thereby making them less attractive to the listening public than the pirates.[106]

While Peters makes a valid point concerning the complexity of the current licensing process and suggests a drastic reformation of section 115, such a dramatic change could cause even more confusion for those seeking out these licenses.[107]

Supporters of statutory changes argue that such alterations should be made to streamline the Copyright Act.[108] In *Reforming Section 115: Escape from the Byzantine World of Mechanical Licensing*, Skyla Mitchell identifies record companies as being affected by amendments to

---

[106] *Music Licensing Reform: Hearing Before the Subcomm. on Intellectual Property, Comm. on the Judiciary*, 109th Cong. 120 (2005) (statement of Marybeth Peters, Reg. Copyrights).

[107] For a complete analysis of Marybeth Peters' Senate address concerning copyright reformation and its potential impact on the music industry, see William Henslee, *Marybeth Peters is Almost Right: An Alternative to her Proposals to Reform the Compulsory License Scheme for Music*, 48 WASHBURN L.J. 107, 118–22 (2008).

[108] *See* Welsh, *supra* note 103, at 1530 (summarizing various statutory reform methods advocated by various experts in American copyright law).

section 115 in two major ways: cover songs and piracy.[109]
Mitchell states, "[i]t is questionable how much the
record companies rely on cover songs for income; but
to the extent they do, it is clearly in their best interest to
maintain a compulsory license with a statutory rate
ceiling."[110] The more pressing issue addressed by record
companies is concern over piracy. It would be more
beneficial for record companies to focus on
streamlining the licensing process, which would enable
them to provide new products and media formats
capable of competing with pirated offerings.[111] The SEA
is a textbook example of a legislative push towards
statutory change.

While increasing the minimum royalty rates paid to
composers could positively impact the music industry,
the fact remains that people are still illegally
downloading significant amounts of music in spite of
the copyright laws that are already in place, causing
massive losses in profits to music production
companies.[112] In contrast to proposals suggesting

---

[109] Mitchell, *supra* note 25, at 1260.

[110] *Id.*

[111] *Digital Music Licensing and Section 115 of the Copyright Act:
Hearing Before the Subcomm. on Courts, the Internet, and Intellectual
Property of the H. Comm. on the Judiciary*, 109th Cong. 15 (2005)
(statement of Lawrence Kenswil, President of e-Labs, Universal Music
Group).

According to Kenswil, "[T]he antiquated structure of Section 115,
with its one-song-at-a-time, one-publisher-at-a-time licensing model,
is frustrating the introduction of [new technologies and distribution
platforms] . . . [that] provide superior audio fidelity . . . as well as
improved security to reduce the sting of piracy." *Id.* at 35, 39.

[112] An analysis by the Institute for Policy Innovation stated that
music piracy causes approximately $12.5 billion in economic losses
each year. Additionally, it results in 71,060 U.S. jobs lost, a loss of $2.7
billion in workers' earnings, a loss of $422 million in tax revenues,
$291 million in lost personal income tax, and $131 million in lost
corporate income and production taxes. Stephen E. Siwek, *The True
Cost of Sound Recording Piracy to the U.S. Economy*, INSTITUTE FOR
POLICY   INNOVATION   (Aug.   21,   2007),

changes to the Copyright Act, some statutory proposals suggest changes be made to criminal law, such as making it a criminal offense to download music illegally from peer-to-peer servers.[113] Enforcing criminal penalties would have a radical effect on society. Prosecuting for damages that are grossly disproportionate to the crime of illegal downloading would be unconstitutional, and public protest could make this result exceedingly unlikely.[114] While statutory approaches may appear as the best mode of change, they can only lay the groundwork for reformation.

---

http://www.ipi.org/ipi_issues/detail/the-true-cost-of-sound-recording-piracy-to-the-us-economy.

[113] McGill suggests a warning system, which would alert habitual illegal downloaders that their activities are being monitored. David A. McGill, *New Year, New Catch-22: Why the RIAA's Proposed Partnership with ISPs Will Not Significantly Decrease the Prevalence of P2P Music File Sharing*, 29 LOY. L.A. ENT. L. REV. 353, 360 (2009). Should this warning go unnoticed or, more likely, ignored, then Internet service to the consumer would be delayed or shut off. McGill also believes, regardless of the measures taken to stop illegal downloading practices, the right to file a lawsuit against the alleged infringer should be maintained. *Id.* at 353, 359.

Lawsuits against parties participating in illegal file sharing are rarely effective. However, there also appears to be no manageable way to protect copyrighted music without giving the music industry more power, which would likely lead to a greater restriction to the public in its personal use of music. The Recording Industry Association of America (RIAA) has proposed the Secure Digital Music Initiative, which would require all electronic devices that play music to install new protective mechanics. Such software would prevent users from burning music CDs to or from a computer, downloading music, or transferring music to an MP3 player. While in theory this may seem like a successful approach, allowing the music industry control over what the public hears, what devices they use to listen to music, and how much an individual must pay for each use of a song is frighteningly restrictive. David Nelson, *Free the Music: Rethinking the Role of Copyright in an Age of Digital Distribution*, 78 S. CAL. L. REV. 559, 570–71 (2005).

[114] Boehm, *supra* note 46, at 207 (proposing criminal enforcement as a deterrence method for illegal downloading).

Considering the ease with which recorded music is transferred among individuals online, parties other than the artist are able to reap benefits from the creation of this music.[115] Since this creates high transaction costs, creators want to protect themselves against the threat of free riding by demanding a higher price for their works.[116] While statutory reformation of section 115 of the Copyright Act is a plausible response to this issue, by increasing mechanical royalty rates, SEA reformation would actually add to costs of music production as well as transaction costs. Parties pirating music are effectively avoiding such costs. And, although it may seem counter-intuitive, digital distribution has actually reduced the risk that parties other than the artist will significantly benefit from distribution profits.[117]

B. The Songwriter Equity Act's Limitations on Maximizing the Availability of Diverse Creative Works to the Public

The objectives by which mechanical royalties are established are defined in section 801 of the Copyright Act.[118] While the CRB is responsible for balancing potential benefits to the public and fair compensation to the copyright holder, these considerations must also be balanced against the potential impacts of the rate on

---

[115] Henry H. Perritt, Jr., *New Architectures for Music: Law Should Get Out of the Way*, 29 HASTINGS COMM. & ENT. L.J. 259, 266 (2007).

[116] *Id.* at 267.

[117] For a study indicating the decrease in illegal online file sharing, see *Music File Sharing Declined Significantly in 2012*, NPD GROUP (Feb. 26, 2012), https://www.npd.com/wps/portal/npd/us/news/press-releases/the-npd-group-music-file-sharing-declined-significantly-in-2012/. *See generally* Welsh, *supra* note 103, at 1525 ("[A]lthough the music industry claims otherwise, digital technology has actually reduced the risk of free-riding. It has done so both by reducing costs and by increasing demand for recorded music, making music that much easier to acquire legitimately and thus decreasing the relative risk of free-riding.").

[118] 17 U.S.C. § 801(b)(1) (2000).

the music industry as a whole.[119] While these objectives were followed during the initial fixation of the statutory rate, many practitioners in the music industry feel that recent rate courts have not been so diligent.[120]

The CRB has long acknowledged the importance of allowing consumers access to an abundance of musical options.[121] If music retailers and policy makers follow the intent of the Copyright Act, the royalty rate should provide incentive to create works for the benefit of the public.[122] As with any service, the number and variety of artists represented in any given market will likely dictate its success with consumers.[123] As identified by David Kostiner, "[i]f the mechanical royalty rate paid to

---

[119] David Kostiner, *Will Mechanicals Break the Digital Machine?: Determining A Fair Mechanical Royalty Rate for Permanent Digital Phonographic Downloads*, 27 Hastings Comm. & Ent L.J. 653, 675 (2005).

[120] Abrams, *supra* note 39, at 235–37.

[121] 160 Cong. Rec. S3510 (daily ed. Apr. 25, 2006) (statement of Sen. Dianne Feinstein).

[122] There is no debate that the CRB is charged with the responsibility of providing the public with as many musical offerings as possible. While it is still uncertain how potential changes under SEA would affect music dissemination, independent webcasters are currently combating paralleling issues with webcasting royalties. (A webcast is any media presentation distributed over the Internet to many simultaneous listeners or viewers.) With legislative changes intended to promote Internet usage by webcasters, many fear the decision to increase royalty rates will "stifle[] technological innovation and use, thereby eliminating forums that provide creative works to the public." Sara O'Connell, *Counting Down Another Music Marathon: Copyright Arbitration Royalty Panels and the Case of Internet Radio*, 8 Marq. Intell. Prop. L. Rev. 161, 177 (2004). While the consequences policy makers are currently facing in response to heightened royalty rates for webcasters is not completely indicative of what could happen should the SEA bill pass, there is certainly a possibility for a similar negative response.

[123] David Kostiner, *Will Mechanics Break the Digital Machine?: Determining a Fair Mechanical Royalty Rate for Permanent Digital Phonographic Downloads*, 21 Santa Clara Computer & High Tech. L.J. 235, 247–48 (2004).

composers is disproportionate to the wholesale income realized by record labels, those labels may decide to decrease the availability of their online catalogs, depriving the public of an exciting, economical, and convenient method of purchasing music."[124] If the mechanical rate were to be altered, it would likely make diverse creative works less available to the public.[125]

While SEA proposals are admirable in their desire to more fairly compensate songwriters, a rise in current royalty rates will almost certainly result in higher price tags for consumers, hindering the ability to access inexpensive and diverse music.[126] Major labels, which are frequently owned by parent corporations, generally focus on maximizing profits through the release of only the most profitable works.[127] Considering that a handful

---

[124] *Id.* at 235.

[125] Jenna Hentoff, *Compulsory Licensing of Musical Works in the Digital Age: Why the Current Process is Ineffective and How Congress is Attempting to Fix It*, 8 J. HIGH TECH. L. 113, 126 (2008).

[126] Kostiner, *supra* note 123, at 245.

[127] In today's market, major labels are more concerned than ever with producing enough hits to remain financially stable. According an opinion by Forbes Magazine, "big-business" record labels are in for a drastic change, and scrambling to make changes to meet the evolving music market. Richard Busch, *Major Record Labels as Dinosaurs?*, FORBES   MAGAZINE,   (Mar.   27,   2012,   1:05   PM) http://www.forbes.com/sites/richardbusch/2012/03/27/major-record-labels-as-dinosaurs/. "For decades the industry relied on a business model of selling massive amounts of copies of a few albums to finance the high-cost of producing records, plugging songs to radio, and overcoming the losses from their other projects. Record companies used the clout of having access to recording studios and access to airplay on the radio to their advantage in contract negotiations with artists, which leveled their risk intake of the enormous costs and influence needed to both produce and push a record." *Id.* However, with major changes, mainly technological ones, we may soon be noticing a change in major labels to more closely mirror independent competitors. "The major labels in the '70s–'90s became experts at mainstream marketing in the days of a singular medium of either radio stations or, from the 1980s on, MTV. In the music scene of today there are multiple subgenres and blogs catering to niche

of major labels control 85% of the market—while hundreds of independent labels have the remainder— the distribution of wealth and resources is heavily slanted toward artists with previous mainstream success.[128] In addressing how many songwriters will actually see a tangible benefit from the new legislations, copyright lawyer Raymond Scott noted, "even if you double the relatively small performance royalty songwriters get each time their song is played, that won't matter for songwriters who don't get much of the pie ASCAP and BMI slices up; the real winner will be already successful songwriters whose songs are widely played in prominent places."[129]

Independent labels are continuing to rise in popularity among artists and are therefore also growing in total record sales nationally.[130] More intimate labels are a valuable alternative to major labels, which, due to

---

audiences on the Internet, 500 cable channels, satellite radio, Internet radio, etc. Massive corporations are not built for this type of promotions, but a smaller record label, a small marketing firm or a motivated artist are." *Id.*

[128] Peter Jan Honigsberg, *The Evolution and Revolution of Napster*, 36 U.S.F. L. REV. 473, 477 (2002).

[129] Julia Rogers, *Twitter and SoundCloud, Songwriter Equity Act and Electronic Dance Music News*, MUSICIAN COACHING: STRATEGY & BUSINESS PLANNING FOR MUSICIANS (May 25, 2014), http://musiciancoaching.com/music-news-2014/twitter-and-soundcloud-songwriter-equity-act-electronic-dance-music/.

[130] "Becoming an Indie Label signed artist has become a movement, a trend, some may even say a fad. But indie labels have created a true niche for themselves and their business has been booming. So much so, in fact, that many of the Major Labels are now beginning to embrace the Indie Label methods in order to achieve future growth as a company. While indie labels can't offer the kind of funding for artists that the major labels can, they do offer many other benefits that may be more important to the artist." Johnathan Ostrow, *Indie vs. Major: Which Record Label Contract is Right for You?*, MUSIC THINK TANK (May 16, 2010), http://www.musicthinktank.com/mtt-open/indie-vs-major-which-record-label-contract-is-right-for-you.html.

size and marketing expenditures, require their releases
to appeal to an unrealistically large population in order
to recoup the money invested in the release.[131] Since
independent labels are already more extensively
affected by piracy and file sharing, they cannot afford
to have their profit margins lessened any further.[132]

By increasing the mechanical royalty rate even
further, it is unlikely that independent labels will be
able to afford marketing efforts to promote a variety of
lesser-known artists.[133] A failure to support such artists

---

[131] Kostiner, *supra* note 123, at 256.

[132] Most notably, the greatest downfall to artists in choosing an
independent label is a general lack of funding. "A lack of funding
means a smaller budget for recording, production of physical disks,
packaging, distribution costs, tour support, merchandise, etc. Another
significant issue caused by a lack of budget is that proper marketing
for the artist is sacrificed, making the artists promote themselves if
they want to be seen and heard." Ostrow, *supra* note 130. Not only are
artists somewhat more responsible for self-promotion, since profit
margins are less stable to begin with, it is likely that independent
labels will feel the effects of piracy and file sharing more abrasively.
Id.

[133] The most recent increase in mechanical royalties greatly
affected Internet radio stations of all sizes. Andrew Stockment,
Internet Radio: The Case for a Technology Neutral Royalty Standard, 95 VA.
L. REV. 2129, 2154–56 (2009) ("In 2008, CBS Radio took over the
internet radio services of both AOL Radio and Yahoo! radio. Fred
McIntyre, senior vice president of AOL Radio, said that royalties were
too high to operate the business at a profit even before the CRB
decision."). According to one mid-size Internet radio station owner,
"[t]his royalty structure would wipe out an entire class of businesses:
small independent webcasters such as myself and my wife, who
operate Radio Paradise. Our obligation under this rate structure
would be equal to over 125% of our total income. There is no practical
way for us to increase our income so dramatically as to render that
affordable." *Id.* at 2156 (citing Daniel McSwain, Webcast Royalty Rate
Decision Announced, RAIN: Radio and Internet Newsletter (Kurt Hanson),
Mar.   2,   2007,
http://www.kurthanson.com/archive/news/030207/index.shtml).   While
this result will not definitively occur if SEA increases mechanical royalties
in the music industry, there is definitely a strong possibility of a similar

would likely result in a diminished music variety, only providing opportunities for those reaching a certain threshold of popularity. Many labels, especially smaller independent ones, may decide not to make their music available online because lower profit margins could result from paying composers a statutory fee; this is especially true if the mechanical rate is set too high.[134] To create the most mutually beneficial marketplace, reformation should be focused on creating a system that represents more artists, therefore giving consumers a wider variety of options. In fear of hindering possibilities for less mainstream artists, music labels should be protected from overly burdensome royalty rates.[135]

VI. Alternative Approaches to Copyright Act Reformation

A. Administrative Proposals: Collective Licensing

A substantial number of concerned parties support modifications to copyright law through administrative proposals, which would remedy copyright issues through a collective license informally referred to as a

---

effect. Andrew Stockment, *Internet Radio: The Case for a Technology Neutral Royalty Standard*, 95 Va. L. Rev. 2129, 1254–56 (2009).

[134] Kostiner, *supra* note 123, at 250.

[135] According to Gregory Alan Barnes, who serves as general legal counsel to the Digital Media Association, the potential for a heightened mechanical royalty rate would likely stifle music distribution across all platforms. "[A] key provision of the legislation seeks to raise the cost of doing business for online music stores and on-demand streaming services at a time when both music platforms are engaged in a fierce battle with pirate websites that provide access to unauthorized content for free." Gregory Alan Barnes, *In Debate Over Compensation, Songwriter Equity Act is Off- Key*, CQ Roll Call (Apr. 14, 2014, 5 AM), http://www.rollcall.com/news/in_debate_over_compensation_songwriter_eq uity_act_is_off_key_commentary-232077-1.html.

blanket   licensing   scheme.[136]   Proponents   of
administrative   changes   suggest   implementing   an
organization that would administer royalties for digital
distribution purposes.[137] Under a blanket licensing
proposal, a music service, such as iTunes, would
negotiate and pay for a single license that would give
the service provider the right to distribute any musical
compositions that fall under the "blanket" of the
agreement.[138]

Considering this administrative view is based
closely off the successful PRO model, it appears to be an
appealing   option   in   fairly   distributing   license
proceeds.[139] Additionally, since the rate of this type of
agreement would likely be extensively negotiated
between the parties, there is a much greater probability
that the final cost of a blanket license would more fairly
reflect current market rates than the current statutory
rate does.[140] However, if a collective licensing system
were adopted to remedy the problematic section 115,
the administration of this new blanket license would

---

[136] *Id.* at 1528; *see also* Mark F. Schultz, *Live Performance, Copyright, and the Future of the Music Business*, 43 U. RICH. L. REV. 685, 695 n.51 (2009).

[137] These methods generally track the common model used by PROs, in that they would gather blanket license fees from users, which would then be distributed to copyright holders according to the amount of use. *See* Jessica Litman, *Sharing and Stealing*, 27 HASTINGS COMM. & ENT. L.J. 1, 41–44 (2004).

[138] It was declared in 2001 that PROs (in the initial instance, BMI) had to make blanket licenses available. United States v. Broad. Music, Inc., 275 F.3d 168, 171 (2d Cir. 2001). However, courts had to derive new formulas for the determination of blanket fees. Broad. Music, Inc. v. DMX, 726 F. Supp. 2d 355, 355–56 (2d Cir. 2012). *See e.g.,* Carly Olson, *Changing Tides in Music Licensing? BMI v. DMX and In re THP*, 10 NW. J. TECH. & INTELL. PROP., 276, 282–284 (2012).

[139] Litman, *supra* note 137, at 41–44.

[140] Mitchell, *supra* note 25, at 1264; *see Bigger Than Grokster?*, THE 463: INSIDE   TECH   POLICY,   (June   23,   2005), http://463.blogs.com/the_463/2005/06/bigger_than_gro.html.

need to be evaluated.[141] Additionally, restrictions under the current section 115 require licensing of musical works on a song-by-song basis, which would likely prevent companies from licensing large numbers of works at one time.[142] The logistics of setting up a new, *effective* system of licensing would be daunting and require a significant amount of time and resources.[143] While it may be worth the time and resources necessary to create and maintain such a system, more efficient private contractual solutions exist.[144]

B. Free-Market Proposals

Advocates of free-market proposals suggest taking no action in copyright reconstruction and instead recommend allowing the market to stabilize on its own.[145] Proponents of this theory believe that "as more consumer-friendly technologies develop and lure new users back from illegal file sharing, an economic equilibrium will ultimately occur."[146] However, due to the vast changes to the music industry in the past decade, there is no support for suggesting that inaction would solve problems relating to lack of compensation for composers and financial deficits due to illegal downloading. Even if a balance between copyright law

---

[141] Anthony Reese, *Copyright and Internet Music Transmissions: Existing Law, Major Controversies, Possible Solutions*, 55 U. MIAMI L. REV. 237, 266–267 (2001).

[142] *See* 17 U.S.C. § 115(b)(1) (2006); *see also* Brian Sanchez, *The Section 115 Mechanical License and the Copyright Modernization Act: The Hardships of Legislating Music Industry Negotiations*, 17 DE PAUL-LCA J. ART. & ENT. L. 37 at 64 (2006).

[143] *Id.*

[144] As discussed later in this piece, copyright law is likely not the best approach to a lasting change in the music industry. By forming private contractual agreements, a more sustaining, beneficial relationship will be formed between artists and distribution teams. *See infra* Part VI.C.

[145] *See* Welsh, *supra* note 103, at 1529.

[146] *Id.*

and emerging technology were struck, composers would likely face severe losses in the meantime.[147] A free-market and statutory hybrid proposal has also recently been considered; the proposal would modify the Copyright Act to benefit non-commercial sound recordings of music, allowing the public to share music so long as it is done without commercial profit.[148] While this possibility is obviously appealing to consumers, there is no foreseeable way for the music industry to continue on such a financially lacking system.[149]

C. Digital Distribution: The Answer Today's Music Market Has Been Searching For?

In an effort to cut distribution and promotional costs, many artists have already explored online distribution methods. Record labels may approach online distribution with a justifiable sense of hesitancy. By not selling full albums, there is a potential for some financial loss. However, in switching to an online distribution process, labels are virtually guaranteed extensive savings in packaging and shipping costs.[150] Additionally, transactions should be efficient and nearly faultless.[151] Instead of having to find a record store that carries obscure works to purchase a full record, a buyer can download or stream individually chosen singles

---

[147] *Id.*

[148] *Id.* at 1532.

[149] Johnathan Handel, *Uneasy Lies the Head that Wears the Crown: Why Content's Kingdom is Slipping Away*, 11 VAND. J. ENT. & TECH. L. 597, 633–36 (2009) (discussing the likelihood of potential suffering should the economic imbalance of the music industry continue).

[150] As Kostiner validly explains, "[t]hese costs make the distribution of less popular artists cost prohibitive because a significant investment is required for even the most limited release, especially when shipping charges to the thousands of disparate major and independent retail music outlets across the country are considered." Kostiner, *supra* note 123, at 251.

[151] *Id.*

from services with unprecedented variety.[152] In considering this more affordable option, artists, composers, labels, and consumers would all benefit, likely resulting in more music legally accessed by consumers overall.[153]

While online distribution services of this nature exist, most notably Spotify[154] and Pandora,[155] they provide little to no benefit to artists. Considering society's drastic conversion to online media consumption, digital distribution is very likely the

---

[152] *See* Alex Veiga, *Tough Tactics Give Music Industry New Sales Hope*, INFORMATION WEEK, (Jan. 12, 2004, 10:20 AM), www.informationweek.com/story/showArticle.jhtml?articleID=17300407.

[153] While the current legitimate online streaming market has not yet come close to reaching the profits necessary to recoup piracy losses, it is making a difference. According to a report by The New York Times, "Over the past year, however, Internet streaming services like Spotify, which offer free listening, supported by advertising or subscriptions, have gained a growing following. Revenue from streaming is accelerating as growth in sales of digital downloads from services like Apple's iTunes slows." Even though physical album sales are dropping about 16% annually worldwide, digital source revenue is steadily increasing. Eric Pfanner, *Music Industry Counts the Cost of Piracy*, N.Y. TIMES (Jan. 21, 2010) http://www.nytimes.com/2010/01/22/business/global/22music.html?_r= 0.

[154] Spotify is a Swedish commercial music streaming service, which launched in the United States in July 2011. The distribution site now caters to fifty eight different markets and hosts over forty million users, ten million of whom pay to use the upgraded version of the site. *Information: What is Spotify?* SPOTIFY, https://press.spotify.com/us/information/ (last visited Nov. 4, 2014).

For media reaction to the site's original launch in the United States, see John D. Sutter, *What's this Spotify Thing All About?*, CNN TECH (July 15, 2011, 7:13 AM) http://www.cnn.com/2011/TECH/innovation/07/14/spotify.us.why/.

[155] Unlike Spotify, which lets users select music preferences on an individual basis, Pandora is a "free personalized internet radio." This means music selections are presented to the user through an automated music recommendation service. *What is Pandora?*, PANDORA, http://help.pandora.com/customer/portal/articles/182180-what-is-pandora (last visited Nov. 4, 2014).

answer the industry has been searching for. However, should this be the case, current streaming services need to make some major alterations to provide artists with fair compensation.

Private contractual agreements are better suited than the suggested SEA modifications to address the increasingly low revenues of the music industry. Such an approach would still operate under section 115 of the Copyright Act, in that parties could negotiate royalty license fees for an amount less than that specified by the statutory rate.[156] Additionally, depending on the distribution service, negotiations over a sound recording under section 114 of the Copyright Act may still occur. However, by focusing on private contractual agreements, the industry is likely to save significant time and money. Instead of debating an entirely new structure for copyright law enforcement, the existing structure for online royalty distributions through SoundExchange could be maintained.[157] Most importantly, a proposal of this nature would more wholly address the problems inherent in the current copyright model while still reconciling consumer desires for affordable music selections with the music industry's desire to make money.

Online music distributors would benefit most from adopting a model similar to online television distributors such as Hulu[158] and Netflix.[159] These

---

[156] While advocates for statutory reform may view this negatively, it should not be considered a step back in industry change. If music production companies begin developing long-standing working relationships with online distributors, even negotiating at lower rates may be worth a financial sacrifice to secure a long-term business plan.

[157] *See* Mitchell, *supra* note 25, at 1255.

[158] Hulu is an online subscription service that offers ad-supported, on-demand video streaming of TV shows, movies, trailers, and additional media content created by its affiliated networks. Since its creation in 2008, three of the four largest American television

agencies are the television industry's answer to visual digitalization, in that these agencies provide content for streaming at a minimal price and make up any lost revenue through advertising profits. In mirroring online television models, online intermediaries would earn profits through online advertising, which could in turn be used to pay record companies a negotiated royalty fee, a percentage of their profits, or a greater of the two amounts. Considering consumers are willing to

---

networks (ABC, Fox, and NBC) have privately contracted with the site to provide content for viewers. Additionally, in 2009 The Walt Disney Company announced it would join the venture, purchasing a 27% stake in Hulu. While the website started out as a free service, solely funded by advertising and commercial revenue, in 2010 HuluPlus was launched, which began charging users a nominal monthly fee for streaming access. While this new expense may have alienated some customers, HuluPlus gained more than 1.5 million paying customers within its first year of operation by expanding the content library for consumers. Mike Hopkins, Hulu CEO, reported the company would reach $1 billion in revenue in 2013, and that the online service reached 5 million subscribers over the course of the year. Additionally, in 2013, Hulu reported expanding its "roster of advertisers" to more than 1,000 different brands. Mike Hopkins, *A Strong 2013*, Hulu Blog (Aug. 24, 2014), www.blog.hulu.com/2013/12/18/a-strong-2013/ (discussing the companies successes over the time of operation as presented by CEO Mike Hopkins). For general information about how Hulu Services operate, see *How Hulu Works*, How Stuff Works, www.howstuffworks.com/internet/basics/hulu.htm (last visited Nov. 4, 2014).

[159] Netflix, Inc. is an American provider of on-demand Internet streaming media available to viewers in North and South America, the Caribbean, and parts of Europe. The company originally started out in 1997 as a flat rate DVD-by-mail system in the United States. A mere two years later the company started its subscription-based digital distribution service. By June 2014, Netflix had a reported 50 million subscribers internationally. Unlike Hulu, Netflix negotiates with television companies on a show-by-show basis instead of presenting an entire network's lineup. Netflix has partnered with Paramount Pictures, Lions Gate Entertainment, and Metro-Goldwyn-Mayer, increasing the company's access to a wider selection of feature films. *How Netflix Works*, How Stuff Works , www.howstuffworks.com/netflix.htm (last visited Nov. 4, 2014).

pay for services such as Hulu and Netflix,[160] it is reasonable to believe a similar model could be replicated in the music industry. A digital distribution process could provide consumers with music that is more portable and less costly, both appealing aspects to today's market.[161] Additionally, studies suggest that those who illegally download music are also those who purchase the most music.[162] Therefore, there is a great potential for music distributors to save money while increasing their stream of revenue should the distributor choose to convert their market to a digital realm. By partnering with multiple online intermediaries who could offer advertising-supported, low-cost streaming and downloading, record companies could potentially increase profits while likely skirting further piracy issues.

It is evident that digital distribution methods are far more cost-effective than that of traditional physical retail.[163] Not only would transactional costs to consumers decrease, but so would costs incurred by

---

[160] A 2014 report by *The Huffington Post* suggests that nearly a fifth of American Netflix or Hulu subscribers have "cut the cord" on traditional cable TV services. While that percentage is substantial, the same report states that statistic rises to 1 in 4 consumers without traditional cable services when considering young adults between the ages of 18 and 34. In the past 14 years, average cable bills, not including fees, promotions, or taxes have risen a staggering 97 percent. Therefore, consumers, especially financially strained younger adults, are in constant pursuit of more affordable options. Timothy Stenovec, *Yes, Netflix and Hulu are Starting to Kill Cable*, HUFFINGTON POST: TECH (Apr. 17, 2014, 3:44 PM), www.huffingtonpost.com/2014/04/17/netflix-cable_n_5168725.html.

[161] *See* Perritt, *supra* note 115, at 311.

[162] *See, e.g.,* Ken Fisher, *Study: P2P Users Buy More Music; Apathy, Not Piracy, the Problem*, ARS TECHNICA (Mar. 20, 2006, 1:33 PM) www.arstechnica.com/uncategorized/2006/03/6418-2 (finding in a Canadian study that peer-to-peer downloaders bought more music).

[163] *See* Perritt, *supra* note 115, at 298–300.

creators.[164] Internet-based promotion and distribution are more cost-effective than traditional methods.[165] With the use of current technology, overall advertising and reproduction costs could drastically decrease.[166] A significant advantage accompanying the adoption of this model would be the ease with which the industry could benefit from such online music networks to cut down on promotion costs by relying on consumers to promote artists using grassroots methods.[167] In creating a more interactive online network of musical selections, the industry would have further opportunities to gather consumer information. In turn, there would likely be a vast improvement in the decisions of distributors as to what singles or artists should be further promoted.

The current music distribution market is frequently characterized as a conglomerate.[168] It is increasingly more common for national media companies to purchase local stations, effectively placing all management and programming decisions under one uniform production system.[169] Conglomeration has

---

[164] See id. at 270.

[165] See id. at 298–99.

[166] See id. at 302.

[167] For example, both Netflix and Hulu services allow customers to leave comments about each television episode viewed, creating an open dialogue amongst all viewers. Both sites also allow for customer connection to other social media sites, increasing the likelihood customers will comment on their viewing experiences on a variety of online platforms.

[168] See, Jeffrey Gilbert, The Dixie Chicks: A Case Study for the Politics of Hollywood, 9 TEX. REV. ENG. & SPORTS L. 307, 312 (2008). See generally, Adam J. van Alstyne, Clear Control: An Antitrust Analysis of Clear Channel's Radio and Concert Empire, 88 MINN. L. REV. 627, 627-29 (2004) (explaining how consolidation within the music promotion industry can lead to irreparable harm to other related industries).

[169] This behavior dates back to the 1996 Telecommunications Act, which loosened restrictions on ownership of multiple stations. Telecommunications Act of 1996, Pub. L. No. 104-104, 110 Stat. 56 (1996).

especially impacted the diversity of programming on local radio stations,[170] resulting in concentrated "playlists" made at the national level, which leads to a common tendency for stations across the country to play the same songs.[171] However, shifting the music market to digital distribution could help further the industry's refocus on the singles sale market[172] instead of traditional album distribution. It could also serve the CRB's goal of maximizing the availability of song usage.[173] If consumers are able to access wide selections

---

[170] The trend of music conglomeration amongst radio stations is greatly important to the digital market considering radio plays are still where the majority of consumers are first being introduced to music and artists. If an artist can get on the radio, there is a much greater chance for success. *See Music Discovery Still Dominated by Radio, Says Nielson Music 360 Report*, NIELSON, (Aug. 14, 2012) http://www.nielsen.com/content/corporate/us/en/press-room/2012/music-discovery-still-dominated-by-radio--says-nielsen-music-360.html.

[171] Laura M. Holson explores the relationship between artist research and the narrowing of radio programming in stating, "as the world of radio hardens into an industry dominated by three or four major chains, the use of research is accelerating and has become far more sophisticated, leading to mounting criticism that the quest for ratings is homogenizing music radio and making it harder for a different sound to break through." Holson also reports that a division of Clear Channel, the largest chain of radio stations, reportedly charges record labels up to $20,000 per song to test unreleased music on audiences. She suggests that what was once a simple conversation amongst industry professionals determining what audiences might want to hear is now big business. While it is important for music distributors to cater to their audiences, today's music industry may be taking matters a step too far. Laura M. Holson, *With By-the-Numbers Radio, Requests Are a Dying Breed*, N.Y. TIMES (July 11, 2002) http://www.nytimes.com/2002/07/11/business/with-by-the-numbers-radio-requests-are-a-dying-breed.html.

[172] Services like iTunes and Amazon Prime are already allowing consumers to purchase single songs from many full albums, but by making the trend more widespread there is a greater chance for revenue since consumers appear somewhat hesitant to spend much on music purchases. Boehm, *supra* note 46, at 196.

[173] As explained by one industry expert, "For the most part, each time a song is played on ad-supported Pandora or subscription-based

of music for a standard, low monthly payment, the consumer may be more inclined to seek out new artists.[174] There is a great potential for artists to see abundant financial gains stemming from album sales where consumers were first exposed to their work on digital media platforms.[175] It stands to reason that the music industry could begin to focus more heavily on finding and promoting artists. National Public Radio publicly advocates for online music distribution sites to

---

Spotify, it reaches one person. Each time a song is played on the radio, it can reach thousands of people—but when you turn on a radio station, you don't know what you're going to hear. Musicians expand their audience when new listeners stumble upon their work, which is why getting airplay is so important to them. Neither Pandora nor Spotify currently has anywhere near as many listeners as AM and FM radio—another reason it makes sense for them to pay less—but they also don't present the same kind of opportunities for discovering new music." So while distributing music online might be financially less profitable, new artists will still benefit from exposure that is uniquely accessible to online consumers. Wolk, *supra* note 68.

[174] Sites such as Spotify and Pandora *are* offering this distribution alternative already. However, as will be addressed later in this text, the rates at which both applications are currently running are ineffective in providing profits for the creators of the distributed music. *See infra* Part VI.C.i.a.

[175] A parallel for potential success can be drawn in looking at Netflix's critically acclaimed television series *House of Cards*. While Netflix will not announce the number of viewers tuning in for the program, one CNBC source estimated "some 16 percent of Netflix users on one particular Internet service . . . watched at least one episode of the show." Jenny Cosgrave, *Viewers 'Binge' on 'House of Cards' After Netflix Record High*, CNBC (Feb. 17, 2014, 7:19 AM), www.cnbc.com/id/101421361#. Regardless of the number of viewers, Netflix is seeing notable increases in share prices in response to the program's success. *See id.* But how does Netflix's success with original programming translate into future sales? While the program is continually available on Netflix, the company is now also producing the series on DVD and Blu-Ray format. A similar system could easily be implemented in the music industry. By allowing consumers to sample many artists and albums for a low monthly price, but still retaining the option to sell fans of each given album a hard or digital copy to add to their collections, production companies could profit from more avenues while still conforming to consumer demand.

serve as a platform for music discovery,[176] where
consumers can locate artists they enjoy and then choose
the best method of supporting those artists.[177] Since
there could be increased attention directed toward
singles as an assessment for artist success over digital
distribution channels, it is likely that producers would
save on production costs of unsuccessful works.[178]

---

[176] "Spotify (and/or its many cousins) works well as [a] try-it-
before-you-buy-it discovery engine. You can't discover a new favorite
band if you've never heard its music, so take advantage of the many
different ways to stumble upon great stuff and then make purchases
as an informed consumer." Stephen Thompson, *The Good Listener: Does
Using Spotify Make You a Bad Person?*, NPR (Sept. 26, 2013, 3 PM),
http://www.npr.org/blogs/allsongs/2013/09/26/226468333/the-good-
listener-does-using-spotify-make-you-a-bad-person.

[177] *See id.* "[D]ig into the tremendous array of ways to sustain the
livelihood of musicians whose work sustains *you*. Contribute to their
Kickstarter campaigns if they exist. Go to their concerts and
encourage your friends to join you – and, while you're there, buy a T-
shirt or music directly from the band itself. Champion the music you
love on social media; that word of mouth means a lot, both financially
and for morale." *Id.*

[178] As explained by George Howard, a former mid-size record
label president who currently works as an entertainment firm advisor
and associate professor of music business and management at Berklee
College of Music, "it's now easier than ever to create and release
music, artists are freed from the one-album-every-eighteen-months
cycle that raised the stakes (and the cost of failure) to such a scary
degree." George Howard, *Sign and Fail: How the Traditional Music
Industry Killed Culture*, TUNECORE (Dec. 1, 2011),
http://www.tunecore.com/blog/2011/12/sign-and-fail.html. Howard
finds the gradual switch from old music business where "you
essentially got one shot" to a more flexible system encouraging to the
promotion of a wider variety of artists. *Id.* He further states, "I
strongly believe that this not only results in a higher chance of success
for artists, but also in a more diverse musical landscape. This is
because no one, *no one* knows what the market wants, and for too long
people thought they did. This resulted in a lot of music being put into
the market just because it resembled something else that had been
successful." *Id.*

i. Fixing the Current Online Music Distribution Model

As earlier mentioned, there are financially successful online distribution services available to music consumers.[179] It is easy to identify these services as a viable alternative to statutory reformation. However, under current models of online music distribution, artists are not compensated fairly enough to promote continuation of their work.[180] And while it may appear that online music distribution services are taking financial advantage of the artists they supposedly support, this is not necessarily the case. Online music distribution, as it operates today, is just not profitable enough to sustain adequate artist payment.[181] The online music industry needs to find a way for current

---

[179] For purposes of this article, focus will solely rest on majority distributors. Majority distribution services do little pre-selection for the artists they work with in exchange for the best prices on the music market. *See* Budi Voogt, *The Indie Musician's Guide to Digital Distribution*, Hypebot.com (Nov. 26, 2013), http://www.hypebot.com/hypebot/2013/11/the-indie-musicians-guide-to-digital-distribution.html. Conversely, selective distributors pre-select their clients in an attempt to work only in promotion of a certain type of artist. *See id.* iTunes and Spotify are both majority music distributors. While Pandora is technically labeled as an online radio service, the site still grapples with the same compensation issues as other music distribution services.

[180] *See* David Lowery, *My Song Got Played on Pandora 1 Million Times and All I Got Was $16.89, Less Than What I Make from a Single T-Shirt Sale!*, Trichordist (June 24, 2013), http://thetrichordist.com/2013/06/24/my-song-got-played-on-pandora-1-million-times-and-all-i-got-was-16-89-less-than-what-i-make-from-a-single-t-shirt-sale/.

[181] *See* Paul Resnikoff, *Streaming Services Will Never Become Profitable, Study Finds...*, Digital Music News (Feb. 18, 2014), http://www.digitalmusicnews.com/permalink/2014/02/18/profitless ("'The streaming business has to slowly move from a free economy to a paid economy as the sustainability of an ad-supported revenue model is a big question mark.'").

distribution services to incentivize artists to continue
creating musical works through increased revenue.[182]

a. Challenges Facing Today's Online Music Distribution Model

There is no arguing that online music distribution
services are rapidly becoming integrated into our
everyday lives.[183] With exponentially growing
popularity, it would appear these sites are actually
indicating a rise in artist compensation. However, while
these services are legal, many consumers are unaware
of how artists are negatively impacted by the
staggeringly low royalty payments made to those artists
whose works are accessible on such sites.[184] "It's a big

---

[182] "'The number one concern of the individual songwriters and
composers we represent is getting fair payment from digital services,'
Paul Williams, president of the American Society of Composers,
Authors, and Publishers told Wired. 'Whenever I meet with members
from all genres of music who are struggling to make ends meet, that's
the thing they ask about most. They know that streaming is growing,
and they don't want to be left out in the cold in terms of having their
creative work valued fairly.'" Graeme McMillan, *Is Pandora Really
Short-Changing Songwriters?*, WIRED (July 3, 2013, 6:30 AM),
http://www.wired.com/2013/07/david-lowery-pandora/.

[183] "In 2014, Pandora reached 200 million users, with nearly 70
million active each month. By comparison, Spotify has about 40
million users as of 2014, 10 million of them premium subscribers."
Spotify   vs.   Pandora,   DIFFEN,
http://www.diffen.com/difference/Pandora_vs_Spotify (last visited
Nov. 15, 2014).

[184] Countless artists have published their royalty payment records
from online distribution sites in an effort to illustrate to consumers
the harm of using services like Pandora and Spotify. One such artist is
Damon Krukowski, of Galaxie 500 and Damon &Naomi, who issued
the following statement: "Consider Pandora and Spotify, the
streaming music services that are becoming ever more integrated into
our daily listening habits. My BMI royalty check arrived recently,
reporting songwriting earnings from the first quarter of 2012, and I
was glad to see that our music is being listened to via these services.
Galaxie 500's 'Tugboat', for example, was played 7,800 times on
Pandora that quarter, for which its three songwriters were paid a
collective total of 21 cents, or seven cents each. Spotify pays better:

conundrum," stated Brian Zisk, the founder of SF
MusicTech Summit.[185] "[W]e are never going back to
the days when people can sell tens or millions of CDs.
So then the question is: How does the compensation
happen."[186]

While copyright law has remained unchanged in
addressing artist compensation issues, many industry
experts and performers have publicly spoken out
against the online distribution model. In June 2013,
David Lowery, guitarist for the rock band Cracker,
published his earnings from online distribution
services, creating a significant buzz throughout the
music community.[187] In his public statement, *My Song
Got Played on Pandora 1 Million Times and All I Got Was
$16.89, Less Than What I Make From a Single T-Shirt Sale!*,

For the 5,960 times 'Tugboat' was played there, Galaxie 500's
songwriters went collectively into triple digits: $1.05 (35 cents each).
To put this into perspective: Since we own our own recordings, by my
calculation it would take songwriting royalties for roughly 312,000 plays
on Pandora to earn us the profit of one-- *one*-- LP sale." Damon
Krukowski, *Making Cents*, PITCHFORK (Nov. 14, 2012),
http://pitchfork.com/features/articles/8993-the-cloud/.

[185] "The SF MusicTech Summit brings together visionaries in the
evolving music/business/technology ecosystem, along with the best
and brightest developers, entrepreneurs, investors, service providers,
journalists, musicians, and organizations who work with them at the
convergence of culture and commerce. We meet to do business and
discuss, in a proactive, conducive to dealmaking environment." SF
MUSICTECH SUMMIT, http://www.sfmusictech.com (last visited Nov. 9,
2014).

[186] Andrew Leonard, *The Music Industry is Still Screwed: Why Spotify,
Amazon and iTunes Can't Save Musical Artists*, SALON (June 20, 2014, 6:44
AM),
http://www.salon.com/2014/06/20/the_music_industry_is_still_screwed
_why_spotify_amazon_and_itunes_cant_save_musical_artists/.

[187] *See* Wolk, *supra* note 68. *See generally* Lowery, *supra* note 180
(Lowery's published earnings).

Lowery urged fellow artists to announce their earnings from online distribution sites as well.[188]

After Lowery's initial attack on the online distribution system, Sasha Frere- Jones, a staff writer and pop-music critic for *The New Yorker*, was one of the first to address the issue:

The shortest version is that the Spotify model does not favor new artists. The larger grumbling about streaming services in the musician community is that the various services, which are governed by fluid and complex laws that are changing as we speak, favor nobody but the major labels that helped fund and grow some of them.[189]

While Spotify routinely declines comment on its royalty rates, according to a pool of music executives who have negotiated with the company, Spotify pays roughly 0.5 to 0.7 cents per stream for its paid tier, and as much as 90 percent less for free account holders.[190]

---

[188] *See* Lowery, *supra* note 180. In response to Lowery's commentary on poor online distribution profits, English singer-songwriter Sam Duckworth published proof that one month of 4,685 plays on Spotify earned him less than 20 pounds. *See* Wolk, *supra* note 68. While the artist feels cheated by such low profit margins, author Douglas Wolk does put this statistic in some interesting perspective. "That might well be the case. If we're getting into hypotheticals, though, how many of those listeners might have bought the album, or come to one of Duckworth's shows, *because* they heard the stream and were impressed by what they heard?" *Id.*

[189] Sasha Frere-Jones, *If You Care About Music, Should You Ditch Spotify?*, NEW YORKER (July 19, 2013), http://www.newyorker.com/culture/sasha-frere-jones/if-you-care-about-music-should-you-ditch-spotify.

[190] Ben Sisario, *As Music Streaming Grows, Royalties Slow to a Trickle*, N.Y. TIMES, Jan. 28, 2013, *available at* http://www.nytimes.com/2013/01/29/business/media/streaming-shakes-up-music-industrys-model-for-royalties.html?pagewanted=all.

For artists whose income is reliant on royalties, the biggest concern is whether streaming will put an end to CD and download sales by offering a cheap or free alternative. However, it is best to keep in mind that streaming services are a relatively new offering. As aptly stated by Donald Passman, a well-recognized music attorney, "Artists didn't make big money from CDs when they were introduced, either. They were a specialty thing, and had a lower royalty rate. Then as it became mainstream, the royalties went up. And that's what will happen here."[191] While it is uncertain this hunch will prove true, it is clear the online distribution model is not completely flawed. The music industry needs to search for modifications to the already functional system that will more fairly compensate artists.[192]

b. Solutions for a More Collectively Beneficial Digital Distribution Service

While it is clear that current online music distribution services are not adequately serving artists, the business model is not a lost cause. It may take some time for developers to create an environment that is beneficial to all parties involved; however, there are steps that can be taken to initiate change.

The first alteration in working toward fair artist compensation would be raising service subscription

---

[191] *Id.*

[192] According to one source encouraging change in the online distribution industry, "The key to a future where streaming may be the preferred delivery method is dependent upon more variations and flexibility in the business model than currently offered by Spotify. There are a range of opportunities in exploring business models that allow for streaming rentals, and limited access to different material at different times." *Why Spotify is Not Netflix (But Maybe it Should Be)*, TRICHORDIST (Oct. 17, 2013), http://thetrichordist.com/2013/10/17/why-spotify-is-not-netflix-and-why-it-maybe-should-be/.

fees. Both Pandora and Spotify currently offer a free tier of subscription.[193] While this is ideal for consumers, there is no benefit to anyone involved in creating the music they are accessing. Television distribution sites have recognized significant success with free limited trials, but after a temporary period, rates are always raised to a more fiscally sustainable level.[194]

The online distribution services would also be wise to explore possibilities of transactional streaming.[195] Much like how the iTunes business model operates, there is no reason why every song ever released should be available at the same price point.[196] While we are already beginning to see this trend in other areas of popular music culture, it would be beneficial for artists

---

[193] While both Spotify and Pandora are labeled as commercial services, each program does allow users to access content for free. Where Pandora's $4.99/month premium service allows customers to access music ad-free (as does Spotify Premium at $9.99/month) both payment structures are optional. Customers streaming for free will have to withstand some restrictions, as well as advertisements. However, for many modern consumers this is a small price to pay for free music services. *Spotify v. Pandora,* DIFFEN http://www.diffen.com/difference/Pandora_vs_Spotify (last visited Nov. 13, 2014).

[194] Both Netflix and Hulu Plus (the two most commonly accessed online television streaming services) offer free trials for new users. However, the longest any given trial lasts is thirty days, after which subscribers are forced to cancel access to programming or begin monthly payments. *Netflix vs. Hulu Plus: What's the Best App to Stream TV Shows and Movies?,* HEAVY (July 2, 2014, 1:34 PM), http://heavy.com/tech/2014/07/netflix-vs-hulu-plus-whats-the-best-app-to-stream-tv-shows-and-movies/.

[195] David Lowery, *How to Fix Streaming Music's Business Model,* HYPEBOT (Oct. 14, 2014) http://hypebot.com/hypebot/2014/10/how-to-fix-streaming-musics-business-model.html (noting that iTunes, a transactional music seller, has been highly successful and that a similar model may be worth pursuing with streaming).

[196] There are endless possibilities in staggering online music pricing. For example, new releases could be priced as transactional streams where the consumer can choose between low-cost limited access to a new release, or pay more for a transactional download. *Id.*

to charge an advance for high-profile new releases that will attract listeners to a specific online distribution service.[197]

An alternative pricing proposal to fix current issues in online music distribution would be the implementation of a variety of pricing tiers. Much like cable television and SiriusXM radio,[198] catalogs of music could be organized and marketed towards certain audiences.[199] Similarly, the online music industry would likely see positive change in a decision to implement a release windowing system.[200] Much like the structure

---

[197] For example, country-turned-pop-artist Taylor Swift has released deluxe editions of her past three albums exclusively to Target. While fans can still access the bulk of her music online or from other retailers, the incentive remains to purchase a physical CD from Target stores. Carolyn Menyes, *Taylor Swift New Album '1989' Deluxe Edition to Sell Exclusively at Target*, MUSIC TIMES (Aug. 19, 2014), http://www.musictimes.com/articles/8984/20140819/taylor-swift-new-album-1989-deluxe-edition-target.htm; *see also The Secret Genius of Taylor Swift*, NAT'L PUB. RADIO (Nov. 9, 2012, 3:17 AM), http://www.npr.org/blogs/money/2012/11/09/164742426/the-secret-genius-of-taylor-swift ("[T]he tools Swift didn't use are as important than [sic] the ones she did. By refusing to release her singles on Spotify, or any other streaming site, she pushed her fans to buy the album. Spotify pays the artist pennies on the dollar. Taylor Swift skipped it.").

[198] SiriusXM Radio is commercial-free radio programming, available to consumers at varying subscription and price levels. *What is SiriusXM?*, SIRIUSXM SATELLITE RADIO, http://www.siriusxm.com/whatissiriusxm (last visited Nov. 13, 2014).

[199] "Creating bundled packages adds value to both the end user and the streaming service. Individual packages can be as little as $4.99 a month, and complete access could [be] priced at $49.99 a month." Lowery, *supra* note 195.

[200] Feature-length films are routinely released in "windows." *Why Spotify is Not Netflix (But Maybe it Should Be)*, *supra* note 192. Most films follow a format similar to this:
1. Film Released in Theaters
2. Film Released later on Video on Demand (Rental)
3. Film Released later on Cable and/or Broadcast
[4.] Film Released Later on Home Video (Rental and Purchase)
[5.] Film Released Later on Netflix (Subscription).

the film industry utilizes for its releases, music distribution services could weigh the cost of ownership rights of new albums in relation to the length the albums have been available for purchase on the market.

While forming a model similar to online television distribution may seem appealing,[201] consideration must be given to the likelihood that consumers will conform to a new system. From a distance it seems unlikely that consumers would pay even a reasonable fee for music access when, competing, albeit illegal, networks are still offering music for free.[202] Overcoming the piracy

---

Id..And while this model is not always followed, the general idea is that different levels of ownership of the movie are available at specific points in time and for a range of prices. This model also has potential for success in the music industry. *The Trichordist* suggests an online music distribution windowing system as follows:

1. Single Release Digital Transactional Download 99 cents

2. Single/Song Release Digital Transactional Streaming Rental 10 cents for 24 hours

3. Album Release Digital Transactional Download 9.99

4. Album Release Digital Transactional Streaming Rental $1 for 24 hours

5. Select Songs Released to Subscription Streaming Services, not whole albums.

6. Album Release Subscription Streaming Services.

Id.

[201] Despite charges to consumers wishing to use services like Hulu and Netflix, online television distribution websites appear to be continuing to make financial gains. According to a report by *Equities.com*, an online financial resource platform that combines interactive social networking capabilities for investors and public companies, despite Netflix's recent one dollar per month increase in subscription price, the company is still benefitting from production of original programming content, and subscriber rates are on the rise. Remy Merritt, *How Netflix is Cashing in on Orange is the New Black*, EQUITIES.COM (June 5, 2014, 10:03 PM) http://www.equities.com/editors-desk/stocks/technology/orange-is-the-new-black-buys-netflix-subscribers-respect.

[202] While the RIAA recognizes that piracy will likely forever be an ongoing struggle in the music industry, should artists continue to see such drastically diminished profits, the RIAA asserts it would not be able to maintain itself. "Q: Don't you think some people are always

obstacle appears especially daunting, considering that illegal downloading has become an international habit among the majority of consumers.[203] For an effective change in the music industry to occur, record companies will need to incentivize behavioral changes among consumers. In moving forward to better the online distribution market, audience education will be undoubtedly necessary.[204] If consumers realized services such as Pandora and Spotify are not beneficial to the artists they support, they would be less likely to use these services.

By placing new songs in online music networks where consumers can safely access high-quality music while still supporting both artists and the industry, a change most likely to benefit songwriters may occur.[205]

---

going to download music illegally, even with a graduated response program in place? ... [A:] As an industry, we have lived with street piracy for years. Similarly, there will always be a degree of piracy on the Internet. It's not realistic to wipe it out entirely but instead to bring it to a level of manageable control so a legitimate marketplace can really flourish." *For Students Doing Reports*, RECORDING INDUSTRY ASS'N AM., http://www.riaa.com/faq.php (last visited Nov. 13, 2014).

[203] While music piracy is a substantial—and unfortunately growing—issue in the United States, international markets are seeing an even larger financial hit due to the illegal file sharing. According to a report by *The New York Times*, many critics believe music companies "have been too slow to embrace new online business models that are attractive enough to lure music fans away from pirate sites." Pfanner, *supra* note 153.

[204] "Because of the social norm of accepting digital music file-sharing, the recording industry has attempted to change the norm by educating the public on copyright law, which included the legal strategy of suing individual file- sharers and labeling the act of digital file-sharing as theft and piracy." Schwender, *supra* note 3, at 261.

[205] Spotify is the first music streaming system to see much use from consumers. While the program (which launched in Sweden) is fairly new to the American market, it is gaining in popularity amongst its *paying* users. According to Spotify's co-founder and chief executive, Daniel Ek, the company has high hopes that customers will begin to see the benefit of supporting artists as valid incentive to pay the $10-per-month subscription fee. *See* The Spotify Team, *$2 Billion and*

It will also be crucially important, in following
successful television models, for online music
distributors to invest resources to improve the music
community at large.[206] In return, online distribution
services would hopefully begin to recognize the value of
providing financial and business support for emerging
artists.[207] It will undoubtedly be a long journey for the
music industry to develop a social norm favoring
legitimate avenues of music consumption; however,
this is a change necessary to its survival.[208]

VII. CONCLUSION

While SEA is a valid attempt at reforming the long-
standing difficulties presented in section 114 and section
115 of the Copyright Act, it is unlikely a statutory change
will most effectively create change at the speed it needs
to occur. An increase in mechanical royalties may
appear beneficial to songwriters, but the increased

Counting,   SPOTIFY   (Nov.   11,   2014),
https://news.spotify.com/uk/2014/11/11/2-billion-and-counting/
("We're trying to build a new music economy that works for artists in
a way the music industry never has before.").
    [206] "Netflix in responding to their needs in the marketplace is
actually investing capital directly into content creation in a
meaningful way." *Why Spotify is Not Netflix (But Maybe it Should Be)*,
supra note 192.
    [207] *Id.*
    [208] The music industry is not alone on the receiving end of
financial hits due to piracy. Similar anti-theft precautions are
currently being employed by the film industry as well. For example,
in the spring of 2014, Warner Bros. Pictures U.K. launched an
exclusive trailer for *The LEGO Movie* as part of an anti-piracy
campaign targeting its young audiences. According to Liz Bales, the
director general at Industry Trust for IP Awareness, it is "crucial that
the film industry is connecting them with legal services, making it
easy to choose to pay for official content and less likely that they
would inadvertently or intentionally access pirate websites." Stuart
Kemp, *U.K. Anti-Piracy Campaign Brings 'The LEGO Movie' Trailer to
Life*, HOLLYWOOD REP. (Nov. 29, 2013, 8:33 AM),
http://www.hollywoodreporter.com/news/uk-anti-piracy-campaign-
brings-660726.

production costs will likely burden music dissemination to a crippling degree. By instead modernizing how consumers view the accessibility of music and placing it in a context comfortable to most purchasers, there is a possibility for songwriters to more quickly benefit from the copyright laws already in place. Modifications can, and *should*, be made to online music distribution outlets to more ethically and financially support every party involved in each music transaction.

www.ingramcontent.com/pod-product-compliance
Lightning Source LLC
Chambersburg PA
CBHW021403170526
45164CB00002B/484

9781507803660